Back Porch Wisdom

ROBERT KJAR

ISBN: 1494337061
ISBN-13: 978-1494337063

to Minda and an unknown donor

CONTENTS

PREFACE

Back Porch Wisdom is a bit pretentious for a title. After all, who decides what is wisdom? In this vein, I welcome you onto my back porch. It's a summer evening, and I'm going to tell you a few tales about life in general through the lens of my life experiences.

"Who is he, that he should be telling me his experiences?" your uncle might indelicately ask, leaning back in the faded vinyl rocker and unbuckling his pants to let the digestive juices work unencumbered, and daring your tale to overcome his food coma.

I might say that I am nobody of consequence, no more than anyone else, but the artful telling is the thing. As you sit on my porch listening to me ramble on, you will notice that the tales are not in any chronological — or even, *recognizable* – order. Neither are the tales spun on the back porch.

In these 72 essays you will be taken to a rubbing alcohol scented doctor's office, transported to an oasis in the Negev desert, and you will meet along the way characters like Popcorn Pierre, The Cat With No Name, Sullivan – the Overt Rebel, the fizzling members of Afire, and conventioneer jackals. Some fun, some poignancy, and maybe even a few life lessons to share with others from your own back porch one summer eve.

In the midst of economic turmoil, terrorist threats, and culture wars, I hope that these simple reflections help you consider what makes us who we are – frightened arachnophobes who are yet heroes in training; failed treasure seekers with wealthy memories; sentimental patriots and rebellious kids; imprisoned students and stumped teachers; naïve advice givers and Shakespearean romantics. From the cynicism of the everyday, I hope you will find in these words "tongues in trees, books in the running brooks, sermons in stones, and good in every thing." (From Shakespeare's As You Like It, Act II, Scene I)

1

THE BACK PORCH

Many of us have a special zone in our homes where the family nestles after dinner, where grandparents whisper wisely, and where children swarm for dessert, dispersing when the adult talk begins. At my childhood home, this was the back porch. The first back porch I remember was smallish, covered with green – and later, blue – astro-turf, and it had a psychedelic turquoise and green floral porch swing at one end. The crabapple tree behind it shaded the setting sun and dropped its fruit in the fall leaving a sweet smelling marmalade on one end of the fake plastic grass.

But the porch I remember best was the one that really was more of a stage on the back of our big rambler house during my transition from boyhood to manhood. It was probably fifteen feet wide and spanned about forty feet behind our laundry room and kitchen. It was made of smooth, highly polished white stone with brass panes marking out the two-foot square pieces. On the long side, we had a single stair that stepped down to the backyard lawn, and black wrought iron posts were spaced every ten feet to support the roof that completely covered the porch swing and patio chairs.

We had moved into this house when I was nine, and I immediately became acquainted with every angle and edge around the porch, which served as my battlefield when I played with my G.I. Joe doll. Incidentally, it is really a travesty to call G.I. Joe a doll because he was an icon of masculinity to me, scaling the wrought iron posts with a grappling hook, jumping into the junipers next to the porch to evade the enemy, and then peering over the white castle wall of the porch step to spy out the next secret plan of the conspiring commanders.

Every Memorial Day we welcomed the summer with a grand waterfight in the backyard, and the back porch was always off limits, since dousing someone there meant spraying the patio furniture and further warping the old pine dining table under the lime green vinyl tablecloth. Water also made the porch like a white ice skating rink, and it claimed many victims who dared to make a running leap from the wet grass over its white cliffs to supposed safety, falling flat or sliding into the back door. Injuries always served as a deterrent to further soaking from water balloons or hoses turned on the fleeing coward.

The scent of a dozen lilac trees mixed with the cherry blossoms to create a natural potpourri for the guests lounging on the back porch. Sounds of kids playing on the trampoline served as background music, and the evergreens shaded the last light of day as the melting sun disappeared somewhere in the distance. Uncles, aunts, brothers, neighbors, old friends – all sat transfixed in time, half listening to whomever felt the need to speak while the others agreeably nodded acknowledging the rightness of the moment.

One summer, my parents did a major remodeling job in the kitchen, and they bought an indoor grill with an exhaust fan that went out to the porch. This created a wonderful backyard grill scent whenever someone was cooking inside. The smoke would pour out over anyone relaxing on the porch and the scent wafted around the yard calling everyone to dinner.

We had a German Shepherd for a while, named Noah, an unfortunate name for a dog because I think he always wondered if we were saying "No" when we called him to come and eat his food or any other time we wanted him to come. I think that's why he ran from us so much. He would give us the half-turned head questioning stare from his home on the back porch (see My Dog's Eyes for other interpretations of dog looks) where he was chained up to one of the poles. When we let him loose, he would clear the porch like a prisoner free to spring from the hard prison floor into the green grass of summertime bliss.

The back porch was ice cream and brownie central, where we would listen to the electric ice cream machine's drone finally succumb to the solidifying creaminess inside the metal cylinder. Strawberry and banana ice cream made its way to the adults gathered in a circle in rocking chairs and swinging slowly in the turquoise porch swing, which now enjoyed a spacious home free from the crabapple nuisance of its previous placement. Brownies were tossed on top of the ice cream, like chocolate bricks in sweet mortar.

Winter shut down most of the activity on the back porch, except for the brave soul who went out to look at the wondrous whiteness of the snow-covered shrubs and the soft lines surrounding the porch. Now the porch, dull against the fallen snow, was an extension of nature coming right up to the house. Sometimes the snow was so deep, the step from the porch to the lawn disappeared, like some cartoon trick meant to catch the unsuspecting victim and plunge him or her spread eagle into the pillowy snow. The stark wrought iron, black and straight merely served to frame the scene so that it could be studied in measured panorama.

The winter solitude served as the perfect cover one special Christmas, when my father played the ultimate slight-of-hand gift trick on my brother and I. After we had opened our presents, my father slipped us each an envelope and told us that we might want to see what was on the back porch. Each envelope held a key, and written on the key was the word Yamaha. Never had the distance from the living room to the laundry been covered in so few steps as we practically rocketed to the back door to gaze upon the two motorcycles parked on the white showroom floor of our back porch. For some time afterwards, the porch was marred by the black tread marks of the tires, like kids' shoes on linoleum floors. I think my mother's face must have been whiter than the porch when my dad brought the bikes home, but she had recovered nicely. I still don't know how he convinced her to let these two teenage boys live out their rebel-without-a-cause fantasies on such a sacred stage as the back porch, but there they were.

At other times, even when the weather was warm, the porch served as a backdrop for the chill of bitter news of loved ones who would no longer share the porch on those quiet evenings. Later, the back porch was the venue from which my father announced that the family business was failing, and that financial adjustments would have to be made to keep the house. Over time, it had become a monument to all who passed over its white surface, and had we thought about it before we packed the last moving box on the truck, we might have written a collective epitaph from our many family gatherings and contemplative discussions:

Masculine dolls scaled castle walls here,
Waterfights met breezy nights here,
Scents and sound filled all around here,
Loyal pets launched like jets here,

Ice cream scoops fed family groups here,
Tire marks told of motocross parks here,
Elders au pined while kids dined here,

Now behind us, let this porch remind us
Of the love we shared here.

2

THE SPIDER IN MY METRO

What's your reaction when someone near you says, "There's a spider on you"? Do you experience the cool entomological reaction, "My, what an interesting species – it will make a great addition to my collection!" or is your reaction more like others, who feel like smashing themselves into walls to get it off, or who scream out something to whomever is near, "GET IT OFF ME! WHAT ARE YOU STANDING THERE FOR?!" Or maybe you're in still another category altogether, which is kind of a hybrid of these two, characterized by screaming fits and jumping around, with a dash of rapid breathing and tunnel vision.

Welcome to arachnophobia. Let's embrace our irrational fears together – come along!

A few years back, I commuted to work, roughly just over an hour each way from my home to the office. My car of choice was a little Chevy Metro, which was a selection more about thrift than about style, speed, or just about any other dimension of the driving experience. Although it must have been at the time one of the smallest four-door sedans on the market, I could just wedge my girth into the driver's seat and I was still able to turn the steering wheel, unlike the second choice, the Kia Rio, so that settled it.

In my Chevy sardine can, not only was the steering wheel always very close to me, although not in a fond way, but also the air vents were so close to the steering wheel that with my hands at 10 o'clock and 2 o'clock, I could nearly touch them if I extended my fingers. I had tried this many times on my hour-long commute, just as I had imagined what it would be like to suddenly veer into a ditch, wondering if I would end up squishy side down or whether, like cats, Metros always land on all fours. I kind of doubted it. But I was certain about touching the vents.

So there I am, driving along in a long line of traffic down a very long, one-lane road, when all of a sudden my eye catches a glimpse of something that wasn't there moments before. I know you hear all these stories and people start comparing spider size to silver dollars or the sole of their shoe or the circumference of a Mason jar's mouth. Honestly, my little visitor was probably more of the silver dollar size – and hey, that's pretty big. But what was worse, he had personality. First, he was black with distinct yellow stripes – so I thought it must mean big time venom or bite, because you wouldn't put on such a show if you were just a friendly spider like Charlotte. And second, he appeared to be *crouching*. So I thought, of course, that he was getting ready to spring.

Now I haven't really seen spiders spring, except for the little black ones that sort of pop around – but I think that's just fast walking. But I imagined this fellow leaping from the vent to my face, or running up my sleeve. And then what? you might ask. Well, I don't really know. Would it bite? and if so, would it hurt? and could I find it and kill it? and if I drove into a ditch would I care more about the spider or about getting out of the car before it blew up? It was kind of a toss up on that one.

I looked at him, he looked at me, and I started to consider my options very quickly. Screaming for someone to get it off was out of the question – no one would really care – and maybe the spider would get mad if it heard me screaming. Moving out of its way was equally unlikely, since I was wedged in good and tight, and was more wearing the car than merely driving it. What to do…

I pulled over onto the shoulder and got out of the car, very carefully, so as not to arouse suspicion by the spider. Having extricated myself, I then felt a wave of panic. I have never been to a doctor for panic attacks, so I don't know the medical definition of one; but perhaps the symptoms would read: sudden light-headedness, heart palpitations, heightened sense of dread, irrational feelings of death, and the like.

At this point I had several options: stay there until the spider decided to leave (even if that were hours – I could probably walk the other 20 miles to work!); try to kill it with something (there were no special implements for this at hand, and I felt sure that without special smashing gear to do the job, I might only do it halfway, which is never good when it comes to the animal kingdom); or I could get back in the car and drive to a store to buy some spider spray. I was imagining a spray so lethal and thick that my spider friend would look like a flocked Christmas tree when I was done with him.

I looked in the driver's side window to see if the spider was still there, and he had gone. But *where*? I took a chance and got back in the car, and when I looked at where the demon spider had rested previously, I only saw two spiny legs extending out of the vent from the lair inside. He was watching. Although there was some reassurance that he had retreated to his corner, I still could see, with the grip on the vent like that, how he could spring out and get me.

I drove another three or four miles until I came to a large grocery store. I immediately got out of the car and walked into the store, prepared to spend anything to get a can of spider killer. I found a large can of Raid that had a picture of a spider on the front, and it had a red line through it – no spiders. Perfect.

Returning to my car, I felt like a kid at school who, having lost the first round of a schoolyard fight, returns to the scene with the town bully at his side. Maybe my spider was thinking, "What's that? Can it be? It's not…RAID!!!!" But when I peered through my driver's side window, there he was, back on top of the vent. If I could have peered further into his little brain, I'm sure he was laughing inside, chuckling at me and my can of Raid. After all, he had the whole car as his hiding place – he was using my Metro vents like the Viet Cong had used their network of tunnels in Vietnam.

As I pondered my next move there was a buzzing near my ear, so I jumped, gasped, and dodged out of the way of this new pest of the insect world – a bee was taking interest in me. At this point I would insert a footnote about another bee incident when a killer bee stung my calf and it swelled up to the size of a baseball, but I won't. Why do insects have this thing for me? Did the spider make a few phone calls while I was in the store so that now this bee was standing between him and me? I popped the top on my can of Raid and took a random shot in the bee's direction (after all, if it's good enough to take down a spider, a bee should certainly pose no problem, I reasoned). The bee must have had only limited loyalty to the spider, or maybe it had fulfilled its debt of honor by just showing up, because it left as quickly as it came.

Perhaps this little bee diversion was all the spider had asked for, because when I looked in my window again he was gone. So I went to work. I opened the door (nothing jumped out) and sprayed a five-second shot of

Raid into the vent where the spider had been. Then I shot five-second bursts in each of the dashboard vents, floor vents, and under the seats, leaving just enough Raid for my return trip home. I didn't think he was dead, I just thought it was time to get on to work, and since I had my handy can of spider death, I knew that if he showed up again, I could put the big hurt on him. My bully would step out on the playground for me, and that would be it.

So I drove the rest of the way in to work, can of Raid in my lap, with my finger on the trigger. My heart was still racing, my breathing was shallow, and at every stoplight, I went into high alert searching for my spider. His disappearance had done nothing to ease my tension, and when I arrived at work and made it to my desk, I continued to feel a little jittery the rest of the day.

I went back home at the end of the day in a similar fashion, fingering my can of Raid like a gunfighter ready to draw. No spider. Once home, I decided to take the only logical and reasonable course of action left. I had to bomb my car. The U.S. had napalm. I had a bug bomb; and if it was good enough to kill spiders in the house for up to a thousand cubic feet, it would be perfect for the interior of my Metro, which had to be what...maybe fifty? So I bombed the inside of my car, watching it fill with the white cloud of death, and went to bed.

I don't know whatever became of my little arachnid friend, but the sort of sticky toxic residue left by the bomb was like a warm blanket in winter. Dip me in pesticides I say. Ultimately, the spider had the victory, because the next day I began to secretly look at trading in my car, and within the week I had traded my little arachno-Metro for another used car. I got two thousand dollars on the trade, and in this larger car I noticed right away that my hands were some distance from the air vents.

3

THE OFFICER'S CLUB AND SHIRLEY TEMPLES

When I was fourteen, my jazz band teacher came to me and said that a friend of his was looking for a bass guitar player for a one-time gig playing at the Fort Douglas Officer's Club. A few days later, I got a call from the leader of the Men of Note, a five-piece dance band, asking that if it was okay with my parents, could I sit in with the band on Saturday night. They consented, and on Saturday night, Mr. Stevens came by to pick me up. He drove a Cadillac Fleetwood, or maybe I should say he "piloted" the Cadillac, since it was more boat than car. I loaded my amplifier and bass in the trunk next to his keyboard, and there was still room for the five Men of Note and their wives, I thought.

The drive up to the club was pretty awkward; after all, what did I have in common with this gray-haired man in the Cadillac? He broke the silence and told me more about the gig, and inquired whether I had a chance to practice some of the music he had sent. He had given my band teacher a folder stuffed with bass parts for about a hundred old tunes ranging from "String of Pearls" to "Girl From Impanema," and I had a few days to look them over. They were pretty straightforward for an average bass player like me, so I wasn't too worried about figuring out my parts. I was just nervous about going to the Fort, and I had all kinds of images in my head.

The army was kind of an abstract thing for me growing up. I had seen the images of the Vietnam War on TV, and saw the men who had been prisoners of war coming home, kissing the ground when they walked down the stairs from the jetliners. I watched Bob Barker reunite military men with their wives in the staged ruses he would play on the Truth or Consequences show. I knew my father and my uncles had served in the military during World War II, but they never – and I mean never – talked about their experiences.

In my mind, I imagined arriving at the Fort, checking through a highly secured area to get to the barracks, and then moving on to the Officer's Club, where I imagined I would see starchy stiff men in medal-covered uniforms saluting each other. I was so naïve that I didn't know Fort Douglas had many years before ceased to be an active military post of the kind I imagined, and the Officer's Club was more of a historic building that had been used for military and non-military receptions for years. So I was a little disappointed when we walked in, and the hall was more like a school multi-purpose room filled with elderly men and women dressed in normal suits and dresses.

Saturday nights at the Fort were dance nights. Dinner was served on folding banquet tables, and after dinner, the tables were cleared away while the Men of Note took their seats at one end of the dance floor, in a little raised alcove that looked like it had been made for a five-piece band. Mr. Stevens introduced me to the other musicians, and they all gave me a warm "Welcome young man" and a handshake. I couldn't believe they were trusting me to sit in with them. They must have been together longer than I had been alive, I guessed. They were all about 40 years older than me, just like everyone else in the place.

While the emcee for the evening, a portly older gentleman, welcomed the capacity crowd of about a hundred, Mr. Stevens announced our first ten numbers. Literally, he called out the numbers on the sheet music in the order we were going to play them. When the emcee finished, Mr. Stevens welcomed everyone from his seated position behind the microphone, tickling the keyboard with a few chords as he spoke – a very cool cat. He introduced the band, and gave a special welcome to their newest guest bass player. He turned to me, whispered, "Here we go...", and counted off the first number, "In the Mood."

In my relatively brief life's experience, I had seen a few dances. Typically, the DJ, a former student who couldn't move on in life, spun the records while two or three couples danced. The rest of us hung around the punchbowl or sat on the rows of folding chairs lining the walls. Occasionally the numbers on the dance floor would reach double digits, but dances were more about thinking about dancing than actual dancing. And dancing, if you could really call it that, looked more like attempts to exorcise the demons from your partner through a series of leaps and wriggles that were rarely in time to the music.

So I was surprised, when we cranked up Glenn Miller, that *everyone* danced. Everyone. There weren't even chairs on the dance floor. The chairs were way back in the adjacent room. And dancing? This was the definition of dancing. Men led their wives to the dance floor, and they began lightly stepping in time to the music while others spun gracefully around the room. On "Tenderly," our saxophonist stood and sang, joined by many on the dance floor, "The summer breeze caressed the trees tenderly…."

We took a break after about an hour, and the band members moved to the bar. Mr. Stevens invited me to the bar with him, and offered me some orange juice the way he liked it. It was orange juice, with a touch of grenadine and ginger ale, with a maraschino cherry, a Shirley Temple, although I gratefully didn't know the name until later in life – I don't think my male ego could have taken knowing that the warm glow of this elixir had its origins with "Animal crackers in my soup." I felt grown up, sipping my orange juice in the bar with my fellow band members. They encouraged me and said I was doing a fine job, and we took our places for the second set.

The night passed too quickly, and at the end, we packed our things and Mr. Stevens handed me twenty-five dollars. I was surprised because I hadn't known this gig was a paying job, after all, I was doing this as a favor to my band teacher. I think I was the only one who didn't know that I was being paid. That summer, I played several more Saturday dances with the Men of Note, all at the Officer's Club, and I threw back countless sunset-looking Shirley Temples as I sat among these Men of Note.

The name suited them well. They were real musicians, and often they didn't need to have the music in front of them to remember their riffs. They were also real gentlemen who treated me with kindness and respect, although I felt so undeserving of it, being simply a young rookie among these seasoned performers. These Men of Note were veterans, businessmen, community leaders, and family men who merely moonlighted as musicians, not for money, but for the chance to go back in time every Saturday night to a time when things were simpler and when men were men.

As the gigs continued to come, I began spending less time watching my music and more time looking out at the crowd. Instead of a room full of retirees clearly past their prime, I imagined chiseled young men in dress uniform and tight-waisted women reveling in the peace they helped to achieve, fox trotting, waltzing, and swinging on behalf of those buddies who didn't make it. Sipping my Shirley Temple, watching these members of the greatest generation make their way off the dance floor, it hit me. This was sacred ground. .

4

VIDEO GAMES THAT DELIVERED

The video game industry has exploded in the last thirty years, with games moving from large consoles in public arcades to in-home systems, and from the simple two-dimensional lines of the original Pong game to fully rendered 3-D interactive environments. Given the achievements of the programming wizards and marketing executives who have built video gaming into a major industry, it is easy to forget its humble beginnings, and the ways we evolved along with the games we played.

The first game that I played was the black and white Pong game at our local bowling alley in the early seventies. It was something totally new, and we marveled at the way the ball would come off the paddle, a line controlled by one knob for each player. If you were lucky enough to bowl on a day when two Pong experts were playing, you might see them volley back and forth for minutes before someone lost a point.

Soon, a version of Pong was available for home use, and we were amazed that our large console TV could be converted to render the friendly blips of the game. My brother and I would stay up late at night playing back and forth, learning the new features that had been added, to curve the ball, or to shrink the size of the paddle to increase the challenge. Friends came by, and we were able to play doubles, increasing the appeal and choosing up sides like we were stepping on to the football field for a neighborhood battle.

A few years later, our local Safeway store had a new video game console at the front. It was called Space Invaders, and it quickly turned into the must-see game. Our school was about a ten minute walk from the Safeway, and if you left right at the lunch bell, you could make it to the store to watch – or better, play – the game for yourself.

Space Invaders presented a new summit to scale because it had something unique: levels. That meant that for your quarter, if you were a skilled player, you could stay there playing Space Invaders for several minutes, a half hour, or more. The geekiest kid, Alan Messner, became a hero when the word got around that he owned the high score and could play as long as he wanted to, defeating all levels of the game. I was never that good because I could see that it was going to take a significant investment for me to achieve something approaching Messner status, not only in the quarters that I would have to feed the machine, but also in the amount of time expended to improve my skills.

The other factor limiting my video game rise to fame was the audience. They just weren't with me. Just like any Broadway star, the Space Invaders video game hero was a performer, and would stay for encore after encore once the initial levels had been defeated. It was just showing off after a while, like Pavarotti holding that high note in the Nessun Dorma aria, "...Vin-ce-ro...vin-ce-ro...vin-ce-roooooooooooooooo – ohhhhhhhhhhh." Ah yes, level seven, and Alan steps back from the machine as if nodding to the conductor as he says, "Does anyone want to play my credits?" The consummate performance, as he turns the stage over to the next act, a decidedly less inspiring one.

A few years passed and the home Pong game had been dumped in the trash, replaced with a new Atari system that had a variety of games and levels. That Christmas, my eldest brother, who had been gone on a foreign study, returned home, and we sat there playing River Raid hour after hour. This is where I first came to understand the addictive qualities of video game play. Not having to drop in a quarter and falter in front of an audience, we were able to stay up late into the night, glued to the TV, practicing our bombing raids on the randomly generated fuel cells, depots, and ships.

I remember vividly that River Raid revealed a new phenomenon for me in video gaming, the evil dictator chortle. My brother first manifested this trait one very late night when I went into the family room and saw him, eyes transfixed on the screen, not breaking away to acknowledge my entrance into the room. He was maneuvering his bomber quickly up river creating mass havoc below, and he was laughing. But the laugh was emanating from somewhere deeper, more of a "heh-heh" than a "ha." It was like watching Jack Nicholson in The Shining, gazing straight ahead under the furrowed brow, drool oozing from the corners of his mouth as he types out page after page of "All work and no play makes Jack a dull boy." It was that same kind of evil gleefulness that had now possessed my brother and soon infected me as well.

Console games continued to advance, and arcades thrived, since they had the most advanced games. The audience factor still played out in the high score legends that were made in the poorly lit hangouts. Video game arcades had become the modern equivalent of the carhop drive-in of the fifties. Over there were the Pac-Man girls, and they were flanked by the Mortal Combat gang draped over the machine. In the back were the old school pinball wizards, mostly college guys who wanted everyone else to see the nuances of pushing a game to the limit without getting the "tilt" light.

Around this same time, I had met Annette Simpson. She was more of an old school arcade gamer, as I found out when we went to Disneyland. She asked if we could step into the arcade, and if she would have said, "would you like to drive me to Lover's Lane" I wouldn't have been happier. Wow, a girl who was into video games. Cool! As we stepped inside, I wondered where she would gravitate. She passed the boxing, the race cars – good, just keep going, I thought – and past a Ms. Pac-Man as she made her way to the back, to an older Centipedes machine.

Centipedes had been on my list of favorite games for a while, and when I was working at the local mall, I would slip over to the arcade on my lunch breaks and pop a couple of quarters in the Centipedes, and later, Millipedes, game. To actually meet someone who liked playing Centipedes was a rare find, like two star-crossed lovers touching hands as they reached for the roller ball.

Annette tore up the Centipedes game, earning extra lives and blowing through all the levels as I struggled to keep up. Rather than feeling defeated or emasculated by her performance, I had the deepest admiration, almost reverence, for her. Centipedes incorporated all the elements of the addictive game: good destructive laser blasting noise, a variety of challenges that seemed to exponentially stack up against the player, and best of all, a rolling ball that put the player's reflexes to the test against the onslaught of descending centipedes, sprouting mushrooms, and threatening spiders. This final characteristic may have been the sole basis for my loving Centipedes so much (see The Spider in My Metro).

While it's true that video game technology has far surpassed the days of Pong and Centipedes, there have been few advances in the ways we play. Arcades are still out there, and the most advanced games have become 3-D experiences incorporating actual motion and virtual reality into the game, something approaching a low-grade amusement park ride. But the same evil dictator chortle is there, whether at the arcade or at home with the latest systems. The weaponry has advanced, but not the performance.

I never graduated to the new home systems, or the range of games that came with them because I never saw the payoff of having to learn the new controls. The latest home systems create beautifully rendered environments for game play, but knowing that there are practically unlimited levels, and that people can buy cheat codes to advance more quickly kind of takes away the incentive for me. Perhaps someday new game systems will draw me back in, but until the evil chortle, the public performance, and the aura of arcade love can be improved, I'm staying on the sidelines, content to watch the pinball wizards and play an old Centipedes game whenever I pass one.

5

YELLOW JOURNALISM – MOVE THOSE PAPERS!

My amateur career in journalism started back in junior high school, when I was asked to write several articles for the Maverick newsletter. There was nothing to distinguish it as a maverick publication in reality, and the biting editorials usually dealt with such mundane topics as unsightly locker graffiti, the eradication of bullying, and the merits of eating a healthy meal (in the school cafeteria?!). It was the definition of selling out to The Man.

I sought personal exile from the press corps in high school until one day in my junior year when John Youngblood, the managing editor, approached me about doing a recipe review. Why he thought I was the right guy to enlighten the readers of the Thunderbolt student paper about all things culinary I'll never know because I never asked. I was so flattered that I just said yes, and for the next two years, I wrote a column entitled Rob's Recipe Review. I highlighted recipes that I thought students might like to make, like chocolate covered frozen bananas or English muffin pizzas, and then made up stories and editorial comments to bring a lighter tone to the writing.

Rob's Recipe Review taught me some very important lessons about the world of journalism. First, I learned that journalists could become celebrity figures. After my first recipe appeared, several students came up to me in the hall and said they read it and it made them laugh. I imagined my reviews taped up in school lockers and lunch conversations that focused on my latest recipe:

"Hey Susie, did you catch this week's recipe?"

"Like, ya…English muffin pizzas. Rob's a genius in the kitchen. I'll bet you could never be a real cook like *him*."

"Could so."

"All the girls are asking who he's going to invite to the prom. I wonder if he would make no-bake peanut butter cookies…mmm…."

"Susie? Susie! Are you listening to me?!"

The second lesson I learned was that feature writing really moved the papers, not the news. Who wanted to know about the goings on in student government? Please! They wanted to know what concerts to see, what movies were hot, and what new recipes they could make afterwards (this is what I told myself). In serious journalism the mantra was *if it bleeds, it leads*; but for high school papers the mantra might have been *hard news, big snooze*.

The third lesson I learned was perhaps more important. No writer is truly free to express his artistic gifts as long as there was editorial oversight coming from The Man. In one of my early recipes I wrote *metaphorically* about castrating a cat. I don't think I really understood the meaning of castration, but it sounded like torture, and it had to go in (for more on this, see Cat Hatred). It was then that I was invited up to the desk of Mr. James Flynn, the school newspaper advisor.

"Rob, I was reading your latest review…"

"Yes, Mr. Flynn?"

"In this piece you talk about castrating a cat…"

"Yes, that's right, Mr. Flynn."

"Do you really mean *castrate*?" (This last word was said in a whisper so as not to disturb the sensibilities of the other journalists working at their desks.)

"Sure, but it's all in fun…and it's really more of a metaphor than – "

"Well, I'm sorry, but you're going to have to change the word. How about *tease* or even *terrify*?"

"Well, I think castrate is more extreme, and it's funnier."

It was then that Mr. Flynn looked me in the eye and said something I'll never forget. He said that the school paper was funded by the Administration (I could see where this was going), and that the Administration would not allow the paper to publish anything that it considered of questionable taste. Unfortunately, I would have to change the word. I caved, but I vowed to myself that one day I would have journalistic control to write the words the way I wanted to write them.

Three years later, I found myself sitting at the Managing Editor's desk of the local technical college's newspaper, Points West. I had contributed articles on what the state legislature was doing to change this little trade school to a true community college, and I had written a biting editorial about campus police overstepping their bounds (see Handcuffed By the Man). But I sat there week after week laying out the wax-coated galley proofs, piecing together the columns of text and the rare advertisement, and I thought there had to be a way to move more of these papers.

Each week as we distributed the latest edition and collected what remained of the previous week's run, we noticed that readership was in decline. I had to increase demand for the product if for no other reason than saving the editorial staff from having to collect so many un-read papers. It was demoralizing.

Late one afternoon, when the staff had gone home and the office was quiet, I hatched a scheme working with the head of student public relations, my future wife. It was true that the news staff had occasionally used journalistic tricks of the trade, like throwing out a rhetorical question to the staff and then citing in the article, "other people agree that...." But this new endeavor would take these innocent white-washings to a deeper shade of yellow journalism. We would create a new column called Letters to Lola, our own kind of Dear Abby, and we could concoct some controversial letters from students (me) that Lola (my wife's pseudonym) would answer. If things got ugly, I could simply take the position that the newspaper would never reveal the real "Lola" out of concern for journalistic integrity to protect its sources.

For the next several weeks, Letters to Lola grabbed the headlines, and from the Automotive Trades building to the Administrative Offices, the campus buzzed. The first few letters to Lola were co-authored rants by one female Data Processing "student" against the leering eyes of the Construction Trades guys and the Business school posers. The tone was perfect. We had essentially created a public forum for legitimate debate and then mocked the system by firing off with one name-calling artillery strike after another.

The papers not only flew off the distribution racks, we had students walking over to the student offices requesting additional copies after we ran out. Oh, this was the journalistic equivalent of the O.J. trial. Real students were beginning to write in to the paper denouncing the Lola articles, and some of the letters were signed by multiple authors or self-proclaimed representatives of these smeared groups. It was great. Advertising revenues were up (okay, from the double figures to the triple figures, but they were up nonetheless).

But best of all, I actually had the opportunity to use my editorial last line of defense on one particularly upset student. It was around early afternoon one day when the head of the on-campus veteran's organization stepped into my office demanding to know who Lola was, and asking for an apology to all veterans who had been attacked in a recent article. He was really steamed. I think one of the letters may have poked fun at their dress habits or hairstyles.

I had nothing against veterans, and the paper had been a proponent of the veterans group for ages, providing free advertising and publicity for their campus events whenever they asked. This was more about the right to sling mud in all directions, a kind of equal opportunity attack on all campus groups, official and unofficial; and it was simply the veterans' turn. I thought this ex-Army guy was going to punch me right in the face when I said, "I'm sorry, but it's the paper's position that we won't reveal Lola's identity." He didn't.

As the weeks rolled on, and we approached the end of another academic year, the campus conspiracy had caused all kinds of hate mail for Lola, and I was being pressured by The Man again to tone down the articles or to remove them completely. It had worked. We had awakened the campus from its own boredom, ignited new vitality into campus groups, and put The Man on notice. It was time to let Letters to Lola take a final bow.

The opportunity came when I was asked to make a speech at the campus awards dinner. I was named as the school's outstanding English student of the year – high praise indeed, coming from a *trade* school. I think I was the only student on campus who had attended every English course offered by the school, so I was the winner more for volume attended than for literary contribution. When I rose to the microphone, I gave my best *mea culpa*, acknowledging to the administration, to the editorial staff, and to all students that indeed Lola had been a ruse. To alleviate some of the sting, I also announced that I was engaged to marry Lola, and introduced my fiancé right there on the spot.

I had risen to the peak of my journalistic career, and now it was time to retire. I had been tainted by this form of journalism, yellowed like the nicotine stains on a smoker's fingers, and I had to quit the news business cold turkey, or else accept a new path towards becoming the future contributing editor to the National Enquirer or Star. In the years since, I have come to appreciate truly great journalism, and editorial opinions that present credible arguments that attempt first to *inform* public opinion. I have also joked with "Lola" about the way we really pulled one over on the student body back then, and in the same moment wondered whether we were being played by someone on a news staff or an editorial board of one of the national news outlets – ah, journalistic irony!

6

THE GUY BEHIND THE SCENES

Every summer our church, and others in the area, used to put together short musical skits and perform them in each others' church buildings – and they were judged (yes, I suppose we violated the "judge not lest ye be judged" deal) for best costumes, best music, best actor/actress, and best scenery. To qualify for the grand prize, you also had to stay within your assigned budget and have a high percentage of involvement from those who were in your congregation.

My mother, who could recall just about any popular hit in her lifetime, was the music director and accompanist, and I joined her on my string bass. She was a gifted accompanist who could transpose musical keys on the fly to match the limited vocal range of the performers, and I learned to follow her lead. It was better than acting or working on scenery and costumes.

One particular year I remember that expectations were very high. We had taken the top award the year before, and we were setting our sights on a repeat performance. As we were getting down to the final rehearsals, the costumes and scenery started to show up. Everyone on stage had costumes, and so did the choir just off stage. Our musical was a musical parody based on "Heaven Can Wait"; but ours was called "Heaven Can't Wait," which meant we had lots of cloud scenery hiding concourses of angels in winged costumes. It was an act of divine providence that all this stuff started showing up. Who was responsible? Nobody saw him, but he was there. It was Lynn, the man behind the scenes, literally.

While we were showing up for our weekly or twice-weekly rehearsals, feeling good about our commitment to the show and expecting soon to see Broadway scouts roaming the hallways, Lynn was out making things happen. He had a crew building scenery headed by a boy and his father who never went to church, but who seemed genuinely pleased to be able to participate through their craftsmanship. Lynn had also followed up with the heads of the women's organization to make sure they were circulating the angel costume patterns. If extra fabric was needed, he went to work to find fabric that could be donated or priced at a cut rate, so as not to exceed the budget. He knew everyone, and was a master at calling in favors and dealing to get what we needed and do everything within the guidelines.

Lynn was also the advisor for the young men in our congregation, so I got to know him well in those teenage years, and I began to see just what this man accomplished from behind the scenes. The scout troop needed to raise money, so he came up with a plan to collect newspapers all year, store them in a friend's unused shed, and sell them for recycling in the middle of winter when the buying price peaked. He would drive us boys around the neighborhood every month, collecting newspapers, and it worked – the scouts got the money they needed.

He was like the back-up man in baseball, always there in case someone else dropped the ball or missed an assignment. He was the guy setting up chairs without being asked or arranging lawn care for widows in our church. He was the guy with the truck who would volunteer to haul furniture when someone moved in or out of the neighborhood. In meetings, when the call would go out for volunteers, he was always first to volunteer without hesitation or first looking around for someone else to take the lead. He was active on the school board for many years, and through that service was instrumental not just in creating better policies, but in finding individuals who needed help and providing that help himself, rather than passing the responsibility to others.

Lynn was a great example in my life, and thanks to him, I was able to see some of the great wonders of nature, like Havasu Falls in the Grand Canyon, and the wilderness areas of the Uintah Mountains in eastern Utah. Yes, he was the man who rustled horses from a few old friends so that a bunch of young men could take a weeklong horseback trek into the wilderness. Everyone trusted him, from scout parent to horse owner.

He showed a personal interest in each person he met, and he seemed to know everyone. Wherever we went, he would take time to strike up a conversation to make some connection, even if it was someone behind the counter at a fast food place. He was the surveillance camera in the neighborhood. He seemed to track who was sick, who was having a tough time, and he knew all the gossip (although you never heard him spread it). I remember showing up at church one day and Lynn asked me how things were going between Joanne and me. What? He had seen us talking on the corner, and had found out her name from his daughter. He was everywhere.

I lost track of Lynn many years ago, after moving from the neighborhood; but I have many fond memories of this man who was always there to see that the right things got done. I have tried to follow his example, and when assignments are made, or when the call goes out for volunteers, I think of Lynn and find my hand instinctively going up – the Lynn reflex.

In my life I have seen great acts of service that are hailed in newspapers and on TV. A donor gives a big check to a favorite charity, an outspoken activist raises awareness for some issue, or the mayor hands the keys of the city to a local professional sports star. These are all very public, and perhaps worthy, acknowledgements of service rendered. But give me ten, fifty, or a hundred men, and women, behind the scenes, and they will have accomplished far more in their quiet contributions than those clamoring for the camera.

How do you count the contribution of a caring nurse who eases the physical pain and emotional suffering inherent in that profession? What is the downstream payback for one teacher who inspires a generation? How do you calculate the return on investment for a timely visit to a neighbor whose marriage is suffering, or who is mourning a loss?

It is often too easy these days to sit back and look at the time we spend as a series of work and leisure activities. What about service? Where does that fit?

Take a page out of Lynn's book, and go find somewhere to serve, and just start doing it. Find a need and fill it. If you need an organization to provide some impetus, join a local charity or volunteer group. Better still, look around, be aware of the needs nearest to you, and give of yourself. Help carry in groceries for a neighbor. Go shovel the snow out of someone else's driveway. Help the young mom on the airplane with the crying kids. Offer to take care of a friend's dog while he's out of town. Help a fellow student who is struggling in a subject that comes easy to you. Stay behind and clean up after a community event instead of rushing home.

Finally, once you've helped fix that flat tire and worked the bake sale, keep it to yourself. *Stay* behind the scenes. Those Lynns in your life who were always there for you are probably still watching.

7

OF FIELD MICE AND MEN

The call went out on a Sunday afternoon that Reid Peterson needed help. The fall weather had taken a decidedly colder and wetter turn before Reid could get all the hay bales out of his field. If he didn't get the hay in soon, it would probably have to stay until spring, and the likelihood of recovering any of it to feed his stable of horses was diminishing rapidly. It had to be gathered up and hauled to the barn, and he needed a lot of strong backs to get it done.

Volunteering is always easier when the person who needs help:
a)   has a reputation for helping others
b)   has a legitimate need, and
c)   is reluctant to ask for help and usually does for him-/herself

This was the case with Reid. He had struggled to put food on the table for years, but he and his wife Debbie had found a way to adopt six kids, since they had been unable to have any of their own. They had adopted older children from tough backgrounds and with different ethnicities; but they put them to work on the farm, helping with the horses and attending church as part of the routine. He suffered a heart attack a couple of years earlier, and with the heavy work demands, had been back to the hospital with other related medical emergencies since then. Reid and Debbie were behind-the-scenes people, stepping away from the spotlight, and giving quiet service to others in the community.

Others must have felt as I did about Reid and Debbie, because when I made the long drive out to the Peterson farm, expecting to be one of a handful of guys to help out, there were probably a dozen men gathered together, and many of them had brought their sons along. It was a cold morning, probably in the forties, and a light drizzle was in the air, as if to mock the volunteers, *Are you sure you want to do this?*

We split into two teams. One team had a truck, and the other team had a tractor pulling a wagon; and as they slowly drove along the empty furrows of the field, punctuated here and there with hay bales, two of us would haul the bales into the truck or wagon. It seemed like a reasonable way to go about it, and we set right to work.

On a dry day, the hay bales would have probably weighed in at around seventy or eighty pounds each; but having soaked in the rain for at least a couple of days, each one was double or triple that weight. I stepped up to the first bale and, grabbing the twine that bound it together, gave a tug. It didn't move. I pulled again, and this time the twine broke. This was going to be a long day. With four of us, one on each corner, we lifted it to the bed of the truck. One down.

After a few more bales, we determined that two of us, lifting on either end of the bale, applying a steady force to the middle, could raise it without breaking the twine, and one person could help us in the middle of the bale while the other helped from inside the truck. Just as we bent down and gave a lift on the next bale, several field mice ran from underneath it, scurrying in all directions, and I jumped back from the hay bale at the shock of seeing the mice. Now it was as if the mice were mocking us, *You should have stayed home.*

It was around that point that the mood began to change. The mice had created a stir in the group, and a few of them were laughing at my expense – although I was shocked because I hadn't expected to see mice, not that I was *afraid* of the mice. That no one believed my story didn't concern me in the least, and we all began laughing at the sight of more mice running from hay bales, counting them as we exposed their warm hiding spots.

As we worked, we started to sweat, and we had to take off our outer coats to combat the heat we were generating. The younger boys were having fun jumping in and out of the truck, and directing the older ones in a reversal of authority, kind of our farm version of *Lord of the Flies*. We poked fun, pushing ourselves physically, and counting the mice.

As we went along, we recounted stories of service rendered in the past.

There was the Timpson move, where we had to haul a piano from the second story down an outside staircase. We had to remove the handrail in order to position the piano just right for the move, and the thing had nearly fallen off the balcony. Another piano incident had occurred at the Miller move, when the guys pushing the piano through a doorway had miscalculated, and took out part of the doorjamb.

Each man there had a piano story, it seemed. The Jameson move required us to roll an antique upright piano (the owners said it was antique, but it was just a big old, beat up piano that weighed a ton) out to the patio and up the ramp to the parked U-Haul. The elder Mr. Jameson wanted to get a running start in order to get the piano up the ramp without stalling mid-ramp and risking a collapse. It actually worked, and we only lost a caster off the piano.

As we shared stories and laughed, the drizzle stopped, and I could have sworn that those hay bales got lighter. No one ran out of energy, no one took a break, and it seemed that we were moving much faster after several hours of work than at the beginning. Then we had our own piano moment. The truck got bogged down in the mud as we got to the lower part of the field. We called the other team over to help us unload the hay bales, and then with a bunch of us pushing from the back, and the tractor pulling from the front, we unstuck the truck, with several of us catching the proverbial "mud in your eye" from the rear wheel spray.

We finished the work and went back to the barn, where Debbie had brought out a pot of hot chocolate and some doughnuts. I surveyed the wearied crew. There they stood, most of them soaking wet, with shoes and boots caked with mud, drenched by the rain and sweat...and they were smiling. How was that possible? The early morning rain, the mice, the mud – none of it had dampened their spirits, and perhaps it had only lifted them more.

Such is the payment of service from the heart. Service always pays off in such ways:
- a feeling of brotherhood (or sisterhood) towards the person being served
- reassurance that such things are possible, and a softening of cynicism about the state of the world
- comfort in knowing that you may be qualifying yourself for such help in the future (in accordance with item "a" under the terms of volunteering above)

I have seen the many ways men are portrayed by the popular media of our day. We are led to believe that real men are – or should be – beer guzzling sports fanatics or metrosexual eunuchs seeking smoother skin. The buffoons characterized in popular TV commercials and situation comedies lower the expectations of what it means to be a man in our society. But I have seen real men in the faces of teens and patriarchs who gutted out a rain-soaked act of kindness for a neighbor. These are my role models, my standard by which I measure other so-called men. I take comfort in knowing that the real men will be there, ready to pitch in, when the going gets tough. And I will ask to join them.

8

NORMA AND ME – FULL STEAM AHEAD

First jobs are often our first opportunity to declare our independence, and we bring home that paycheck with pride, knowing that we are on the path to one day leaving mom and dad and providing for our own wants and needs. Often, these first jobs are among the shortest in duration, some lasting just a few weeks or months as we take a break from school or save for some longed-for treasure in the discount store.

My first job was working at a warehouse facility for a chain of retail clothing stores managed by my father and uncles. I had been to the warehouse many times with my brothers. On Saturdays, when the warehouse was closed, we would go there with my dad and get into all kinds of mischief in the back rooms while he worked in his office up front. Our favorite pastime was gathering up all the empty boxes and stacking them at one end of the receiving dock. One of us would stand "surfer-style" on a flat-bed cart for transporting merchandise, and the other would push the cart, speeding across the shiny cement floor while the surfer launched himself into the pile of boxes.

I was looking forward to working at the warehouse, although I figured that box surfing might not continue once I began working there. Little had they known that they could have said, "Work here, and for every eight hour shift you will be entitled to three box surfing runs," and that would have been enough. Maybe if work were more like play, we could pay our workers less and still keep turnover low, instead of trying to pay people more to shackle them to the organization, to convince them to give up things that they consider valuable beyond the work alone.

I didn't know what my job would be at the warehouse, but upon arrival, my dad said that he would start me on the steamer with Norma. He took me to the corner of the warehouse and showed me the big green steam press, a closet-sized chamber where unboxed and hung clothing shipments were fed through in a continuous line to steam out the wrinkles. Steam was whisping from all four sides, as my father introduced me to Norma. I couldn't tell anyone was there, behind the machine, but there she stood, a regal-looking woman with white hair and a grandmother's eyes. She was wearing a blue smock, and, leaning across the table to shake my hand, she welcomed me with a smile.

My training lasted about ten minutes as Norma showed me how to take the empty hanger out of the box, hang up the clothing, and send it through the steamer. She was careful to note the way I was hanging the clothing, to make sure I wasn't stretching the collars. It was from Norma that I learned how to hang a shirt that was already buttoned when it left the factory, by inserting the hanger completely through the neckline, and then easing the shoulders into place.

Norma told me that on a good day one person working on the steamer could process about fifteen hundred articles of clothing, but she said that with my help, we could probably double the rate for our steamer. It had a counter on it that clicked every time an item passed through, so we were able to track our progress. She would call off the numbers to me throughout the morning, "Okay, we're at five hundred...now a thousand...we might be able to hit fifteen hundred by lunchtime if we keep it up."

By lunchtime we had cleared sixteen hundred, with a whole afternoon to go. Since we had only really been working for about three hours, we could easily hit the three thousand goal by the time our shift ended. My dad came and got me for lunch, and we went to the cafeteria together, and I told him all about what Norma and I had accomplished so far. He seemed pleased, and told me to keep it up.

Returning to the steamer after lunch, Norma and I moved even faster. I wasn't slowing her down anymore, having to ask where to get more hangers or how to do the paperwork to process more merchandise sitting in the dock area. She was happy to have someone to lift the heavy boxes onto the conveyor, and to transfer the steamed garments to the sorting area. We slowed a bit when we got to several boxes of lingerie that was difficult to hang; but we picked up speed when the men's shirts were back. "Okay, we're at two thousand two hundred," Norma said when we took our afternoon break. The steamer was starting to make things uncomfortably warm as we closed out our shift with a final flurry, but we finished the day at just over three thousand two hundred pieces of clothing.

I felt like big John Henry defeating his steam machine to poke through the tunnel he had carved through the mountain. My big green steamer sat there looking satiated from the day's feeding. We did it. We passed three thousand. Norma congratulated me and said we worked well together. I was so proud. I had done something that I didn't know anything about when I woke up that morning, and by the end of the day we had beaten the record.

Unfortunately, the next morning, when I reported to the warehouse, the head of Personnel came back to the steamer to tell me that due to my young age and labor laws preventing child labor, I would not be able to work on the steamer effective immediately. I was so disappointed. I was looking forward to breaking new records with Norma, and then going on to achieve greatness in the warehouse operation. I had imagined people passing me and commenting under their breath, "Do you know who *that* is? That's the boy who beat the record on the steamer!"

Despite my one-day stint as a professional steam lineman, I had learned some valuable lessons that stuck with me:

- Work is fun when you get to experience something new and fresh
- Enjoy the people you work with, and try to learn as much as you can from them
- Set high goals so that when they are achieved you can look back down the road you just traveled and take pride in the sacrifice it took to get there
- Periodically measure what you are achieving, rather than waiting until the end – it can be the motivation to push you over the top
- Find ways to improve your own productivity through small changes (like moving the hanger box closer to the clothing box to improve speed)
- You can set all the production records you want, but if you violate government regulations that shut you down, the price isn't worth the victory

From this auspicious beginning, I was transferred to the landscape crew at the warehouse. In fact, I *was* the landscape crew, and it was an ignoble fall from the big green steamer to brooms and shovels. I now worked for the head of maintenance, Bruce; and I soon learned more lessons about the nature of work and one's relative importance in the wide universe of work (see Dispensable You).

9

POE IN THE AFTERNOON

In the last few years if you have had kids or grandkids in the public school system you have noticed that elementary school classrooms have become more alike in their steady diet of political correctness. Christopher Columbus was run out of town over Native American guilt. Martin Luther King is the new Lincoln. The earth is dying, so write on both sides of the paper before you turn it in. All kids are gifted, all are creative, and all have the right to win awards for their attempts at art, even if the poetry stinks, the drawing is ordinary, and the musical expression is vapid. If recess is allowed, it is just for a few minutes a day, so the little ones can develop social skills. In other cases recess is excused away because the camp commandant doesn't need the injuries ruining another afternoon of administrating – and who needs the additional inconvenience of breaking up fights, or the covering the mounting costs of playground balls and hopscotch paint? After all, that extra ten minutes of copying notes off the board could spark the intellectual Big Bang for the next Einstein. Kids are so incredibly brilliant that teachers no longer lead parent-teacher conferences; it's up to the kids to render their professional teaching opinions in something called "student-led conferences."

"So Bobby, what did you do this quarter," Mom says.
"As you can see here, I have a firm grasp of all the technical aspects of my writing. I just need to develop my inner voice," Bobby says.

In many schools, teachers are still called "Mr." or "Ms." (You can't use "Miss" anymore, didn't you get the memo?), but the distance between student and teacher has narrowed to this last formality. Teachers are expected to be friends with students, mere guides along a path of learning, handing out papers, making corrections, and managing the classroom. Learning? Discovery? Those were once very quaint ideas, and students may find the need for such things in their own paths of learning one day before graduation. But right now, we need to know all there is to now on the subject of saving the whales, overcoming the spread of AIDS in Africa, or stopping the polar ice caps from melting, now that's what *really* matters.

It is against this backdrop that I want to return to a classroom of fifth and sixth graders. We were mixed, I suppose, because they had extra kids they didn't know what to do with, so they put us together and gave us to Mr. Chase. Mr. Sidney Chase was about six foot seven inches tall, a great red-headed giant who cast a long shadow on the playground. He had an entourage that followed him on the playground just to see what he had to talk about as he walked the grounds. Sometimes the talk of current events was temporarily halted while Mr. Chase stopped a fight from breaking out or booted a stray playground ball back to its field of origin. Perhaps some hiding under the folds of Mr. Chase's tweed overcoat were simply there for protection, figuring that the bullies would stay away, not only during recess, but also once kids returned to class. Protection by association was a nice preventive draw for Mr. Chase.

I had Mr. Chase for both the fifth and sixth grade, and I really loved him. He was bigger than life to me, not only in stature, but in his intellectual capabilities. He was a disciplined man who also demanded discipline from his students. Class was usually quiet, but it was common for students to be lined up at Mr. Chase's desk asking for special help. He reciprocated with thorough explanations and encouragement to do better. If someone like Kevin Jameson was acting up, Mr. Chase, with his bullhorn voice would call, "Kevin...!" and it shook the tables. I could just imagine little Kevin's bony knees knocking under his desk, trembling with fear.

Mr. Chase had a simple disciplinary system based on rewards. He never made one student write a hundred times on the chalkboard. I don't recall him ever sending a student to the principal's office, and I don't really remember him being genuinely cross with a student. We students would work hard during the day, many of us moving ahead to future lessons to get as much completed as possible.

What was his secret? Was it intimidation? No. It was Poe. Mr. Chase would promise to tell us stories from Edgar Allan Poe.

Mr. Chase was a masterful storyteller. He was good at reading stories, and he dutifully sat on his stool in front of the class and read books like *The Black Stallion* series to us to help us check our reading comprehension. He would read, and then pause to ask questions about what he had just read. Following this simple method, we learned not only to love the books he read to us, but also how to ask questions about our own reading, a wonderful meta-cognitive technique that I learned years later when I was studying to become a teacher.

Mr. Chase was a good story reader, but he was the penultimate story*teller*. What was the difference? When Mr. Chase told a story, he never sat down. He never read, except briefly just to keep himself on track with the events in the story, and as a result he would look us straight in the eye for effect. His voice echoed off the tiled floors and walls as it would rise and fall with the action. We could tell something awful was about to happen when he would dramatically pick up the pace or diminish to a whisper, or he would use his voice to startle someone who wasn't paying attention (although this was rare).

Fridays were usually Edgar Allan Poe opportunities, but we could only earn a story by completing our work during the week and by acting as good citizens. By giving or taking away Poe, Mr. Chase created a dynamic in the classroom that controlled negative behavior, because no one wanted to be the one responsible for the loss of Poe, and peer pressure controlled the troublemakers who were silenced by the overwhelming majority who wanted to hear the twisted tales from our own oracle.

I have often wondered what would the school administrators of today's public education system say if one of their teachers was in the habit of telling scary stories to his students. And Poe, it was commonly believed, was a habitual opium user and alcoholic. Administrators probably wouldn't have a problem with that so much if it were in the pursuit of creativity, but the graphic and grizzly nature of Poe's stories to anyone familiar with them would at least raise the ire of some in the babysitter's club of teachers today.

On Friday afternoons we would sit there, like scouts around a campfire, while Mr. Chase would relate in detail the murder-mutilation in *The Tell-Tale Heart*; the gore of reanimated flesh in *The Monkey's Paw*; the strength with which the throat and sinews of the neck were nearly severed in *The Murders in the Rue Morgue*; or the gleefulness with which the sadistic author places the final brick in the *Cask of the Amontillado*. Often, particularly for the longer tales, like *The Masque of the Red Death* or *The Fall of the House of Usher*, the story would be told over two Fridays, heightening the anticipation during the week.

I'm not sure whether this type of storytelling goes on today in any of the school districts, although I doubt that it is, not only because of the fear of reprisals from parents or school boards, but because I suspect that today's teachers would find the subject matter objectionable and that the literary vernacular with which Poe constructed his art would be too far above the abbreviated textiness of today's student. Or would they find it as compelling as the preceding generation? Maybe *literature* is that which worthily survives such tests.

Here's my challenge to educators. Instead of rewarding idiocy and fawning over mediocrity, provide a literary bar high enough to stretch the imaginations of the truly gifted or the merely curious. Help them aspire to *be* great, not just to *feel* great.

10

INTROVERTS UNITE!

I would like to say a few words on behalf of a crowd who rarely gets attention. Chances are, if you're reading this, instead of talking on the phone, having lunch with friends at a coffee shop, or meeting buddies at the local bar, you're one of us. If you are drained by the mere thought of small talk, chit chat, or friendly banter, you're one of us. Welcome to the club: you're an introvert.

For those who belong to our club, a fairly loose affiliation that none of its members will openly acknowledge, I would like to offer a few words of comfort and encouragement. For those who worry that this association is a front for some conspiratorial force rising in the world, I would like to offer a few words of enlightenment and elucidation.

We introverts don't spend a lot of time running on with the mouth, but we have a lot to say to you of the extroverted clan. True, we may not want to blurt it out; we may not want to risk damaging our shallow relationship; and we may not have a good grasp of empty glib phrases with which to meet you on common ground. So I will ask you on behalf of my introverted brothers and sisters, to bear with me as I describe a few things that really bother us, as well as a few recommendations on how to cope with our silence.

(If you find yourself growing anxious at the thought of reading on, without talking to someone about it first, please excuse yourself, call a friend, and then come back to reading in a few minutes.)

First, it might be helpful to begin with a common point of reference, a persona – or perhaps a caricature – that typifies the extrovert model member: the used car salesman.

Seen in his natural environment, this extrovert exemplar uses a variety of techniques to coax out conversation or elicit engagement. As a way of illustrating where the attempts might fall short, and why we introverts collectively roll our eyes at you, allow me to introduce a few simple situational tips for starting up with an introvert.

Extroverted Greetings

For example, the call of the extrovert might sound something like this:

"Hey Buddy…(also, Sport, Guy, or Man)!" or "Hun, Love or Sweetie" for females of the genus extrovertus. These greetings are often shouted across the room at a decibel level better equipped for a crowded convention hall rather than the hallway or the quiet office. "I'm Larry (or Rick, Terry, or Billy). What's your name?"

To an introvert, we hear the final question as the equivalent of throwing your hands in the air after failing to guess our correct name. It also puts us on our guard to have someone asking our name so early on. We grow suspicious, like being the recipient of a telemarketing call, worried that this is an "approach" for a longer conversation. Instead, try just diving right in to the conversation, and we'll let you know whether we are comfortable exchanging pleasantries and contact information later.

Also, this greeting doesn't have to be shouted in your hail-fellow-well-met way, from across the parking lot. We introverts will wait for you to walk the distance to get to us. If we are walking away from you, it's because you looked like you were about to speak, and we were worried about the delays that might be caused by stopping to chat. If we are shopping for a car, and we are not making eye contact, it should be a signal for you: we also don't want to make *vocal* contact. Also, when you introduce yourself with some equivalent of, "my friends call me Bob (or Sammy, Skip, or Sharkie)" this is useless information to us. We *aren't* your friend, and we don't want to know your friends who call you that. We really don't. Remember, we're not buying *you*; we're buying a car, something that we will invest a great deal of time and money in, once we have had a chance to see it, touch it, and drive it. Stop interrupting us in this quest.

Other forms of greeting are more intrusive and annoying, such as the insincere hug or kiss. We are not in Europe, and we have to think about where your extroverted lips have been, so please stop, even if you're just smooching the air by our ears.

Extroverted Rapport Building

Once the extrovert and his silent partner have moved past the awkwardness of the greeting, the extrovert makes the attempt to build rapport:

"That's a fine jacket (or hat, sweater, tie, hairdo, baby, surgical scar or tattoo) you've got there."

We introverts generally want to be left alone, and we don't want to have *parts* of us or our extended family invited into this conversation. We know what you're looking for. You're looking for a story – an *in* – to get to us thinking that if we respond with something like "Oh, I got this jacket from my trip to Durango," you might say, "Oh, I've been to Durango too." Of course, when we respond to your inquiry about our lovely baby with, "Yes, his name is Ernest Theophilus Xavier, *the third*," you are going to be hard-pressed to meet us halfway. Or when you comment on our rather ordinary sweater with "Now *that's* a great sweater," we simply know it's not true. As introverts, we know we're a bit plain, and we're comfortable.

Other forms of rapport building occur while waiting in line, such as, "You look all dressed up, what, are you goin' to a funeral?" tend to suck the life from us. If we were, we wouldn't tell you. And what business is it of yours? Just wait there quietly, okay? Also, describing the food that we're eating is also in poor taste, so when you run into us at the local dining establishment, you don't have to say, "I had the fajitas too, they were great, weren't they?" We don't care about *your* meal, and we don't want you to get so excited about our meal that your spittle ends up landing in it. Comments about what we drive, what we read, what we listen to, or what we are working on is all out of bounds. Stop looking over our shoulders. If you are genuinely interested in these things, try a little softer approach, like, "I'm just naturally nosey, and I can't help myself. Do you mind if I ask you a few meaningless questions?" just so we know where you're coming from.

Extroverted Probing

Returning to our used car salesman prototypical extrovert, often the attempt is made to take the conversation to a deeper level through probing questions:

"So what are you in the market for today? How much do you want to spend?"

To an introvert, the answer seems quite obvious – we are at a used car lot, and you sell used cars. We are in the market for a used car. How much we want to spend is exactly zero, since you're asking – we really would – but since that's unlikely, how about you just hold off for a few minutes before your probing proboscis sniffs out more details. If we are walking towards something, like a used BMW, that's *probably* what we're interested in, and we are going to be willing to spend what we think a used BMW should cost. Speaking for other introverts, we know that we are asking you to read a bit more from the context of the situation, so if you feel the need to seek confirmation, just ask us something like, "I can see that you are looking at this very expensive BMW. Is that what you are interested in today?"

"Why yes, it is. Could you tell me more about this automobile?" See, we'll be very civil.

Probing done poorly can occasionally make even the most well-insulated introvert ignite in an extroverted rage, so use caution if you are a food server and you ask us if we want to hear the specials of the day, for example. Is there any possibility that we will say no, or that you aren't going to tell us anyway? Just say it, "Our special today is a scintillating veal cutlet cradled in sautéed spinach greens with a hint of saffron. I'll leave you alone now, and I'll be back for your order." Perfect. Leave us alone. Now we're getting somewhere.

Probing comments about the weather, while it must ease some tension you feel, are hugely unhelpful to we sentient introverts. When you say, "Sure is warm (or humid, sticky, desert-like or blistering) out there, isn't it?" we would be more than happy to confirm your uncertainty if you are unable to see or feel for yourself what are the present weather conditions. However, if your intent is simply to pass your time and annoy us, please refrain, or try texting your comments to yourself.

Extroverted Posturing

There are times when your society intends to bring us to some sort of conclusion, an enticement to close the deal, against which we might bristle. In the case of our model salesman, he might say, "Let me go crunch the numbers with my boss and see where we land. I really went to bat for you and here's what I've got."

We know the drill. We have kicked the tires, taken the test drive, and asked all the technical questions that allow us to mull over the decision, and you feel that we are ready to go for the close. We were waiting for that. Go ahead. Talk about the price, the finance terms, the extra delivery charge floor mat warranty – it's really okay. Just don't insult us with the quasi business speak and the flowery language. Don't dramatize it for us; just give us the cold hard facts. Instead of "crunching the numbers," just say, "Let me go crunch some chips while my accountant puts together a laughable offer for you." Or maybe, "I was watching people at bat back there on the TV, and here's this piece of paper that was handed to me by my accountant, an insane person who believes in sticking it to you introverts." Believe me, we're okay with that kind of world.

What we can't tolerate from the extrovert tribal leaders, such as company CEOs – who were once salesmen – are quasi-business expressions such as, "We are the world leaders in first-to-market, turn-key, B-to-B, thought leadership." They really aren't, he's just saying, "We are the world leaders in shoveling extrovert excrement upon our introverted investors." Walk away, Sport.

Also, attempts to ingratiate yourselves to introverts – something that you feel compelled to do – are mostly unnecessary. Pretending to go out of your way for us has become a bit tiresome. The Ming Dynasty vase that you found for us on your last trip to China, where you also claimed that you were interrogated in your hotel room by gun-wielding PRC police, and on which occasion you barely escaped with your lives while the authorities ravaged through your luggage for the missing artifact, is a recognizable pitch. But we can see the Pottery Barn label on the bottom. We get it. You need to tell a story, but we would be just as happy knowing that you went to the store and found something nice for us.

Trying to impress us with your verbal resume is something we have tolerated long enough. "My commodities business is just getting off the ground, and I expect to be doubling my plant this year," we know just means that you're in multi-level marketing and your plant is just a houseplant. We were just being polite by letting you go on.

These are just a few examples of why we want a refund for all the time we have invested in our relationship with you. It's not that we dislike you. We find you extroverts entertaining. At times, we find you incomprehensible, but not like a piece of ancient text; more like a Ziggy cartoon that we don't understand. We ask ourselves, "Why does she think that is funny, interesting or important?" We are dismayed at the attention others give you, wondering if we are somehow failing to grasp the importance of your rant about fashion, sports stars, celebrities, and so on. No, we don't agree that People magazine's list of most hunky guys constitutes contemporary non-fiction.

So next time you see us across life's parking lot, don't speak. Walk on up to us and stop. Look at us, consider where we are, consider the weather outside and the song you just listened to, and don't ask us for confirmation. Now, what do you want to talk about? It's okay, we'll wait for you to think. Take your time.

11

HANDCUFFED BY THE MAN

I have never been much of a rebel. During the seventies I was one of those "squares" who looked at the hippie movement as just a bunch of lazy potheads with nothing to do. I guess today people look on that period as a time of experimentalism and as a necessary rite of passage to adulthood. Of course, those are the same people who *were* the lazy potheads who are now justifying their illicit drug use. See, I'm a square, man.

In the classic battles between police and demonstrators, I usually came down on the side of the police. Of course, this staunch support for "the authorities" was severely challenged during the Nixon Watergate hearings. I couldn't watch any of my after school shows because they were pre-empted again and again by those hearings. It nearly made me draw up a picket sign and take to the streets: "Hey-hey, ho-ho, your Watergate hearings have got to go…hey-hey, ho-ho…," but I was conflicted about what I would do if "the authorities" showed up – I would likely have just walked away, embarrassed.

Many years later, when I was a college student attending a small community college, I had my first real run-in with the stiff arm of The Law. Well, okay, it was a campus cop; but he was at least a symbol of real authority. If you were once a campus cop, you are now hurling this book across the room cursing uncontrollably. Campus cops were always a little sensitive when it came to their quasi-cop status. A cop who calls a cop was no cop at all, I thought. In fairness to my faux fuzz, I was a student body officer, the editor of the school paper – so I was sort of a quasi-journalist, reporting about reports by other reporters. No hard feelings.

So one fine morning I drove onto campus and headed towards the student union building where I usually parked, only to find that barricades had been set up blocking about twenty parking stalls. A little sign was placed at the entrance to the row that read, "Spaces blocked due to Board of Regents meeting." Board of Regents? Why should they get reserved parking? True, they handled all matters related to higher education for the state schools, I understood; but didn't students matter? Shouldn't tuition-paying students have a right to park in front of their own union building without being given the boot by a bunch of state bureaucrats? My head was spinning, but I did the only thing that my conscience would allow, and I drove into one of the spaces, avoiding the orange cones placed there by the campus cops.

I exited the vehicle (it's not called a car when you're dealing with *any* form of police) and got my backpack out of the trunk. As I closed the trunk, I saw the imposing figure of the navy blue campus cop heading my way.

Campus Cop: "Didn't you see the sign?"
Me: "I'm sorry?"
Campus Cop: "You can't park here. These spaces are reserved."
Me: "I'm a student, and these are student parking spaces. I have a right to park here."

Of course, the minute those words, "I have a right," left my lips I knew I had joined the anti-Man crowd, and I felt bad that it was over something as petty as a parking space. But the weather was pleasant and I didn't have to be to class for a half hour, so I thought I'd let this drama play out. I suspect many a rabid activist is really just in it for the diversion – maybe some of them are just bored, or enjoy being outdoors. I empathize.

I felt pretty strongly about students having to sacrifice all the time for the administration. The administration never took a ten percent pay cut, but tuition went up by that amount nearly every year. Fees and add-ons to tuition were mandatory, but they paid for little pet projects that the administration said would benefit all students. Ordinary procedures, like registering for classes or requesting transcripts, required multiple forms of ID, and the students were always presumed guilty if there were any problems. In my case, the campus cop had already tried and convicted me, and was just considering what kind of sentence he had the authority to pass.

Campus Cop: "Didn't you see the sign?"

Me: "Yes, I saw it, but these are student parking places."

Campus Cop: "You are going to have to move your car. There is parking spaces over at the business building."

Campus cops often had poor grammar, but you couldn't call them on it without risking additional enforcement "issues." "I'm sorry officer, it's 'there *are* parking spaces,'" is translated in the law enforcement brain as, "I would like an additional fine for failure to cooperate, officer."

My course was set, and I wasn't going to move. This was also during my Letters to Lola phase (see Yellow Journalism – Move Those Papers!), when I was reveling in my journalistic freedom of expression. Obviously this fellow didn't understand who I was. I was the Managing Editor of the campus paper – not that I was asking for a free parking space because of it.

Campus Cop: "If you don't move your car, I'll have to handcuff you and take you in."

Me: "I've got a right to park here."

Campus Cop: "I'm going to give you one minute to move your car."

Me: "This is a student lot and I'm parking here."

That was it. He told me to turn around, and he put on the handcuffs. He had a bit of a tough time putting on the handcuffs because of my thick wrists. I had always thought of this physical trait as advantageous for tennis and golf, but now it was a bit of a liability. The cuffs were really digging in, and when I was ushered to the backseat of the unit (campus cop car), the awkward position made things worse. He could have put the cuffs on their last setting owing to my freakishly large hands. I wasn't about to slip the cuffs over these meat hooks; but I think campus cop was just upset at my protest. It was cutting into his time, and he would have to fill out reports, and this may have been just the diversion that campus terrorists were planning for months. So he made the cuffs a little extra tight for me.

He left me in the car while he went out to talk on his remote audio device (or walkie-talkie). I think he was talking to his superior about what options he had, and where he might take me. He was out there for a while, and the cuffs were really starting to hurt, but he finally returned to the car with his ultimatum. I could move my car or else he would take me into the campus police office and a hold would be placed on my student record.

Someone unfamiliar with bureaucracies would say, "A hold? What's the big deal about that? What a wimp!" But I was thinking that a) class was going to be starting soon; b) I would hate to think about how many forms of ID I would have to come up with to remove a hold; and c) these cuffs really hurt. I half considered calling campus cop's bluff, but opted instead to move my car.

After parking across the street, I went right to my office and wrote an editorial describing everything that had just happened. I used campus cop's name, and gave a play-by-play account of what went on. It ran in that week's paper, sort of a personal vendetta for my red wrists.

Within minutes of the article hitting the newsstands, the Dean of Students called me in demanding an explanation. He was upset that I hadn't gone to him first, and that this attack on The Man appeared without any warning. He reminded me that the campus paper was funded by the administration, and that going around the system this way really put a lot of people (him) in a bad position. He acknowledged that this campus cop's name had come up before and that other students had complained about his intimidating style. He explained why going to him first would have been a far better option, and that he still would have supported some kind of editorial. Looking back on it, he was a reasonable man, and he probably stuck his neck out on my behalf; but I was just too focused on "my rights" to see things objectively.

So who was the offender in this case, and who claimed the victory?

If I were a *professional activist*, I would have claimed victory at being able to raise my voice despite threats of police violence, showing that no one was going to trample on my rights. Power to the people, and all that.

If I were a *campus policeman*, I would have claimed victory that some punk kid who could have been a potential disturbance for the Board of Regents meeting was shut down and the car was moved without further incident. I might have even expected a promotion.

If I were the *Dean of Students*, I would have claimed victory at expressing the situation to the rogue campus paper editor to help him see his error in judgment, and thereby alleviate further action against him or further embarrassment on me.

If I were the *rest of the students* who saw the signs and just parked in another place, I would have thought this was all blown out of proportion, if I had bothered to read the one-sided editorial in the campus paper.

If I were the *Board of Regents*, I would have not known a thing.

I'm not a professional activist, but I'd say that claiming a moral victory for being handcuffed, embarrassing yourself and others, and wasting everyone's time for nothing should be characterized as simple melodrama. Next time I'll just get to class.

12

DISPENSABLE YOU

Occasionally, in our careers, we end up taking a step down before we can take a step up. For example, a sales manager might move into a lower position in the marketing department in order to gain that experience in preparation for a move into senior management; or a seasoned worker might be laid off and have to accept a lower position in order to become employable. Such is the nature of jobs and business.

In my case, I had my first job as a steam press operator, for one day (see Norma and Me – Full Steam Ahead!) before I was transferred to another department, maintenance; but for me, this felt like more of a permanent step down rather than something that would prepare me for future greatness. My father had arranged for me to work at his warehouse, so it was with a sense of obligation that I began applying my recently acquired press operating skills to more mundane tasks such as weeding the gardens, trimming the shrubbery, and sweeping the parking lot.

I worked for a guy named Bruce, who was probably twenty years older than me, and whose father also worked for the company. He was the head of maintenance, not just for the warehouse, but for all the stores in the chain. Bruce was a kind man who looked like a body builder, and seemed to be able to fix anything. He had all the answers to questions like Where's the tool closet? How should I clean the bathrooms? and What should I do next? Most of the time I felt like Bruce was wearied by my constant questions about what I should do next.

One day Bruce offered me some career advice. It was as I was preparing a bucket with some cleaning solution so that I could mop the floors in the bathrooms. I made an off-handed remark about what would the company do without me to perform these menial tasks, and Bruce jumped on my comment right away. He brought the bucket over to where I was standing and with an intense look on his face said, "Let me tell you something about how important you are."

I was expecting a discussion about my budding skills and future promotion to Senior Maintenance Specialist, but it was just the opposite. Bruce looked at me soberly and said, "If I fill this bucket up with water and stick in my finger, and then I pull my finger out, what happens to the hole where my finger was?" I thought, this must be a trick question, and so I began thinking of my response. Let's see, finger goes into the water, and then comes back out, but there's really no whole in the water, it just rushes right back. Hmm...

He must have sensed that I was about to answer his rhetorical question with something that was clearly not going to further his object lesson with the bucket, because he followed up with, "Think about it, *that's* how indispensable you are." I *was* thinking. Was I the finger or the water? I understood what he meant, but I couldn't understand why he said it. Had I offending him somehow? Had I been acting like I was going to take his job in the future? Was I about to be transferred again, after just a few weeks as landscape specialist, and would it be for a better job?

I was puzzled for weeks after this exchange with Bruce, and his sage advice had the desired effect. I was considering my indispensability on a regular basis. I'm dispensable, meaning someone else could easily replace me. Right. It wouldn't take much to get rid of me and get someone else who could do just as well. Okay. The water goes back to just the way it *was*, only you're not there. That's true, I supposed, but it would take a while for the weeds and the shrubbery to grow back to the way it was when I showed up.

The more I thought about it, I didn't mind the concept of being replaceable. I often looked forward to the idea of being replaced one day with someone less qualified. My career, I decided, was more than this summer landscape job, and as I extracted myself from the bucket of water that was my job, I knew that Bruce would still be there, the water where I – the finger – once was inserted. It was all becoming clear.

In the years since Bruce's bucket full of career advice, I have thought a lot about this idea of being dispensable. About ten years after this discussion, it all became too true as the company reorganized and then finally succumbed to bankruptcy. Suddenly everyone was dispensable, from the landscape specialist to the steam operator to the company executives. It was as if the company, a finger in the retail bucket, had been extracted, and the other retailers just closed in around the hole that was left.

I saw lots of good people lose their jobs, their careers, and their retirement accounts. All were dispensable.

I decided at that time that I would do what I could to make myself as indispensable as possible. It became my mantra throughout my college years and was a great motivator when I went back to work on my Master's, and later, PhD. Specialized knowledge, specialized jobs, in companies who were hungry for the type of skills I possessed – these seemed to be the keys for my developing career. Keeping my options open was the counter-offensive to companies who could lose their profitable place in the market and end up laying off its workforce. If there was to be no corporate loyalty to employees, then it was incumbent on the employee to be ready with the right educational background, the right set of skills, and a willingness to flex with the changing conditions.

Bruce's bucket analogy taught me about playing good career defense rather than passively sitting back and waiting for the worst to happen. It also taught me about the nature of companies and organizations. They operate on a macro scale with many of the same attributes of the individual employee, hedging a new product line with solid legacy products, hiring new talent to improve its capabilities for expansion and growth.

Ultimately you are dispensable, your organization is dispensable, and you have to plan for the worst while working vigorously to improve yourself and the organizations you belong to, whether you are a small business owner or the head of a non-profit community group. Someone or some other organization is waiting in the wings to take your place, and your absence will hardly be remembered. Bruce was right, it was worth thinking about; and coming to terms with my own unimportance has been an important and guiding principle in my own career aspirations.

13

CHEESE FISH AND JOINING IN

Occasionally, when we find ourselves in a new cultural experience, whether at a friend's home or while visiting another country, the desire to go along in the spirit of cultural sensitivity can motivate us to new and challenging epicurean heights – our own personal Everests. If you have ever had to swallow something without chewing, fearing the inevitability of the gag reflex would take over, fear not; what I am going to tell you now might just bring newfound empowerment to your life.

I spent a little time in Japan, in the Osaka region, for business. On one occasion, my Japanese host invited me to join in a manager's meeting at Lake Biwa, the largest freshwater lake in Japan just north of the historic city of Kyoto. I saw the lake from the train, and from the shuttle bus just before dark, and I saw it again when I left the next morning.

Why would we have this meeting at the lake, but not really spend time *seeing* the lake or *doing* anything at the lake? I imagine many executives in large companies have asked themselves the same question, "If I'm simply going from the airport to the hotel meeting room, and then back to the airport in the morning, why are we having this meeting at this beautiful location?" Why don't they just hold the meeting in the parking lot in one of those temporary classrooms we had growing up? Maybe they could just hire a limo to drive them around for an hour and put them at a local hotel, where the shuttle could drive them to their parking lot meeting. Perhaps a couple of hundred bucks could be spent to buy some really nice framed pictures of exotic locations, and then do some trim around the pictures so that they appear to be windows looking out on Bora Bora or Paris, for example. But, for whatever reason, that was not the case with my Lake Biwa meeting.

We stayed at a pension hotel, a beautiful Western-style hotel right on the lake (I could tell from the sound of water lapping the shore as I walked to my room). To get into one of these hotels, you have to be affiliated with the labor union. You have to know someone. I only knew my co-workers, but that was enough to get me in the door. I was quickly conscious of the fact that I appeared to be the only non-Japanese guest at this place, so I sat quietly in the lobby waiting for the room to be arranged.

I like to think of myself as a pretty tolerant and open-minded guy, but I'm sure none of us who harbor such sentiments have a very clear view of our own biases and prejudices. Okay, maybe you do – I don't. So I began thinking about my fate if the hotel wouldn't let me in. Would I be like the droids in the first Star Wars who couldn't get into the bar at Mos Eisley with Luke and Obiwan? "We don't serve their kind here!"

Japan is a wonderful place. It's clean, people are generally friendly if you keep the rules, and people operate in mostly quiet tones in conversation. Knowing your place in Japan, especially if you're not Japanese, is something that is held in high regard. So for me, I knew that I was the only non-Japanese guy, that I was obviously not a member of any Japanese unions, and that my host would be the right one to negotiate my stay. The agent behind the check-in counter looked at me several times during the conversation as if sizing me up – are you *sure* he's part of your group? I kept thinking my host would at some point either produce a blaster from under the table and say "No deal, Gweedo!" or else use the old Jedi Mind Trick: "He's one of us and you will be rewarded for granting him entrance to this fine establishment." It must have been the latter, because the agent gave me a room and ushered me to the elevator.

Hotels in Japan are wonderful places to discover your own language, if you are a native English speaker. In Tokyo you are more likely to get a very nice translated room guide, but out in the Lake Biwa area you end up with English instructions like this:

- It is the swimming pool which can be relaxed while thoroughly enjoying rural district scenery and setting sun in the summer
- No sripper (slippers) outside of pool area
- A warm and harmonious atmosphere arises whenever people get together to enjoy each other's company with smiling face and warmhearted talk

- Come enjoy original Japanesque meals at traditional restaurant to recall the memory of dining experience from bygone

I was looking forward to the Japanesque meal, and so I showed up at the converted ballroom at the appropriate hour. Seated around a table with the whole management team, about 12 of us, we spent the next hour enjoying smiling face and warmhearted talk, I suppose. There were many stories about Lake Biwa, and about our host's boyhood memories there. The conversation then abruptly shifted from our lauded host's personal history to Mr. Watanabe, a younger member of the staff, whose youth and inexperience were fodder for jovial jibes at times like these. It was apparent from our senior executive host that Mr. Watanabe was a complete rube when it came to all things Biwa-esque, or it may have been that Mr. Watanabe was taking it on the chin in order to save face for his boss. Either way, the banter about Junior was a nice complement to the timing of the multi-coursed meal. Just as he was about to get skewered again, the next plate would be revealed, diverting the guests' attention like a lone wildebeest loping by momentarily stirs the gorging of hungry lions, who look up briefly before returning to the gutted prey's body.

Kaiseki ryori, the multi-plated traditional meal is a wonderful opportunity to see the artistry of the chef at work. Colors of pickled radishes, fish paste shaped into unique shapes, and other jellied things are placed one-by-one in front of the guest as if to say, "How 'bout this?" or "Have another?" I suspect that Mr. Watanabe was being offered up as a sacrificial lamb for my own ignorance about the various Japanese delicacies, so I think I didn't laugh quite as hard as my colleagues at Mr. Watanabe's expense. He vicariously tasted the presented fare as the lions taunted him, and seeing his survivability, I took courage and foraged on through the dishes.

Soon the conversation turned to one of the particular delicacies to the Lake Biwa region: *funazushi*. I knew where this conversation was going to go, so I played along, fully aware that I was about to be served something that might make someone else wretch uncontrollably at the mere description. I hope that doesn't happen to you here.

Host: "So have you ever heard of funazushi, Rob-san?"
Me: "Why no, I haven't."
Host: "It is a very popular food for Lake Biwa."
Me: "Really?"
Host: "It is a cheese fish. Do you know cheese fish?"
Me: "Cheese fish (putting on a smile)? Why no, I don't know."
Host: "Would you like to try it?"

Me: "Thank you, it sounds wonderful."

I have often uttered those words, "Thank you, it sounds wonderful," upon being offered many other strange dishes such as ox tail soup, liver carpaccio, papaya pilaf, natto (fermented beans), or fugu (the puffer fish that kills you if not prepared properly), so it rolled out so easily I almost sounded like I meant it.

A few minutes later, the funazushi made its appearance. At first sight one is repulsed not so much by the smell as by pity. What must they have done to this poor little fish to get it to look and smell like *that*?

Me: "What kind of fish is funazushi made from?"
Host: "It's made from the…uh…Mr. Watanabe will know…Mr. Watanabe?! What is this fish?"
Mr. Watanabe: "Eh?"
Host, louder: "WHAT IS THIS FISH, MR. WATANABE? He doesn't know. He's so stupid."

Mr. Watanabe had just taken a bludgeoning for my lack of knowledge about funazushi, and since he had been taking the lead with all strange foods, I figured I owed him one. I was in the zone, nothing was going to get me to admit that this was the foulest-looking fish I had ever seen, even worse than the dreaded sea cucumber or pickled herring.

Me: "It looks delicious."

It's time to reveal one important rule about fine dining in Japan: It may look bad, but it has probably been prepared by professionals in clean kitchens, so it is very unlikely that you'll die by eating it (even fugu, if eaten in fine restaurants, doesn't pose much of a real threat). The other thing I can take comfort in is knowing that since I'm about twice the size of my Japanese counterparts, anything that might kill them, will probably take longer to kill me, or it might just make me violently ill. That this may have been happening with my stand-in, Mr. Watanabe, and that a slow and painful death from ingested fish products could be just a few hours away, didn't really occur to me at that moment. Funazushi? No problem, I thought.

Picking a particularly large chunk of the orange-colored pungent fish from the saucer, I put it in my mouth and chewed it once before letting it slide down the hatch. I didn't even drink my water. It tasted like I would imagine dirty socks would taste if they were worn by forty different track

56

stars on the same day. Knowing it was once a fish, now just a smelly fish, made me think about going boating as a young boy and seeing the dead fish floating near the shore. Perhaps this fish had been one of those along the shores of Lake Biwa, rotting from the inside out, and finding its way to this plate in front of me. Wonderful. I had them just where I wanted them, and I was ready for the next exchange.

Host (now smiling to himself): "How do you like funazushi?"
Me: "It's very good. Wow."
Host (now surprised): "Really?"

Others at the table were fixated on my face and my now empty chopsticks at the ready for another bite. I reached for another large chunk and put it in my mouth, chewing and swallowing, holding the rising gag reflex at bay. A few of them looked surprised, and one of them even looked uneasy. What was about to happen?

Me: "Yes…it's delicious…oishii…really."

Here it comes. I had them. Ready…aim…

Me: "I think everyone should have some. It's great!"

No one at the table seemed happy with the suggestion, but my host – in order to save face – ordered a dozen stinky cheese fish for the whole table. Gleefully, I watched as my co-workers tentatively picked at the funazushi, and put it to their lips more out of obligation than out of desire, like the obligatory kiss of a corpse at an open-casket funeral service. The punching bag, Mr. Watanabe, also appeared to be smiling now that the lions had were chewing on fouled meat.

So be brave, fellow travelers. Practice your lines until you can deliver them with the coolness of a professional, and you can spread the cultural delight of sharing exotic foods with those who love to run taste-tests on their colleagues like gross-out fraternity pranks. Just remember these three magical lines:

"Thank you, it sounds wonderful."
"It's delicious."
"I think *everyone* should have some."

14

CAT HATRED

Warning: This contains an account of cruelty to cats. Although no cats were killed, they were certainly traumatized. And if you care more about that than the trauma of a young boy who has lost his friends, fine. Don't read any further. Go hug your cat, and I hope your allergies kick up big time; or I hope that it claws you in the face causing damage that can't be repaired even by expensive plastic surgery.

I would like to object to the many thousands, perhaps millions, of indiscriminate cat haters out there who are repulsed by all things feline. I hate cats, but with good cause. I'm willing to accept that many of you have simply joined in my cat hatred because you are dog lovers or because cats don't play fetch. Fine. But let me explain myself and then you see if you're worthy to call yourself a cat hater.

You might want to read about the pigeons in Quiet Places before you read about this incident. It will heighten your cat hatred beyond what I am able to achieve here.

My cat hatred has several focal points, or centers of gravity, around which spin all the felines who have entered my solar system: Max, then Ryu, and then the Cat With No Name.

Max was a stray cat in Japan, who was taken in by our American friends in a neighboring town. Max was a large white cat with black patches and big chubby cheeks. He used to lay on the sofa and lick himself. Oh yes, that obsessive licking. Sure, it makes the cat clean, but isn't it a little too much? I used to sit in the same room as Max and think, hey, relax, there are no female cats around, and you won't let anyone within five feet of petting you without sounding a warning, so what's the point of being clean? If Max were a person, and he primped all day long, you'd say he was a bit of a dandy; but cats get a pass. Oh, they're so clean. Right.

What about the litter box? It's a box of cat urine and feces right there in your house. Yummy. Oh, but it's contained to one *place* in the house. Let me ask you, if someone – let's say, a good friend of yours – had a box in their house where they went several times a day to deposit their fecal matter, what would you say? "Oh the Johnsons are so clean and waste-friendly, and they only go in one place in the house!" Goody. But Max was mostly harmless, choosing to run away rather than stand and fight, a typical scaredy cat. Or maybe he just didn't want his fur mussed.

This brings me to my second cat, reaching back a few more years. This cat was Ryu, also, coincidentally, a friend's cat in Japan, on another occasion when I lived there for an extended time. I use Max and Ryu especially to point out that the feline species is the same on two completely different sides of the world. Ryu belonged to the Shoji family, and he used to sit on top of the refrigerator. Whenever a stranger would enter the room, Ryu would lash out with his razor claws and try to kill him or her. Nice kitty.

Ryu was evil, and so I returned this evil with a little game of my own. Ryu was deathly afraid of the Shoji's tank type vacuum, and so I would often borrow a vacuum and sneak up on the unsuspecting Ryu, prodding him in the rump with the corner attachment and waving it over his head while he cowered and hissed loudly, striking out at the vacuum attachment mercilessly. He would get very upset, of course, kind of like the way I felt upon entering the room and feeling the swipe of kitty claws near my head. Was it traumatizing to poor Ryu? I certainly hope so.

Going back to my youth, there was another cat, a feline specter who roamed among the shadows – the Cat With No Name, or CWNN. He was gray and fluffy, really quite a nice looking cat, and I'm sure he made some little girl very happy. But this cat harbored a secret. By day he was probably Fluffy the family cat, but by night he was the Shadow of Death. This no-name cat was always hanging around our yard, and I chased him away from my pigeon coup several times. I would scare him off by throwing a tennis ball at him or by flinging a marble from my handy wrist rocket slingshot, and he would run off to a distance, turn, and glare at me as if in some Clint Eastwood western, "Oh, I'll be back, so you best be ready, son!"

One day I went out to see if my pigeons had come home from their day in the clouds. I had let them out on my way to school and was expecting to see them perched comfortably on the broomstick that ran from one end of the coup to the other. Instead, when I looked in the door, it looked like the scene from a Godfather movie. The mob had come and riddled my pigeons with a Tommy Gun. Blood and feathers were everywhere, but no other trace of my birds. Then, in the distance, the CWNN strutted across the yard. I went in the nearby shed to grab my bow and arrow, but when I came out, he was gone. I knew he would come back, and I was going to be ready. He was going to *pay* for what he'd done.

Well, a few weeks passed, and I went out and bought another pair of homing pigeons. They were great, and soon I was recovering from the carnage of my two lost friends. This new pair had even produced a couple of squabs, who were growing and starting to show some feathers. I had sealed up the entry hatch where the pigeons would enter the coup, and had latched the larger door to the coup with a big stick to keep it shut tight; but once again, when I came home from school, it was the Godfather sequel. The CWNN had knocked the stick out and had entered the coup, destroying everything inside and leaving another trail of carnage.

I was devastated, but I redirected my anger at a scheme to get CWNN. I am an animal lover at heart, and would never kill any creature – except spiders and bees and animals who intended to kill me (see The Spider in My Metro) – so I wasn't planning to kill CWNN, just make him suffer. That's why it was fortuitous that just a month or so earlier, my father had come into possession of a large wooden food dehydrator. It was a box with sides about three feet wide and about four feet tall, with tracks for screens that could be inserted with all types of food, and it had a small fan in the bottom to move the warm air around the food to suck out the water in a few days.

Nobody was using it, and the screens were out, making this the perfect size to trap the gray ghost. I put it in the backyard near my pigeon coup, and left the door ajar. Then I waited. I had determined to trap the cat with no name and simply *begin* the process of dehydration.

By some act of Fate, CWNN was poking around the new wooden "coup" attracted by the food I had placed inside, and he went in. Slam! I stepped from behind the shed and closed the door on him. I *had* him, I *had* him; and somewhere deep inside CWNN, my pigeons were cheering. I wheeled the dehydrator out of sight, and went in the house, content to let the process begin. The next day I went outside and heard the mewing cries of CWNN, like a cat in heat, which I suppose was literally true for him. Ha!

Day two was a little harder. CWNN was still in the dehydrator, but since it wasn't plugged in, he was just upset, hungry and thirsty. I began to feel guilty about killing him, despite the lives he had claimed. I had pronounced sentence on CWNN and he was going to meet his doom. But then the thought crossed my mind that somewhere there was an owner who would come looking for his evil cat, Fluffy the Fierce, Fluffy the Assassin, Fluffy the Terrible. I couldn't let CWNN die. I decided to let him out. It must have been the same guilt that Colonel Saito felt in "The Bridge on the River Kwai" when he at long last decided to free Sir Alec Guinness whom he had locked in the "oven" for failing to make the British officers work alongside the other British prisoners of war.

So I resolved to let out CWNN, and I opened the door. He sprang from the dehydrator like a cat delivered from the gallows. Seeing him so healthy after two days was actually a little discouraging to me, so I chased him, and I was able to grab his tail and in one motion, flung him over the fence. He must have landed on his feet, because when I looked through the fence, he was gone.

I never saw Cat With No Name again; and I never kept pigeons again. Pigeon slayings had to stop, and CWNN, who had paid some measure of justice, had deserved a general amnesty. Harmony was restored, and I suppose if it had been a Hollywood movie, rain would have come to wash the blood from the pigeon coop and flowers would have sprung anew from the crimson soil. But the next year we took the coup apart and burned it in the garden.

Thus my hatred for cats. I had lost two sets of birds and two squabs to the cat, and his having no name only served to generalize my hatred for their species. So what's your excuse for hating cats? Is it the litter box? Their finicky eating habits? Their aloofness? Come on, please. Don't insult the rest of us who hate with a cause deeper than yours. And if you were the owner of CWNN, and he came back a little thinner and with a new-found gratitude for being alive, now you'll know why.

15

YELLOWSTONE STARS AND STRIPES

Old Faithful, the geyser that blows its top like clockwork, spewing super-heated sulfur spray from deep below the surface, has been the icon for Yellowstone National Park from the beginning; and the park is celebrated by tourists domestic and foreign for its wonderful nature hiking trails in the summer and challenging snowmobile trails in the winter. Nearly thirty summers ago if you were one of those tourists wandering the boardwalk around Old Faithful you would have seen around a hundred high school students in royal blue dresses and navy suits posing for a photo in front of the simmering geyser, waiting for the moment when the nature-made fountain would shoot skyward, and the photographer would snap the photo.

Each summer, the Granite Youth Symphony, a group comprised of students from several high schools in the school district, boarded school buses and set out for the two-week summer concert tour. This road trip was usually confined to three general routes, the plains states tour, the southwest tour, and the western Canada tour. Two of the district's largest school buses, decked out for the trip with red flames coming off the wheel wells – the contribution of one of the regular summer tour drivers – would haul the students, their gear, and the instruments six to eight hours each day before stopping at small towns along the route to perform.

Concerts were usually at a local church or recreation center, and audiences ranged from the infant to the incontinent – both ends of the diaper continuum. Sometimes the conductor, a stickler for stagecraft, would wait for what seemed like hours while the audience would quiet down before raising his baton. At other times, particularly if the audience was a little sparse, he would push the tempo, turning adagios into andantes or allegros. Maybe this was to show displeasure with the low turnout, and by so doing, get things over more quickly; but more likely, it was his opportunity to stretch the musicians to the breaking point and then pull them back before things turned disastrous. As our conductor-coach, it was his way of making us do the musical equivalent of wind sprints at a football practice to see who would collapse first.

After the concerts, families from the area would collect several students and put them up for the night. This made for great story telling the next day:

"You won't believe what we ate last night!" (This particular phrase was used with equanimity to express disgust or delight – if only they would have learned the three phrases from Cheese Fish and Joining In…alas.)
"We had a pool!"
"Our dad was a jerk."
"We each had our own room."

In addition to the cellos, tubas and bass drums that packed the belly of the bus, a few members of the symphony also stored amplifiers, electric guitars, and a mixing board used for post-concert dances at some of these venues, replacing Bach with Bachmann-Turner Overdrive. It was an effective way of bringing other teens to the concerts, although most of the time they were late, and had that "when-is-this-going-to-be-over" look on their faces. Still, mingling with the locals was great sport, and also made for good storytelling:

"She was hot."
"He smelled."
"We're going to write to each other!" (This was around the year 28 P.T.E., or pre-texting era, when people would write things on paper, put them in envelopes, and send them to an address. It used to take several days to arrive, and for a response to be composed.)

On some nights, the yellow bus brigade would pitch camp at a local Motel 6, where rules about disturbing other guests gave way to road-weary students letting off some steam from the day's journey. Despite the occasional shenanigans – like flushing symphony uniforms in the head, piling up motel mattresses like Princess and the Pea, or staying up late spreading gossip about the scandalous TRs (Tour Romances) – the audiences seemed grateful to have the group pull into town.

One feature that made the northwest and Canadian tour a big enough draw to drag students out of bed to the early morning practices was the opportunity to play at Old Faithful Lodge. It was the last stop on the tour before returning home, which made it the grand finale, the final performance which capped off the season and relegated all previous performances to mere dress rehearsals. It was the Carnegie Hall of the tour. The hall was large enough to accommodate the symphony comfortably, with capacity for several hundred audience members on folding chairs as well.

On this night, the symphony members were in place and ready just as the last of Old Faithful's droplets hit the sandy ground outside the series of double-door entries. The doors were blocked open to carry the sound out to the masses, a kind of audience baiting technique that must have suited the old trapper spirits still whistling in the pines. At the concert mistress's nod, the oboe sounded a long "A" as the symphony tuned up. With bows at the ready, reeds saliva-soaked, and lips puckered, the conductor hit the downbeat and the kettle drum thundered a roll. On cue the symphony burst into "The Star-Spangled Banner" and the growing crowd rose to its feet, many of them singing along.

By the time the last note reverenced the home of the brave, the audience had doubled in size to perhaps a hundred. By the time Bizet's toreadors had pranced, Stravinsky's Firebird had risen from the ashes, and Bach's Little Fugue had echoed through the large hall, the crowd had swelled to standing room only. After a flurry of the Brandenburg Concerto played at hyper speed, thanks to the wind sprints practiced in another small town days before, the crowd granted a standing ovation, and a several shouts of *Bravo!* and *Encore!* echoed from the rafters. The symphony members stood, bowed in time with the conductor's exultant wave, and returned to their instruments. As the applause started to die, the symphony members fixed their gaze on the conductor's eyes and coiled around their instruments for the encore. As the conductor lifted his baton, the final applause gave way to a crescendo of silence, tension growing as the horns, strings, percussion and woodwinds collectively inhaled.

With a stroke of his stick, the conductor unleashed the strains of "Stars and Stripes Forever", as cheers erupted and applause returned in an instant. Piccolos and flutes stood when it came time to dance out their reverie, and the applause that followed momentarily buried the bluster of the horns as they rose and fired a salvo of their own into the audience. Cymbals crashed, the bass drum boomed, and it was over. The vacuum of the final orchestral attack was filled immediately with cheering and applause, falling into perfect cadence and then bursting out again as the symphony took its final bow.

As the concert ended, and the equipment and instruments were covered, cased, and readied for loading back on the buses, audience members, one after another, filed up to thank the musicians. This had been one of our best concerts, but why did they linger? And why all the gushing praise? What had moved them? Of course, the audience appeal of a good march couldn't be discounted. But this was different. Could it have been – dare we say it – *patriotism*?

Rarely do we get the opportunity to reflect on our own patriotism. Perhaps every couple of years we see glimpses of it in our fellow citizens who strive for Olympic gold. We look in the faces of the military men and women as they pass among us on their way to defend the nation, and we feel pride or gratitude for their service. We place hands on hearts as the flag goes by or doff our hats at the playing of the National Anthem.

How about cheering or feeling a lump in your throat like the Old Faithful audience? Is that emotion okay nowadays? If I say "I love my country," will someone ask me to lower my voice or take exception to that sentiment citing the old "America-is-an-imperialistic-exploiter-of-people-around-the-world-for-the-sake-of-oil" argument or the "we-were-oppressed-so-we-can't-get-over-it" argument, or even the "Europeans-get-more-time-off-work" argument. These arguments arise more out of spite for the institutions of government, a kind of post-hippie redux – hating The Man because it's fashionable. It's okay, they thought fringe and tie-dye were fashion-forward too.

I love my country. Agree or disagree – it's your First Amendment Right to express it. I would just like to say that it's okay for us to feel pride in our country, even though it's not always fashionable. And as a favor to those who want to stand up and cheer, but who have been silenced by the opposing voices among us, I'm going to lay out fifteen occasions when it's absolutely okay to feel outright awe, deepest reverence, or sincere gratitude toward these United States of America. Feel free to join us on these occasions. Consider yourself entitled to lay down your cynicism at these times and join with the rest of us as fellow Americans. Here they are, with a nod to the Granite Youth Symphony for the first three:

1) When you hear the Star Spangled Banner's closing lines, "Oh, say does that Star Spangled Banner yet wave, o'er the land of the free, and the home of the brave?"

2) When you hear the band strike up "Stars and Stripes Forever"

3) When you visit a National Park like Yellowstone, Yosemite, or the Grand Canyon
4) When you see a small flags placed lovingly next to tombstones at a cemetery
5) When you see a line of veterans marching in a parade
6) When you return from an extended overseas visit, and the wheels of the airliner touch down again on American soil
7) When you walk the hallowed grounds of Gettysburg, Arlington National Cemetery, or the U.S.S. Arizona
8) When you see the executive, legislative, and judicial branches come together for the State of the Union address
9) When you see fighter jets flying in formation
10) When you see our citizens rush in to help each other, whether it is in the simple act of a kind visit to a neighbor or to rebuild a devastated town
11) When you witness a great 4th of July fireworks show with close family and friends
12) When you hear a choir sing "The Battle Hymn of the Republic"
13) When you experience a chance meeting with another American in some remote part of the world
14) When you hear the words to the Pledge of Allegiance
15) When you cast your vote

Go ahead; you have permission to say it out loud, "Wow, what a great place this is!"

16

THE LIMITS OF CUSTOMER SERVICE

My wife and I were raised by parents who worked for many years in retail, particularly in the department store business; so it was natural that we both ended up doing time in that industry. At the time of our marriage, my wife was working for a large department store as the lead fashion consultant in the petites department, and she was always much better at making commission than I was. I worked for a competing department store as the men's department manager.

That we were working for competing companies might have been a big deal if we were in the aerospace industry or the pharmaceutical industry, but in retailing, there are few secrets to guard. The difference between making great money in retailing and just getting by was the store's ability to attract customers and keep them coming back. Sure, there were volume discounters and stores that catered to niche fashions; but department stores were destinations for the discriminating shopper, someone who wanted attention and was willing to pay premium prices to get it.

We used to swap stories all the time over dinner, when our schedules happened to match. Her favorite story was of the woman who returned worn swimwear, which is nearly like trying to return used underwear. According to my wife, the suit looked like it had been sold in the spring and worn all season. At that time, few department stores were still asking the reason for the return – that was left to K-Mart – and my wife, probably figuring it was less risky to appease the insane swimsuit abuser, proceeded to give her a fifteen-dollar in-store credit. Then the woman asked, "So what are you going to do with the suit?" My wife explained that the suit would either be returned to the manufacturer or destroyed, at which the customer said, "Well, if you're just going to do that, can I have it back?" Perhaps the store should have just adopted a "money for nothing" campaign handing out in-store credits and used merchandise.

Most of the customers, the vast majority, were great to work with, and I never got tired of helping the guy who was going in for his first job interview or the executive who needed a new pair of shoes. I enjoyed learning about the way the clothes were made, and learning the way different brands fit, and showing off a great bargain.

About a year after our marriage, the department store where I worked went into Chapter 11 bankruptcy, and then into liquidation. Not only was this the loss of a future for me, since I had been there for several years and was beginning to learn the business; it also meant the loss of an enduring family tradition. My grandfather had founded the company that was now headed by my three uncles and my father. The same company gave me my first job, and had employed other family members over the years. I had grown up knowing the people in the warehouse operation as well as the tailors in the store (see Norma and Me – Full Steam Ahead!).

Bankruptcy meant that my father's retirement plans were over, as well as a number of others who were nearing retirement, anticipating their golden years with fond memories of their lifelong contributions to this family institution. Their dreams were dying a slow death as they watched the company hemorrhage and then go on life support. For others, like me, this turn of events had a short-term gain. I was promoted to assistant store manager to help manage the day-to-day operations of a shrinking business. I was happy for the bump in pay, temporary though it was, but I felt the burden of my co-workers more acutely than ever. At its peak, this 50,000 square foot store employed close to 60 full- and part-time people. Many of them had already left to find work elsewhere, and the skeleton staff that remained was understandably not in the best spirits.

Bankruptcy meant a loss of control, and each week seemed to bring new and unexpected changes for the workers and for customers. The store – or more properly, the liquidators and the bank that had seized all assets and was running the show – stopped allowing merchandise to be transferred from one branch to another. Later, they stopped allowing any returns. Soon the company's charge card was suspended, followed by the refusal to honor any previously issued store credits or gift certificates.

Each morning, before the store would open for business, the usual practice was to get on the store's speaker system and greet the employees, make a few announcements, and give a few words of encouragement. During this liquidation period, the morning announcements were devoted to updating the latest policy changes and mentioning what employees had left. I tried to encourage our employees to remain professional despite the challenges, and to honor the kind of company we had always been, where customers received our best service.

The week that the bank stopped allowing us to accept our own gift certificates, I had spent a lot of time at the Customer Service desk explaining the new policy to people who walked in with their twenty-five or fifty dollar gift certificates. Of course they were upset, but there simply was no way to redeem these for merchandise or cash.

In addition to these small amounts, other gift certificates were trickling in from other sources. The company had for many years traded on-air advertising with local TV stations for gift certificates, since the newscasters needed to be well dressed. These gift certificates were usually for five-hundred dollars each, and they were among those that were no longer redeemable.

On one occasion, I was called back to the service desk to handle an irate customer. I knew before I arrived that it was probably one of the big dollar gift certificate holders, a fact that was soon confirmed as the well-dressed woman waved a stack of them at me from across the counter.

Me: "I'm sorry m'am, but we have been ordered by our bank not to redeem these gift certificates as of this last Monday."
Irate Woman: "What am I supposed to do with these?! You mean to tell me that I'm not going to get anything for these? This store used to be a great place to shop – boy, no wonder you went out of business with customer service like this!"

She slammed them down on the counter and stared at me. Yes, truly it was unjust, and yes, truly the bankrupt store had diminished as a great place to shop. The racks of fur coats and designer suits had long ago been replaced with liquidation merchandise that was of inferior quality and design. Instead of helping customers pick out new wardrobes for special occasions, our employees were being asked to negotiate on everything, from a pair of nylons to a piece of display furniture. The employees at the customer service desk had gone from wrapping beautiful Christmas packages to deflecting customer complaints on behalf of the bank, like this one in front of me.

It was enough. The rant had pushed me over the top, and in a quiet, even tone, I said to I.W., "M'am, I *am* sorry that I won't be able to help you with these gift certificates. I would really like to. And I know that it's not fair. You were promised merchandise for these, and now they are not worth the paper they are written on; but I would just ask you to stop and look around for a moment."

My voice rose a bit, as I continued my version of the soapbox, more of a laminate counter rant, "Each of these employees you see is going to be losing his or her job in a few days or weeks. Now, you are welcome to file your own complaint or lawsuit to collect your damages; however, you will stand at the end of a long line of creditors who are unlikely to recover a dime in the process."

I.W. had a look of utter shock and horror on her face. Never in her life had anyone talked to her like this. Was she actually being told no? I had now worked myself into a low roar as I put the final punctuation on this speech, "So, m'am, you can wave those gift certificates at me all day long, and it's not going to change the fact that they are worthless. You're not getting anything today. You can scream and yell all you want, but we're done with this conversation!"

She threw them at me and walked out in a huff. If she hadn't left so quickly, she might have heard the cheers go up from behind the customer service desk.

What is acceptable customer service, and how far should we expect the man or woman behind the counter to go in our behalf? How many times should we send that steak back before we just eat it? Why does our special order take precedent in our minds over the masses who just buy off the rack, who settle for what is there, or who are happy with something that isn't in a color they really wanted?

In our world of have-it-your-way food service, of monogrammed towels and personal shoppers, when does it become enough? When will our expectations finally be met? Will it be when the sales person offers to drive that new line of outerwear to your house and hold it for you as you try it on? Will it be when the restaurant manager comes out and offers to pay for your meal, and everyone else's meal in the restaurant for the injustice done to you by failing to keep your glass filled? Maybe you will declare your satisfaction when the customer service person on your telephone starts crying into the phone.

Perhaps when you have negotiated a better deal on your lawn furniture because you spotted a stray thread – maybe then you'll get the reputation you seek as a shrewd shopper. For me, and for the workers who lost their jobs trying to serve you, I would just beg a little more consideration and ask you to put yourself in their shoes. Expect to get a fair service for a fair price, and then sit back and enjoy yourself rather than counting the ways you could have shaved off another nickel here or gained a concession there. Be a loyal client, be grateful to someone who goes the extra mile, and reward those who serve – we'll return the favor.

17

DIVINE SHAKESPEARE

Although I went to school for a long time, I rarely felt changed by what I learned, especially in my undergraduate years. I couldn't wait to get out of class, to sell back my books at the end of the quarter, and to check another required course off the slowly shrinking list of prescriptions I had to swallow before the university declared me cured of my ignorance.

The exception to this torture was Shakespeare. When I first bought my three-inch thick book of the Bard, I was a little intimidated. Would reading this force me to adopt a stuffy British accent? Would I have to go to parties with people who spoke in iambic pentameter? It felt inaccessible to me because I remembered my days of suffering during the winter of my discontent known as high school English class. Our study of Romeo and Juliet was something more like reading the ingredients on a cereal box – *bran* cereal – than it was coming to know taste of words, the sweetness of syllabic honey that Shakespeare represents.

This all changed when I picked up Shakespeare in my post-graduate studies. I had a professor who loved to teach Shakespeare, bubbling with sheer delight as he would hold the three-inch book close to his chest and paraphrase different passages. He spoke about the characters as multi-dimensional studies on the human condition, personifying all that is divine and devilish. Through this professor, I came to appreciate the relevance of Shakespeare, and his ability to do with language what others did with paint, or musical notes, or chisels.

I recently pulled my three-inch collection of Shakespearean works off the shelf again – no I didn't sell this one back at the end of the quarter – and found illumination once again.

Quiet times cause us to reflect on our place in the universe. As we stare into the infinite expanse of the night sky or as we sit by a fire staring at the embers, we might take along a few words from *As You Like It*:

All the world's a stage,
And all the men and women merely players;
They have their exits and their entrances,
And one man in his time plays many parts...[1]

Or we might look to the timeless query posed by Hamlet, *"To be or not to be, that is the question,"*[2] or by King Lear, *"Who is it that can tell me who I am?"*[3] In Shakespeare's plays, we find the answers on his stage, the world into which he thrusts villains, heroes, poetic commoners and vapid aristocrats. We see our own fears and foibles carried to their tragic heights. We see our pride and deceitfulness turned back on ourselves in comedic, or tragic, fashion.

Consider the psychology of fear through the diminishing king, Richard the Second, and imagine the armies arrayed against us in the battlefields of our own minds:

To fear the foe, since fear oppresseth strength,
Give in your weakness strength unto your foe,
And so your follies fight against yourself.[4]

Occasionally in our own lives, we find the spoiler, the scorned lover, the aggrieved debtor, or the vengeful youth, and we see the transformation from prince to villain as in *Richard the Third*,

...since I cannot prove a lover
To entertain these fair well-spoken days,
I am determined to prove a villain
And hate the idle pleasures of these days,[5]

In recent decades we have seen the rise of such villains in the masked faces of terrorism and in the growing thunder of our enemies, looking not for power or position, but our annihilation; sentiments articulated with chilling clarity by Aaron, in *Titus Andronicus*. When asked, *"Art thou not sorry for these heinous deeds?"* He replies,

Ay, that I had not done a thousand more.
Even now I curse the day – and yet I think
Few come within the compass of my curse—
Wherein I did not some notorious ill:
As kill a man, or else devise his death,
Ravish a maid, or plot the way to do it,
Accuse some innocent, and forswear myself,
Set deadly enmity between two friends,
Make poor men's cattle break their necks,
Set fire on barns and haystalks in the night,
And bid the owners quench them with their tears...
...But I have done a thousand dreadful things,
As willingly as one would kill a fly,
And nothing grieves me heartily indeed,
But that I cannot do ten thousand more.[6]

As a counterweight to doctrines of devils, our minds are lifted heavenward when we see acts of compassion, bravery, or nobility, and we hear the echoes, as if filling a stony Danish castle's cavernous hall, *"What a piece of work is a man, how noble in reason, how infinite in faculties, in form and moving, how express and admirable in action, how like an angel in apprehension, how like a god!"*[7]

Of course, Hamlet had his own demons to exorcise. We might find ourselves in the downward spiral of self-pity or self-deception, as if our lives are a sieve into which is poured all that is good and evil. As it washes over us, we taste the bitter taint of sorrow and the tartness of joy, and in choosing what remains in us, we might do well to recall the words, again from *As You Like It,*

Sweet are the uses of adversity,
Which like the toad, ugly and venomous,
Wears yet a precious jewel in his head;
And this our life, exempt from public haunt,
Finds tongues in trees, books in the running brooks,
Sermons in stones, and good in every thing.[8]

For some, it seems, hardships multiply on hardships. *"When sorrows come, they come not single spies, but in battalions,"*[9] says the artificial king to his grieving queen in Hamlet. We might choose to respond to life's challenges by constructing excuses of what might have been, as if erecting scaffolds to obscure the façade of what might have been a glorious palace. *"This is excellent foppery of the world*," says the erudite bastard son of Gloucester, in *King Lear*. He continues,

> *that when we are sick in fortune – often the surfeits of our own behavior – we make guilty of our disasters the sun, the moon, and stars, as if we were villains on necessity, fools by heavenly compulsion, knaves, thieves, and treachers (traitors) by spherical predominance; drunkards, liars, and adulterers by an enforc'd obedience of planetary influence; and all that we are evil in, by a diving thrusting on.*[10]

Others of us might spin tales of noble deeds from our past, like virtuous statues set in blighted urban enclaves.

> *Let not virtue seek*
> *Remuneration for the thing it was;*
> *For beauty, wit,*
> *High birth, vigor of bone, desert in service,*
> *Love, friendship, charity, are subjects all*
> *To envious and calumniating Time.*[11]

Perhaps the equalizing effects of the hands of Time are Shakespeare's penultimate theme.

> *The end crowns all,*
> *And that old common arbitrator, Time,*
> *Will one day end it.*[12]

How we have lived our lives, as cowards or heroes, is up to us. How our lives are memorialized is not up to us, as exemplified by Othello, who, after committing murder in a jealous rage, and in a last suicidal gasp commanded,

> *Speak of me as I am; nothing extenuate,*
> *Nor set down aught in malice. Then must you speak*
> *Of one that lov'd not wisely but too well;*
> *Of one not easily jealous...*[13]

No, our lives will be remembered by others; and we pray that they might be such tributes as those paid by Mark Antony for the fallen Brutus,

> *His life was gentle, and the elements*
> *So mix'd in him that Nature might stand up*
> *And say to all the world, "This was a man!"*[14]

NOTES

1. *As You Like It*, Act II, Scene vii.
2. *The Tragedy of Hamlet, Prince of Denmark*, Act III, Scene i.
3. *The Tragedy of King Lear*, Act I, Scene iv.
4. *The Tragedy of King Richard the Second*, Act III, Scene iii.
5. *The Tragedy of Richard the Third*, Act I, Scene i.
6. *The Tragedy of Titus Andronicus*, Act V, Scene i.
7. *Hamlet*, Act II, Scene ii.
8. *As You Like It*, Act II, Scene i.
9. *Hamlet*, Act IV, Scene v.
10. *King Lear*, Act I, Scene ii.
11. *The History of Troilus and Cressida*, Act III, Scene iii.
12. *Troilus and Cressida*, Act IV, Scene v.
13. *The Tragedy of Othello, the Moor of Venice*, Act V, Scene ii.
14. *The Tragedy of Julius Caesar*, Act V, Scene v.

18

MY DOG'S EYES

I'm a dog owner (see Cat Hatred for further background on this declarative).

Dogs have many good qualities, but I suppose the thing that endears us to them is that they love to be loved. Sure, they are loyal to us; but aren't we also loyal to them? We feed them, give them water, give them a place to sleep, and scratch them behind the ears once in a while just to see if we can get that old back leg reaching up to help us scratch.

I have wondered many times what my dogs were thinking behind their eyes. I didn't really wonder much about this when we had Cricket, a hyper Sheltie who used to run a circuit in our home. One day I moved a piece of furniture in her regular circuit, and it slowed her down a little; but I could never really *see* her eyes – she was always running.

Then there was Goldie, our first Golden Retriever. She used to look up waiting for any signal that you were paying attention to her, and she'd find a way to rub up under your hand to sneak a pat on the head or to snuggle side by side if you were lying in bed. She would look up as if drawing energy by looking at you. "What is it?" I found myself asking her most of the time.

I'm convinced that Golden Retrievers are something of a higher order of intelligence than other dogs, like poodles or beagles I have known. Somehow, the Golden is more of a regal creature, sharing your thoughts and trying to run alongside, figuratively speaking, more in parallel step than at right angles. Now, if you're a beagle or poodle owner, it's nothing personal, it's just my opinion based on personal experience – I'm sure they have a proclivity for fine arts and quantum math when I'm *not* watching.

We also had Alpine, a big yellow lab who was so named because of the valley where he had been found. My wife had rescued him from a shelter where he had stayed for nearly eight months. He was the one to replace Goldie, who died prematurely of cancer, and Alpine was an odd substitute, I thought. Compared to Goldie's frolicsome face and wavy coat that practically shimmered as she trotted, Alpine was nothing but skin and bones. He was tenuous around home for the first few weeks, and he couldn't walk up and down the stairs either because he hadn't had stairs in his prior home, or had forgotten how to navigate them during his kennel confinement; or perhaps his muscles still hadn't gained enough strength to attempt the task.

Then one day, after several days on a strict regimen of good food, water, and rest, my wife let Alpine out the back door to take care of his business, when she noticed that his usual measured walk and occasional trot had given way to a full out scamper. Alpine ran the length of our fenced yard, and then ran circles, and he kept on running. Stairs were no problem, and he seemed to clear them two at a time. It looked to us as if he were smiling, and his eyes seemed bright with hope.

Before I go much further, let me just insert a disclaimer to all of you non-pet owners, or cat people. No, I do not think that dogs are human, and no, I do not think they should be dressed up in clothing, taught to potty train on the toilet, or to eat human food. They should not suffer the humiliation of wearing antlers at Christmas, absurd super hero costumes at Halloween, or sunglasses, hats, or jewelry. I think they hate that, and they'd rather just be "naked" to run around the yard doing dog things. They're dogs.

That brings me to Xavier, another Golden who became good buddies with Alpine, and Zoe, a Bernese Mountain Dog, who took Alpine's bed when he had to be put down. Xavier was by my side many times when I was relaxing on the bed or sitting at my desk working late hours on my dissertation. All I had to do was look at him, and he'd get up, come over, and nuzzle my hand for attention. I would stroke his ears and scratch under his chin, and he would look me in the eye and give my hand a lick as if to say, "Hey, thanks, that feels great," and he'd go lie down watching for his next opening.

Zoe, the Berner, was a massive black dog, with the markings of a pedigreed pup. Her eyes were hidden as part of the black mask she wore permanently, a small ridge of white fur running from her nose up between her eyes, and ending in a patch of white between her ears. Zoe would lie on the floor and stare up to see what you were doing. She would waddle over and curl up into your legs, almost cat-like (for which I forgave her) as she warmed to the slightest touch on her coat. When sitting next to you, she would crane her neck backwards at you, head almost upside-down, as if to say, "You still there?"

I've wondered with these dogs, what if they really are sent to us with some greater sentience? Sure, they understand a few commands and hand motions to signal a response, but what if they *think* in the way that humans do, or at least is it beyond mere instinct? I've wondered about this, which is the main reason why I am bothered by cruelty to animals (not that I was always so kind to them in my past – see Cat Hatred). I think it is their innocence that inspires such feelings in me. There my dog sits, looking up at me, and I wonder what he's thinking.

My dogs' eyes send many messages my way, but most often I find them saying,

"I love being here with you."
"Keep petting me—ooh, that feels good." (This one is usually followed by eyes rolling over into eyelids.)
"Where are we going? Can I come too?"
"Don't feel bad, I understand."
"Are you alright? You don't seem like yourself tonight."
"I heard you yelling (or laughing, or crying) – what was that about?"
"How can you watch the stuff on TV, I can't even keep my eyes on it!"
"Were you calling me?"
"Was that someone outside? Let's go see."
"Aren't you forgetting...dinner?"
"What do you want to talk about?"

My dogs' eyes tell me that he/she is always there for me, listening to me, ready to go with me. I hope my eyes say the same thing back.

"I'm here for you."
"Don't worry, you've got a home with me, pal."
"I'm not leaving you."
"Stay, and share this fire with me."
"How do you like those beef scraps?"

"Same time tomorrow?"
"What are you *doing?*"
"You're a good dog."
"Thanks for the lick."

Maybe, just maybe, they are thinking of you behind those eyes. If so, make them proud. Be a good human. Cruel people are easy to spot in the way they treat their pets, and in the way they talk to them. If you're considering marrying a person who kicks their dog, or leaves them alone for long stretches without food, water, or shelter, you might want to reconsider. You might be next to be abandoned. If you pal around with a buddy who abuses his friendship with a member of the canine family, you might consider what you have in common with Fido as both of you wonder what happened to your human friend.

And if you belong to a fanatical pet's rights group, stay away. I'm no activist, and people are ultimately more important than animals. There I said it. But as long as we're going to keep pets, whether they are dogs, cats, pigeons, goldfish or even snakes, I just think that our animals deserve our best for the time they are with us. Take a minute to lean down and give old Butch a scratch behind the ears.

"Hey, thanks, I love you to," he says from behind his eyes.

19

REJECTED GIFTS, REJECTED LOVE

When the Christmas season rolls around again, and I consider how I might make this one of the best of the seventy or eighty Christmases I hope to experience in my sojourn, I am weighed down once more by the prospect of gift giving and gift receiving. We all experience it. The thoughts go through our heads, "I wonder if (insert name of friend here) will get me a gift..." and "What do they *need*?"

Of course, in the ideal world, not yours or mine, we should probably give without regard to reciprocation. For me, it's as much a practical decision. I don't want to spend more than I have to in order to keep harmony with the loved ones in my life. But when I do open my wallet, I want to buy something of quality and meaning, and yet something purposeful.

This has led to a number of gift giving mistakes that I hope to explain in an attempt to alleviate needless suffering from the lives of others.

My cousins lived down the street from my childhood home, and this made for close kinships and endless hours of playing Little Men (playing with little toy armies, knights, or cowboys), Big Men (dressing up as army men, businessmen, or spies), or Blue Blob (a game of tag played with a sleeping bag over one's head). I wasn't quite sure, being of such a young age, what was the protocol for gift giving to cousins who were at times "the enemy" in these games.

My confusion turned to clarity one Christmas day when a knock came on the door and a gift was left secretly with a card from my cousins. It was a nice Christmas version of ding-dong-ditch, and I appreciated the sporting aspect of their gift. Of course, my mom knew that this meant a return gift was needed. I think we ended up repackaging a box of chocolates and dropping it on the doorstep. I remember how I felt, and the guilt that invisibly waited by my package as I rang their doorbell and ran away.

I hadn't understood the closeness rule: If they are family, that's close. If they are family that lives down the street, that's close. You must give a gift. So now I know.

Another tragic mistake in gift giving occurred during the first Christmas with my new bride. We had moved from our tiny apartment to a slightly larger one, where we were paying higher rent, but we enjoyed the little storage space we acquired in this step up. Ever since then, it seems that home buying has been mostly about finding more room to put our junk; but I suspect that we will go through a corresponding reduction in old age, when many people sell off, donate or dispose of things that never really mattered anyway.

As my wife and I exchanged gifts on this newlywed Christmas, I gave her my gift, which was undoubtedly something that she picked out; and then she prepared me for her gift. "Close your eyes," she said, as she placed a heavy box in my arms. When I opened my eyes, I saw that it was a new desk chair. It would replace the one that I had leaned into, causing the back – and me – to crash to the floor weeks earlier. It was a thoughtful, yet pragmatic gift, and the balance was sublime. She watched eagerly as I opened the box, removing the parts of the new chair.

As I began assembling the chair, she went into the other room to put a few things away, and I considered the parts in front of me. They didn't look solid enough to hold me, and I wondered out loud if this chair would break prematurely like the other one. I could only imagine being impaled one day as I leaned back and the back of the chair would give way. My wife entered the room and sat down on the floor with me, looking concerned. I made a crass remark about the lightweight chair's construction, forgetting my newlywed niceness governor. But there it was, and she broke into tears, mourning that she hadn't been able to spend more money for a nicer chair for me.

I felt lower than the casters on the chair as my wife's sobs, like knives, pierced my heart repeatedly. My comment was a boorish gaffe that made me feel instantly lower than the lowest height setting on my new chair. It was as if I had just been given a homemade chocolate birthday cake with my name written lovingly on top and I was complaining that it wasn't yellow cake.

The perfect example of gift giving in O'Henry's short story, *The Gift of the Magi*, told of Della selling her flowing hair to buy a chain for her husband Jim's pocket watch, a watch that he had sold to buy a set of coveted combs for her. In my complaint about the unstable-looking chair, it was as if I was saying to the angelic Della, "Boy, you shure look funny with that haircut," or "Well, whole lotta good a durn watch chain's gonna do me now!"

Which brings me to the memory of perhaps the best Christmas great gift I received once – a comb.

Growing up the youngest of six kids, I was often the recipient of all the hand-me-downs except when it came to clothes. I was bigger than my two older brothers, so more often I passed my clothes to them with some symbolic sibling irony, a hand-me-up, as it were. My oldest brother had gone through some tough years growing up, and during my early teen years the sight of his car in the driveway meant that we would face the inevitability of a parent-child battle.

Most Christmases during that time, he wasn't there, or was physically present, in his dingy mustard robe, while his troubles took his mind somewhere else. This particular Christmas he was absent, but for one small package under the tree addressed to me from him. It was a ridiculously large green plastic comb, like the kind found in the toy aisle of the local grocery store. A gag gift, to be sure; but I couldn't tell the intent of its giver until I read the hand-written tag on it: "To my biggest, little brother." It was so much more than a comb to me. It was a peace offering, a reconciliation, an honest capitulation from across the bloody battlefield we shared. His was a sweet offering – a handshake through the fence that had divided us so often. I ran the giant comb through my hair and thought of his fingers tousling my hair as an older brother would do to his junior apprentice if he were there. It was enough. He was more present on that day than in many Christmases.

Maybe gift giving and receiving should follow some basic principles.

The Bible speaks of the widow casting in her mite, the smallest of all possible alms, and the rich man who offered much in the eyes of those taking notice. Nevertheless, in this parable of giving, it was the widow's offering that was received because it was given in her poverty and need; it was given from her heart as a token of devotion.

As gift givers we have certain obligations. For example, we should take into account what are the recipient's needs. Woolen mittens are just hand coverings to some, but to bare hands brushing snow from a car or to child's hands who are rolling out a snowman, they are thoughtful remembrances and lasting memories. Cookies delivered to a friend suffering from depression remind him or her of the sweetness of life, of simple pleasures to experience, and of caring hands ready to share a treat or a warm embrace. A letter of appreciation penned carefully by hand on parchment paper signals the giver's sincerity whether or not the words are poetic. The price is in the thought paid to match the gift to the recipient.

Gift receivers also have certain obligations. We should remember that the giver intends the right thing. They don't usually mean to offend. So when we get woolen mittens, we shouldn't put them on wondering if the giver can't stand the sight of our hands. When our friend brings cookies to our door, we shouldn't assume that they know about our health ailments and so intend to kill us with these sugary sweets. And when we receive a letter in the mail written on parchment paper, we should stop and read it, looking for expressions of the heart rather than the smudge of ink or the garbled sentence.

As I think of the gifts I have given, I can do a much better job of putting the other person's needs ahead of my own guilt or sense of obligation. A little thought in advance will help fit the gift to the person, and forge a lasting memory of the exchange long after the gift wastes away. And I vow to appreciate gifts dropped on my doorstep or handed to me when my eyes are closed. Someone took the time to think of me, to spend time or money considering my needs. I hope that I will always retain the memories of these gifts from loved ones long after I forgot where I put them.

20

THE BAND TEACHER

In junior high and high school I was in the jazz band. It was the cool place to be. Sure orchestra had its merits, and I was loyal to my friends and teachers who gave mostly comical imitations of the great composers: Mozart, Beethoven and Bach. We were even a joke to ourselves – a few cellos short of a full orchestra, one might say – but we believed in the music and in the importance of bumping up our grade point averages with music classes. But jazz band was a prestigious club, the elites of the high school music scene.

Transitioning into high school jazz band was a personal Everest for me. I played the bass guitar, and considered myself lucky as the second chair apprentice to Martha, who seemed able to play anything. I had to practice hard just to be able to play along on a few of the easier numbers. I looked at the other band members with awe. Evan, the son of our band director in junior high, was the best trumpet lead in the state; Mike, on guitar, was legendary for his stylistic riffs reminiscent of George Benson or Herb Ellis; Mark's trombone improvisations were so furious that his hair was ratted afterwards; and Diane's pure musicality on the drum set brought the entire band to life. Legends all, I was humbled just to sit in with the band.

Our band teacher was a guy named Kendall; not Ken, or Mr. Newman. Kendall. He had a Groucho Marx moustache and Harry Potter glasses, and actually looked like a conductor's baton, a dark black head on a narrow body – kind of an upside down exclamation mark…with a moustache. He was a geeky, nerdy young guy and no one could explain the source of his cool-ness. It was as if he had eaten Miles Davis and didn't have an extra pound on his frame to show for it.

Having the privilege of playing under his baton in orchestra, I was able to experience the discipline of his rehearsal regimen. If he heard a sour note, he stopped, found the source, and corrected it, often to the sheer horror of the offending violinist or cellist who was publicly exposed. But the public humiliation tended not to matter so much after a while as we were able to hear with our own ears the results of Kendall's fine tuning.

When he led the jazz band, Kendall would stand on the side, the classic bandleader position near the rhythm section where he could keep watch over the ensemble while subtly cuing the soloists. Instead of the stiff-backed, baton-wielding figure rising above the sawing strings, he stood beside the ride cymbal slump-backed, snapping his fingers in syncopation on the upbeat, the picture of cool. He was no less demanding in these rehearsals, and with his occasional scoldings, we joined in his pursuit of excellence.

That year we challenged ourselves with complex pieces at our competitions, and we started picking up awards. Kendall decided to enter us in a national competition about halfway into the school year. We had to send in a recording of the band, and Kendall knew of a recording studio that could accommodate us. The studio experience was intimidating because we were recorded one section at a time: first the rhythm section, and then each of the horn sections in turn. But by the end of the very long night, we looked more like rock stars, strewn over sofas and mixing boards while we listened to ourselves through monster speakers in the sound engineer's booth. We sounded...wow...was that us?

Our recording took first place, and we won a set of jazz albums for the band, which did nothing to alleviate the debt we had created for the school by our extra-innings recording session. Kendall cooked up a way for us to pay back the school, and he came to us with the proposal. We could go play community dances and church gigs, doing all the big band classics from our parents' era. Of course, we wouldn't get paid individually, but it would help discharge the debt, and we might just have fun doing it.

We did have fun. We had our own zoot suits, with pinstriped, double-breasted coats, and we kept folders full of oldies, from "Moon River" to "String of Pearls." I think these local jobs did more to unify the band and develop our improvisation skills than any of the rehearsals and regular performances did; and we were eventually able to repay the money owed to the recording studio.

As we were preparing for our final challenge of the year, the big statewide jazz ensemble competition, Kendall came to us with another proposal.

"Okay, guys, we are playing better than we've ever played, and we can win state this year if we go and compete with the easier pieces we already have under out belts. They sound great, and you can play them flawlessly; but we could also go to state and play the Chick Corea piece, Pictures at an Exhibition. It isn't what the judges will be looking for because it is technical and contemporary, and they are either going to love it or hate it. Ultimately it might mean the difference between taking state and taking second place."

We had been practicing the Corea number for a few weeks, and it was pretty rough, but it was an incredible ensemble piece, incorporating non-traditional uses of congas, bongos, flutes and a bass clarinet. It included a long percussion solo and a unison riff that left no room for error. One player missing one note, or stepping into the multiple holes of silence we created, would be forever noticed.

"So you decide," paused Kendall. "Which piece do you want to take to state?"

It was unanimous. We picked the Corea piece, and after weeks of refinement, there we were, on stage at the state competition. On cue from Kendall, a second trumpet player screamed, and thus began our performance of Pictures at an Exhibition. We were so excited to showcase the piece, our giddiness overcame nervousness, and we laid down a perfect performance. And yes, we took second place in the state competition to a band that had made the conservative play; but we were happier than if we had taken first. We had pushed for excellence and we had achieved it together. I don't recall since that time when finishing second was ever quite as glorious.

These experiences gave me a special feeling for the unheralded school band teacher. If I could, I would give the good ones a special bonus to stay on and to keep inspiring their protégés. As it is, I have only been able to contribute my voice to those of the other parents who plead with school districts to let their music programs survive one more year.

My boys played in the school band, and they were lucky enough to have a teacher who was a Kendall in spirit. One day my ninth grade son, a trumpet player, said to me, "Dad, you know, Miss Wyeth is really tough. She gets on our case when we don't sound good. But we sound so much better than we did with Mr. Roberts, who let us just get away with stuff. He didn't really care." I smiled and told him the story of Kendall and the second place state competition.

In the pursuit of excellence, we often find ourselves at a crossroads. Take the road to the left, and there we will find a downhill slope well suited for coasting. It is a well-marked path that leads to a predictable destination. Take the road to the right, the uphill one, and we will find self-doubt nipping at our heels as we make the push to get to the other side of the mountain, uncertain whether we will succeed, or what lies beyond.

Ultimately, each of us has to decide whether easy victories – racking up "Ws" on the record book of our lives – are more personally rewarding than losses in epic struggles. Lessons learned in losses are often the catapult to future greatness. As I consider the greatest losses in my life, I am grateful for a band teacher who taught me the importance of setting for ourselves worthy challenges, and relishing victories over our own acceptance of mediocrity.

21

TOPAZ HUNTING – GLINTS OF LIGHT

When I was a Boy Scout, the scout troops in my area used to go on overnight excursions to Topaz Mountain. We didn't really know what topaz was, until some of the older boys told us about how the ground sparkled with crystals everywhere. As young boys we immediately thought of a mountain of diamonds, and that we might each bring home a pack full of treasured gemstones. We were certain that good fortune and lives of luxury were ahead, and dreams of living in a mansion playing on our own Space Invaders video arcade game were instantly within reach.

The funny thing about young boys is that we never really thought about the logic of this.

Posit: there exists a mountain of precious gems just a three-hour drive away. Anyone can go there and collect as many of these crystals as they can carry. They sell the stones and become embarrassingly wealthy, having to leave the neighborhood because of their newfound fortunes.

Conclusion: there are no valuable gems at Topaz Mountain.

Of course, it never occurred to us that we knew all the boys who had gone to Topaz Mountain in previous years, and none of them was wealthy and everyone still lived at home. But regardless of this obvious truth, we packed into the scoutmaster's truck and headed out for Topaz Mountain.

"There it is!" someone shouted, excited to be the first to make out a mountain on the horizon, but obviously not smart enough to know that it *couldn't* be the mountain. It wasn't shimmering from all the topaz, I thought.

"No, that's not it," said someone else who – like me – was looking for the equivalent of the Emerald City.

It turns out that it *was* Topaz Mountain. We were certain that the big crystal finds were just around the next corner as we drove to our campsite.

"Hey look, there's some topaz right there!" cried out an eager junior patrol member, caught up in the excitement of the moment.

It was then that the scoutmaster told us the truth that we didn't want to hear.

"Boys," he said in a fatherly tone, "you can't see topaz in the daylight. You have to see it at night, when you shine your flashlight on it."

Oh, right. Night. We silently wondered if we were the only boys within the surrounding towns who had fallen for the Topaz Mountain gag. Had we been the victims of another cruel gag, like the famous snipe hunts we all remember, chasing imaginary varmints through mud, sand and tumbleweeds as the older boys snickered to one another? The snipe hunt was right up there with the famous jockstrap-is-a-nose-warmer lie told to gullible boys by their seasoned teen lords. We were wary this time.

Night came, and the treasure hunt began. We were all in a line, flashlights at the ready, as we struck out from camp, our minds full of anticipation. How far would we have to hike before we came to the pile of gems? Should we bring our backpacks to haul the goods back to camp?

At the edge of camp, our scoutmaster had parked his truck, and as we came upon it, he stopped us and climbed in. He popped the switch for his headlights, and exited the truck. "There it is, boys," he said pointing in the direction of the beams.

"?" thought the scouts. If we were dogs, our heads would all be cocked a quarter turn, nonplussed, like dogs do when they think their "master" has gone out of his or her mind (for more dog translation see My Dog's Eyes).

Following the beams, as we walked out into the brightened landscape, the ground sparkled as if a thousand ant armies had lit their torches and were marching on this mechanical monster lying in their path. It almost looked like the truck had impacted an invisible wall, shattering its glass headlights and windshield on the ground beyond.

Stooping down and reaching for the sparkling lights, we noticed that the sparkle disappeared just as our fingers closed around the tiny pebbles. We put them in our pockets anyway, thinking perhaps that in the morning light we would see the jewels sparkle like wedding rings encased in dirty shells that we could wash or chip away.

The topaz hunting continued for several hours after dusk, as boys with flashlights walked the surrounding hills, ravines and parched riverbeds. Several of the boys were like Troy, who greedily stuffed his pockets full, as if all the Halloween candy baskets in the neighborhood were left on the doorsteps with a sign, "Please take one." The boys who joined Troy in this faction soon rated the quality of their finds, certain that the best topaz gems were just over the next ridge. I found myself in that group for a while, until I admitted to myself that I couldn't tell any difference between what we had gathered nearer the truck and what we were now putting in our pockets a mile away.

I had become a member of the other emerging faction led by the chief complainer and heretic, Danny, who was the first to suggest that topaz hunting was not all that had been promised. The boys in this group talked about going back to the campfire to toast marshmallows. They strolled, some of them with their flashlights off, looking occasionally at the finds made by the boys out ahead, generally unimpressed. While the noise on the front line was punctuated with sounds of delight and disappointment, the boys farther back fell in beside one another and began chatting and laughing, soon drowning out the Eureka-cries out ahead.

As the night wore on, and as eager topaz hunters left their searchlights for the camaraderie of the swelling crowd in the Toasted Marshmallow Faction, I was surprised to see the relative value of the once-prized pebbles drop so precipitously. On the way back to camp, several of us turned our pockets inside out, spilling our fortunes on the ground.

Troy never really did give up his search. The next morning, as we gathered around the campfire in the dawning day, Troy's disappointment revealed itself as he held out his handful of brownish-gray gravel. His treasures turned to stone, Troy sat through breakfast downcast, moping over his loss.

Like hunters who return empty-handed but full of stories and good cheer about the hunt, we topaz hunters returned home with plenty of tales for the rookie scouts to be. They too would get their chance to go to Topaz Mountain to find their treasures.

I have found myself in many other hunting parties since then, from tour groups to corporate klatches, and I have seen the emergence of the Troys out ahead. They scurry about, looking for the glints of light just beyond their reach, while farther behind, their comrades are snapping photos together or laughing at an impromptu potluck luncheon. Eager to find that elusive fortune, like Tantalus reaching for food just beyond his reach to sate eternal hunger, these Troys seek into the night just beyond the campfire. With pockets full of designer goods or prized collectables, they too find disappointment and despair in the dawning.

Come join our faction. Turn your pockets inside out, take a seat by our campfire, and lick the stickiness of the toasted marshmallow from your lips.

22

DO YOU LIKE THIS JOB?

While I was finishing my undergraduate degree, I worked at a department store near the university to pay for school and to help put food on the table for my new bride and myself. She worked too, and we were just able to afford our small apartment and the most basic of life's expenses. I had just enough time each day to complete the three verses of my daily song: school, work, and study.

I worked in a variety of departments, from shoes to accessories and even domestics, where I learned such vital information as thread counts and loops per square inch. I worked with some wonderful people, several of whom were also students, and we were always good-natured in our competition for commissions. Becky was the forty-something Taiwanese shark who always made commission, prowling the waters between pillow and comforter fixtures waiting for an unsuspecting customer to enter. Kelly was the college student with the asymmetrical hair, a real rebel in those days, but her quirkiness was endearing to towel shoppers. Melodie was the manager who cared more about sheets and tablecloths than anyone I had ever met. I was starting to learn just how important these coverings for beds and tables could be to the right person and the vast differences between one hundred eighty and three hundred thread count sheets. To me it was the difference between making commission or not, so I learned from Melodie and the Taiwanese shark.

Among the many tales of life in a department store, one that I remember well was the night I got locked inside the store after hours. It was late in January when Becky and I were doing inventory counts deep in the recesses of the stock room. We lost track of time, and we were locked inside the department store for several hours until the store manager could let us out. It was something you would see in a movie, and we toyed with the idea of going up to the demo kitchen and cooking a bite to eat; but we knew we were already in enough trouble.

On another occasion, I learned an important lesson about work when I was helping in the men's department on the first floor. The store was right downtown, and so we were prone to getting traffic from the local convention center nearby. We could spot conventioneers from a mile away. Their cheesy badges, logo hats, and canvas tote bags were dead giveaways. That day, a national convention was being held by one of the leading multi-level marketing firms, a household name associated with chiseling your neighbors and scheming against your family members to make a few bucks in cleaning supplies.

There I was, innocently looking over the racks of pants and shirts, when two conventioneers came up to me and struck up a conversation – selling, as it were, to the salesman. Only multi-level predators would have been so bold; but I saw them coming, like a prairie dog sees the jackal in the distance, and decided to hold my ground rather than retreating to the stockroom. Boredom has a way of inviting a challenge.

"Hey, how ya doin' there guy?" the first jackal cackled. For some reason he figured that "guy" was an excellent substitute for learning my name (See Introverts Unite for more on this). This was going to be fun.
"I'm great, how are you two?" I replied.
New jackal circles in.

"I'm Bill, what's your name?"
"Rob."
(Hand extended) "Hi Rob, it's a pleasure to meet you. How are sales today?"
"Oh," I said casually, "they're going along fine, a little quiet, maybe."

First jackal, sensing the prey was distracted, went for the hind leg.
"Do you like this job?" he asked, as if planning his next sentence. He really deserved some credit. He had probably learned this standard approach at one of the convention seminars, and was out there pitching his way to a six-figure salary.

It took exactly .017 seconds to think of the whole conversation that I

94

was about to sit through, and about that long to determine that I would see it through to the end, and just be myself. This conventioneer had crossed the line from customer to annoyance, and I followed suit, crossing from salesman to antagonist.

"Yes, it's okay," I offered. It was like saying, "Here chew on this leg."
"Don't you wish you could be making more money?" he said.

I paused for several seconds rather than answering out of hand. I wanted to throw off his rhythm a bit, "No, not really. I have enough for what I need, and it pays the bills," I rejoined. Now I saw something new in the jackals' eyes: fear. This was a new animal in the herd they hadn't encountered before, and it made them uneasy and skittish as they came in for a new bite.

"Wouldn't you like to *double* your income," he said, emphasizing the word double, "and be able to work out of the comfort of your home?"
I replied, "No, I'm fine. I'm going to school, and I have a small apartment. It's not bad, but I wouldn't want to work there."

"—You married?" the other asked.
"Yes."
As if smelling the scent of fresh blood, "Wouldn't it be nice to be able to afford some nice things that you've always wanted to get her?"
"Well," I hemmed pensively, "she works too, and buys what she needs. But I think she's happy."

I was toying with them a bit, and they seemed happy to try out their shtick on me, although they seemed disappointed at my apparent ignorant bliss. After a few more exchanges like this, the pair of jackals, with their Hello-My-Name-Is badges, walked away to search for a weaker member of the herd.

I have reflected on that encounter, and the first question many times since then: "Do you like this job?"

So often we see advertisements and portrayals on TV of people who hate their jobs that we come to believe that the best job lies just around the corner at the other store. We are told not to be content with what we have so often that we become neurotic about building our own resumes or padding our job titles or salaries in front of friends so that we're not embarrassed.

What would be the danger of living one's chosen profession with greater appreciation? That dismal job at the fast food restaurant may not be your ultimate career choice, but isn't it great to earn a paycheck to cover movie money or a dinner out with a friend (preferably not at a fast food place)? Can we feel satisfied that someone else is enjoying the benefit of our work, whether it's in a house we helped to construct or a child who has a newfound love of math because of our teaching?

Of course, earning money is one of the main reasons for work, and I don't know anyone who ever refused a pay increase – except for incumbent politicians *prior* to elections (we all know what happens afterwards). But are we all so universally unhappy with our wages that we become easy prey to unwise investment schemes, corporate headhunters looking for a commission, or "sure-bet" work at home fiascos that fail to deliver promised wealth?

We hear sermons about money being the root of all evil, but what about money just being okay, neither good nor bad? After all, it's not that the money is evil on its own; it's that our desire to be filthy rich soils our souls. As we plow the ground with our downward glares, justifying why we ought to be the ones to win life's lottery, we rob ourselves of all that is joyful and fulfilling in work.

To all of us, I would ask, "Do you like this job?" Does it provide the means by which you enjoy a drive in the country, a warm coat on a cold day, an adventure novel you share with a friend, or a night out at the movies? Does it give you somewhere to call home – a warm glow to welcome you back? Does your job give you something to hold to when life's struggles come along, a welcome routine that clears your mind?

You had better think quickly – the jackals are coming!

23

CIGARETTE BURNS ON THE TROLLEY

I recently returned to San Francisco on business, and I recalled an incident that taught me something about tolerance; and, like so many of those early memories, I still don't know who was right, me, or my parents.

I was nine years old, and as a family, we had decided to visit my grandparents in Oakland, California, a kind of springtime birthday trip for my two brothers and me. The trip was one of those occasions when so many more questions found their way to the surface of my emerging conscience than were answered. It was the first time I encountered Led Zeppelin music up close, watching my oldest brother and my cousin air guitar to music I recognized only as disturbing at the time. Perhaps this had made a bigger impression on me because it was contrasted so starkly with the sleep-inducing sounds and candy-apple sweetness of the Lawrence Welk show, which my grandparents watched religiously. Zeppelin was loud and obnoxious to my nine-year-old eyes and ears; but the bubbly blonde chorus girls singing "Good night, sleep tight, and pleasant dreams to you," were actually more frightening in a way. It was like they were the militant wing of a fascist Barbie doll state singing us to sleep while they peppered us with another attack of accordion torture. So many questions.

After enjoying the peaceful suburban hills of Oakland, my parents decided to take us into the city for a day of sight-seeing. We crossed the big orange bridge, disappointed that it was not golden at all. We drove through the city – including the parts where I had to keep my hands over my eyes – and parked near Fisherman's Wharf. Walking to the wharf was a real challenge because of the rain-soaked pavement and steep inclines. My Keds had a hard enough time holding the ground, and the innocent sidewalk felt more like a sheer granite face beneath my sneakers, rain-slicked and treacherous. I'm sure native San Franciscans are more like mountain goats, because they walked briskly by us as we clawed our way up and skidded our way down to the bottom of their hills.

We decided to take in a trolley ride, which looked like some fun from a distance. Up close, it was more like an over-crowded death sled where people hung off every possible foot-hold and hand-hold while a lean man in the middle, working a piece of wood, kept everyone from sliding to a human heap at the bottom. Hop on, kids!

I didn't know where to sit, and we all scrambled to find space. I finally ended up sitting on one of the benches facing out from the trolley; and while it was a little more relaxing the standing, from a purely physiological point of view, it was a tension-inducing ride for me because there was no railing to grab if I suddenly slid off the bench. I imagined myself sliding off the bench and into the street, and then being crushed by the oncoming trolley. Hey, but at least it would be able to stop, I thought.

I was wedged in next to a woman in a beige trench coat. As we started our ascent, she lit up a cigarette and pulled a few long drags, and as she did, a piece of ash fell onto the back of my hand. It was hot, but I didn't want to make a scene by immediately pulling my hand back and brushing it off. She didn't mean to burn my hand, after all, and she would probably be embarrassed. It was just then, just as the pain was starting to break my chivalrous silence, that she looked down and saw what had happened.

"Oh, did that fall on your hand? Are you okay?" Her voice was the sound of sandpaper, a desert of raspiness against the damp day, but I could hear her concern for me, although I kept my eyes forward to make sure I wasn't slipping off the bench.

The stinging on my hand was growing worse, but I said, "Oh, no, it's fine."

"Are you *sure*?" she asked as she attempted to brush the rest of the ash off, although the ash brand on the back of my hand had already begun to redden as a permanent souvenir of this trolley ride.

"Ya," I said, not making a big deal of it, although if my hand had known sign language at the time, it would have been cursing profusely.

When I got back in the car, after our adventurous mountain climbing, death-sledding day, my mom saw that I had a burn on my hand, and I told her what happened. "Didn't you *say* something, honey?" she asked rhetorically, knowing my shy nature better than anyone else did. I didn't answer, figuring it wasn't needed, but I was trying to answer that question in my mind. Why didn't I say something, and what should I have said? Should I have been angry with the arid-voiced smoker? Should I have inched her off the perch where we were seated, sending her into the oncoming trolley instead? She would be dead, and my hand would still have been as burned as before.

Sir Isaac Newton told us that for every action there is an equal and opposite reaction. We live in a world of action and reaction. All around us there are societal examples of this physical law. The businessman at the airport whose plane is grounded due to bad weather goes ballistic on the airline representative, as if she were the Divine in a little red vest, intent on changing the climactic conditions just to upset the Blackberry-starved, blue-toothed electric man. The woman in the grocery store express lane snipes at the shopper in front who has exceeded the posted item limit, forcing everyone to wait and extra five seconds while the cashier swipes the smuggled item through the scanner.

On a grander scale, we see this action-reaction law played out along our national borders, where the fleeing seek refuge and the encroached seek relief; in mahogany boardrooms, where executive mismanagement contemplates the next round of layoffs; in the courts, where the aggrieved seek retribution for the irreplaceable; and in the classrooms, where the teachers, fighting on the front lines in the War on Ignorance meet the immovable minds of videogame junkies. The cynical among us see these as stand-offs, inevitable stalemates of will, where only the tough survive, where nice guys finish last, and where the meek inherit nothing.

I'm taking a stand for meekness. I'm standing up for sitting down, for sitting on your hands before they ball up into fists and start flying into someone's face. I'm for parking the car instead of speeding up to feed the road rage. For first-strike weapons, I prefer debate, reasoning, parody and satire.

At the same time, I am not a pacifist. There is a time when words no longer do, when the consequences are so severe and so weighty that inaction serves only to strengthen the will of those enemies of justice and free will. But perhaps we could be more tolerant of a few, unintended mistakes before pulling from our own arsenals rockets of retaliation.

I don't know what I should have done back on that trolley. We are told to despise the smoker, cast him out, sequester him, tax him, and vocalize your disgust with him. We are told to stand up for ourselves, to forbid others from trampling on our rights, to demand respect for our gender, race, wealth, title or status. If I were to take that trolley ride again as an adult, what would I do differently?

First, I don't know if people can still smoke outside in California. I'm not a smoker, but it seems to me that smoking in the open air is probably okay for others to do. I suppose that if the situation occurred today, I could raise a tirade over the ill effects of her smoke on all the passengers on the death sled, drawing the entire crowd into the argument and isolating the offender, shaming her into stamping out the cigarette. Maybe I could pull the cigarette from her nicotine-stained fingers and ram it into her cheek, one-upping the ash-burn on my hand. Alternatively, perhaps, like a modern version of the ancient stoning rituals I could incite the crowd to throw her from the trolley, sealing her fate for daring to waft ash onto my hand.

On the other hand, I could just let it go, brush the ash from my hand, and put it in my pocket.

24

MUD FIGHTS AND LIGHTNING STRIKES

The summer of 1977 was a glorious time for any teenage boy. We crowded in to see Star Wars – most of us for the third or fourth time – and we hung out at the local arcades, the new jousting grounds that equalized bully and brainiac in virtual battlefields. It also happened to be the year for the National Boy Scout Jamboree, a quadrennial event where scout troops from all over the country came together in one sprawling campsite to meet other scouts, work together on merit badges, and engage in cutthroat patch trading.

My older brother and our three cousins packed up our gear and joined about twenty-five other boys for the adventure. We purchased special red, white and blue duffle bags to haul our gear, each with the boy's name emblazoned on the bottom in iron-on letters. Since we were going to be inspected by the national boy scout leaders, we made sure that our uniforms were pressed, that our patches and awards were sewn exactly where they should be (snug to the seams), and that no one forgot his official green belt or the green tasseled garters that held up our official green socks.

The Jamboree was held in Moraine State Park in western Pennsylvania, and our troop was scheduled to arrive there in the early part of August after touring a number of historic sites in that region of the country, such as Niagara Falls, Gettysburg, Washington D.C., and New York City. We stood at the base of the newly completed World Trade Center towers unable to bend back far enough to see the top as our eyes followed the converging lines toward the heavens. We enjoyed *parts* of a baseball game in

Yankee Stadium – our seats were right next to the main walkway, so we mostly watched fans passing back and forth on their way to alternating beer and bathroom breaks. In Washington we felt the substantial cold marble chair of Lincoln's Memorial and pressed our noses against the glass vault containing the Declaration of Independence and Constitution at the National Archives.

These were times of emerging independence for us as well. We stayed at hotels, and in the evenings we struck out on our own, usually with one of the senior patrol leaders guiding us to convenience stores for a snack run or out for a stroll near the sites we had seen during the day. Wherever we went it was in full uniform, and often we would meet up with other troops on their way to various events. In Washington, our converging sea of green scouts actually caused several public escalators to give up under our combined weight, a fact that was a surprising source of pride for many in our group.

After nearly two weeks of sightseeing, we arrived at our destination, a spacious clearing on one side of Moraine State Park where several hundred tents had been pitched by the other scouts who had arrived ahead of us. We set up our camp in a roped off area designated for our troop, and we posted our banner with the troop number and hoisted our American flag. We were on what appeared to be the outskirts of the scout city, but by the time another day had passed, over ten thousand scouts had arrived, filling the tens of acres in our portion of the camp from one tree line to the other.

That first weekend, we enjoyed a sing-along evening with the king of folk music, Burl Ives; and then we huddled in small groups to begin the patch trading ritual. Patches with more colors, more figures, and more complexity – like the shark and sea creatures of the Malibu district patch – fetched a higher value than those colorless, ordinary patches of the unfortunate junior scouters who would undoubtedly return home with the same boring patches they brought.

We awoke the next day to the sound of thunder and the skies opened up with seven inches of rain in the span of a few hours. It was a deluge, an upside down tidal wave drenching the canvas camp and turning everything from green to brown. Getting to and from the makeshift showers involved trudging through so much mud that showering was the only time our feet were clean. We laughed as we skidded and slid in impromptu mud Slip-n-Slides through the newly re-named Camp More-Rain. School buses that were serving as camp shuttles, bogged down in the mud, and they stopped running with any regularity, so we were cut off from most of the scheduled activities on the itinerary.

In Camp 480, we began digging trenches to channel the water, and my cousin and I spent the better part of the day trying to divert the river running through the middle of our tent with little success. Elsewhere, the camp became a tribute to scout ingenuity as boys lashed logs together to make bridges across new rivers and to pave the main paths like boardwalks – or logwalks. If there had been a merit badge for public works projects, we would have earned it after all the canals, dams, and bridges we fashioned in the mud. Finally, the civil authorities called in backhoes and earthmovers to dig yard-deep trenches and spread new paving material where roads had been washed out.

The next day we were playing cards in camp, wasting time waiting for the quartermaster to deliver the day's ration of peanut butter and jelly. Just up the logwalk from our camp was an open grassy area where boys would go to play flag football or assemble their latest log projects. It was an island of green amidst the rising brown tide. On this afternoon, the rain continued to fall, with occasional rifle shots of lightning splitting the sky in the distance.

Then we heard it, a loud crack that sounded like the earth had just split in two. This crackle lit up the entire camp and seemed to send a static spark through all the tent poles and stakes. We all looked at each other. One scout had quickly pulled his hand away from holding onto his tent pole because he said he felt a charge. Where do you run when your only shelter is a nylon or canvas tent with a river running through it? We stayed put, trusting the reassuring looks of our scoutmaster.

It was then that we noticed a stir coming from the open field. A few minutes later, we ran up to investigate. A crowd of leaders had gathered around a figure lying on the ground, making it impossible to see who it was or what had happened. We were told to get back to our camps and stay inside. A life-flight helicopter landed in the field and took the boy to a nearby hospital.

Within the hour word had spread through the entire tent city that a boy had been struck by lightning.

As the afternoon wore on, we were encouraged to offer prayers in the boy's behalf, and accounts of what had happened made their way to our ears. This boy had been playing catch with a Frisbee and the lightning had traveled along the ground passing through the dog tags hanging around his neck and stopping his heart. He had died instantly.

Suddenly our mud-caked shoes and rain-soaked tents turned from symbols of a grand adventure to somber reminders of the elements that had claimed our comrade. The tone in camp was noticeably subdued, and boys passed to the latrines and showers in haste. We recalled our mud-induced giddiness, remembering how lightly we had treated our surroundings, irreverently passing under Nature's threatening cover, skipping through Her minefield.

Of all the memories from the scout jamboree, this juxtaposition of muddy mayhem and solemn solitude remains with me. In the years since, I have seen tragedies, many of them closer than the adjacent field in camp, and I have been struck by the contrasts of life lived to the fullest but seldom appreciated until the moment following the tragedy. The scout playing Frisbee with his buddies was laughing and running and in an instant transported to his grave. The towers in New York where I craned back by head in 1977 were full of the buzz of business twenty four years later, a hive of activity in the instant before the first plane struck.

Perhaps it is these contrasts that make such memories so lasting, so vivid in life's repository of recollections: joy robbed by grief; fullness rent with loss; laughter silenced by anguished cries. In the years since the jamboree, I have tried to reflect less on the morbid details of the aftermath and more on the richness of life enjoyed in the moments just prior – and I picture the Frisbee-playing boy. Tragedy will eventually touch us all with its grim interruption. Enjoy this moment.

25

DRIVING AWAY FROM 9-11

September 11, 2001 is a date carved deeply into the American conscience. Each of us has a story to tell about where we were on that day. I would like to humbly offer my own account in the spirit of remembrance, and with the hope that others might write about the events on that shocking and sobering day. This is our collective journal, our memory we pass to our kids to remind them that evil exists, that life is precious, and that goodness abounds in millions of unknown fellow Americans.

The ride from LaGuardia on this Monday evening was beautiful. It was near twilight, and I looked out the taxi window, leaning closer to take in the view as we traversed the Triborough Bridge. Beautiful. Lights began to sparkle on the distant Manhattan shore as the sun sank behind the skyline casting its warm glow on the backs of those driving home from their long day at work. Unlike the recent business meetings I had enjoyed downtown, I was going to be spending the next day at our Paramus, New Jersey office, and I felt a little disappointed that I wouldn't be able to continue into Manhattan this time.

The next morning I arrived early to prepare for the meeting that was to start at nine o'clock. Just prior to the meeting one of the attendees said he had overheard a news report in the office that a plane had crashed into one of the World Trade Center towers. We couldn't get any clarification from our co-workers about the nature of the crash, but naturally assumed it was a small aircraft that had tragically strayed off course. Then came the news that a second airplane had crashed into the other tower. This time we understood from the office staff that it was a commercial airliner. Stunned, we all crowded into a cramped office to listen to the radio.

Within minutes the shock turned to panic, and the reports from the World Trade center suddenly became dismally clear. America was under attack by a terrorist group probably connected with the same organization that attacked the World Trade Center in 1993. The office was closed as a precaution, although we couldn't understand how it was supposed to make us safer to leave this three-story building in the suburbs. The news we had to that point originated from the office radio, but no one had seen any news footage.

Across the street from the office was a hotel with a bar, and thinking that they might have a television, several of us ran across the street to try to get a glimpse of what was happening just over our horizon. The bar was dark except for a big screen TV, surrounded by fifteen or twenty guests and staff, all eyes fixed on the glowing screen. As I approached, peering through the group to get a view of the report, I understood for the first time how dreadfully understated had been the reports on the radio. Both towers were on fire, and I stood aghast listening to the reports and estimates of the number of people potentially trapped above the conflagration, watching as several of them, in utter despair, leaped to their deaths. I tried to imagine what would drive a person to jump, tragically settling in their own minds the question of survivability, leaping free from the burning threat into momentary blue sky.

A camera had caught the second airliner impact on tape, exploding in a ball of fire that exited the opposite side of the tower, leaving a flaming gash across the width of the building. It was a massive wound in the side of the tower, yet this appeared to be all that remained of the airliner.

Around the room there were hands on faces in stunned disbelief.

Then it happened. The first tower fell, as if it were a great ocean liner sinking into the billowing surge below.

Heads lowered, hands dropped, eyes winced, and the room went silent except for whispers of "No...no..." and "Oh, God." The tension of what we all feared was replaced with grief for the countless lives extinguished in that moment.

We continued to watch, not knowing what to say, saying nothing. Horrific scenes filled the screen: smashed cars and rescue vehicles, and replays of crowds fleeing the shadow of the falling tower. In the continuing mayhem, the other tower fell, and grief turned to shame. We were powerless to stop its descent, and no force rose to steady its mass. As if mocking the scene, sunlight now peered through the gaping skyline casting its fresh light on the gray rubble as the sky began to clear slightly.

My mind went back to my colleagues back in the office who were listening, but not witnessing, the broadcast images we had just seen. Two of us returned to the office and told the sad news of what we had seen, trying to convey the scale and scope of the tragedy, like two street preachers crying repentance from the ignorance of the earlier frivolous assumptions we had all made.

Our minds had seized upon the certainties amid the confusion, and we began to consider how we were going to get home. The airports were closed, as well as all tunnels and bridges in and out of Manhattan. With the background reports continuing to come in about the attacks on the Pentagon and crash in a field in Pennsylvania, we assembled in the conference room to consider our situation. We began to list our names and the names of those who had cars or who lived in the area who were willing to provide shelter. Some felt that if we waited, we would know more about the airports or bridges and we might be able to get back to the airport or to a car rental facility.

Amidst the indecision, small groups began to form up. I saw that one woman, Sue, had a rental car, and that she was heading for Ohio, but she was willing to give the car to another man, Jim, and me so that we could continue on to Chicago. She called the rental company and we were gratified to hear that we could take the car wherever we needed to go and they would sort out the situation with her later. The three of us agreed on our simple plan. Leave now, and drive west.

We loaded the car and began driving, with Sue and Jim in front and me in the back seat. We turned on the radio and listened to the grim reports as we made our way to the freeway. We assessed our fuel and on-hand cash, and determined that we could make it for several hours before we needed to stop. The radio reports said that as many as ten thousand could be trapped or killed under the rubble of the two fallen towers. As we made our way onto I-80, heading south and west, about ten miles from Ground Zero, we looked out our windows to the left to see against the clear blue background, just behind the low hills, a column of smoke rising from what could only be lower Manhattan.

At that moment, gazing at the smoke through my backseat window, I felt a compelling pull toward the disaster site. So powerful was this feeling that I shifted in my seat, suddenly uneasy and quickly considering whether my new friends could drive me in a little closer so that I could go dig through the rubble. Could I stop them, and if not, could I walk the distance in time to help? I thought what words I would use to explain this emotion and began planning how.

Just then the radio reported that scores of people had showed up to help, and authorities were requesting others to stay away so as not to interfere with the heavy equipment and rescue efforts that were underway. I thought of my wife and three boys who would worry for me, and I needed to be there to comfort and help explain what had just happened. Despite the tangible pull towards the unknown thousands who were suffering, I knew my first duty was to get home.

The freeway turned to the west, and we drove away from the column of smoke, watching it diminish in our rear window. My thoughts were of Ground Zero, and I fought back feelings of cowardice as we abandoned those behind us, trying to focus on those ahead of us.

We stopped for gas at a small town in central Pennsylvania, while about seventy-five miles to our south, investigators were combing the site of the ill-fated Flight 93 that had pierced the earth outside Shankesville. As I filled the tank, I looked at the sky. Since the FAA had ordered all planes to land at their nearest possible airport, the blue sky was unmarred now by jet contrails, as we were now exposed to heaven's wide view. As I went to the window to pay the cashier, I caught his gaze and he nodded. No words were said, but the feeling was clear – mutuality in grief.

In Youngstown, we drove Sue to the regional airport where she had parked her car. The airport gates were filled with planes of all sizes, clearly straining capacity, with jumbo jets peering down on the regulars at the gates, uninvited guests of the tragedy, much like our friends we had left in New Jersey, grounded with their co-workers. Jim and I drove on, finally arriving at a hotel outside Chicago where we parted company with few words, and my wife met me. Warmed by her embrace, welcomed by her longing eyes, I could only guess at the pain I would have caused her had I remained in New York; but my heart stretched back across the solemn freeway we had just traveled to that turn west.

Like the millions of others on the following day, I stayed riveted to my TV looking for signs that the rescuers had found survivors. I read the

Leonard Pitts column in the Miami Herald[1], circulated widely on the Internet in the aftermath. The words captured our collective rage: "You *monster*. You *beast*. You *unspeakable bastard*." Days passed and images flooded our conscience, from the reconciliation of an embrace between President Bush and his rival, Senator Daschle, to the thunderous applause when the president made an appearance to throw out the first pitch at the delayed World Series. We watched as our enemies danced in the streets, and we reverenced the fallen in the flags unfurled across the nation.

As I drove down the country lane from my house days after 9/11, I saw a couple outside lashing a giant American flag between a basketball standard and a parked RV. Our eyes met, and they waved enthusiastically. The American spirit had been reborn in newfound patriotism, or at least stirred from its slumber.

As days and years passed following that tragic day, it has faded in our rear windows much like the scene I remember on I-80 outside Paramus. Every September 11, and occasionally in the intervening months, I recall the heartache and helplessness of driving away, and I vow to remember. Remember.

NOTES
1. Pitts Jr., Leonard. "Sept. 12, 2001: We'll Go Forward From This Moment." Miami Herald. 12 Sept, 2001.

26

LIKE TALKING TO GRANDPA

Like many other young couples across our land, my wife and I spent a year living in her grandfather's basement while I went to school. His wife had recently passed, and this created a mutual need – he in his loneliness and we in our poverty. Our basement home consisted of Pepto-Bismol pink walls and an ancient paneled basement where I set up an impromptu office, featuring a particleboard desk and a floppy disk-drive computer.

Our lives in the post World War II bungalow basement were harried as we drove from work to school to the occasional night out; and grandpa's back door might as well have had double-hinges like the doors from a short-order kitchen as we passed through life at a decidedly quicker clip than did our octogenarian watchman, and his stiff-legged fox terrier, Jake. Grandpa's mornings consisted of a Danish cringle warmed in the toaster oven, sharing an occasional piece with Jake as we threw back a bowl of cereal without sitting, and flew out the door. In the evening, I would return from school and work to see grandpa cooking up something in the kitchen like boiled calf's brains or toaster oven pizzas from the frozen food section at the market.

He had worked for Coca Cola for over thirty years, delivering mixes to vendors in town, so his house had a few reminders of those days – Coke trays, toy trucks, and bottles that once contained the brown elixir. One particular bottle, a gold painted bottle, remained unopened, as if somehow this were a fine wine to be enjoyed after another decade or two had passed. Other memorabilia included an old trunk under the stairs full of Samoan artifacts and black and white photos of great-grandfather's missionary service to that part of the world, and the garage and basement were full of old hand tools bearing at least two generations of wear on the wooden handles and grips.

I was so rarely to be found on the main floor of the house that I couldn't blame him for not knowing who I was. He often called me by the other in-law's name, or substituted "Rock" or "Rod" for "Rob." When referring to my wife and I in the plural, we were usually "those people who live with me" or "those people who are trying to steal my car." I certainly hadn't lived up to my part of the bargain to keep an eye on grandpa. With one eye fixated on work and one on school, I had already acquired that cross-eyed misalignment in my young life common to so many trying to move up from the basement.

My wife's two eyes were more often in grandpa's service. She worked too, but found more time to be with him to cook or help him with cleaning when I was at school. She would make time to take him to the local Wendy's for a chocolate frosty, or to accompany him on a trip to the market. On Sundays, he would don his tweed hat and we would go to church together and then return to a beautiful meal, when we weren't running out to visit our parents to forage in their kitchens.

Mealtimes with grandpa were usually pretty quiet, although he would occasionally comment on the fine food and care given to its preparation. Sometimes he would launch into conversations about family members that would put my wife immediately on the defensive. Each was certain of his or her position, and they dug their foxholes deep, preparing for battle.

I need to interrupt this part of life with grandpa to mention that this dear man was suffering from the onset of dementia. His shuffling walk became more pronounced as the neural pathways seemed to take longer to send their signals, and once-vivid memories became clouded, like a cataract was spreading its cover over his clear mind. The occasional pot left on a hot stove became more a more frequent occurrence, and the number of sacrificial Danish cringle pulled smoking from the toaster oven rose with corresponding and increasing regularity.

For those who care for the elderly, they witness the great injustice of life's journey towards what Shakespeare called "second childishness and mere oblivion," as the collection of life's memories are robbed by the thief of mental deterioration. Those who provide care are at once the parent and the child, often caught in the no-man's land in between, unwilling to agree and unwilling to scold. This is where my wife occasionally found herself with grandpa.

These dialectic duels usually happened when I was out of the house, so I would only learn of them after the fact, while staring at the Pepto-Bismol walls, as if I were the acid in a giant churning stomach, wondering if the house would win or if we could ever eat our way out of the smothering basement. Her arguments with grandpa were never really arguments, but were more like a series of battles in clarification. He might start talking about how someone owed him money or took his money, and my wife would rise to the defense of her parents and siblings.

Finally, after hearing about one of these incidents, I said, "Does it really matter if he's wrong? Why do you care so much?" In the back of my mind I was thinking that he, being closer to death, would soon be able to learn the *actual* answers for himself and end all speculation. But I don't think this was any satisfaction to my wife. She wanted to win, and she admitted it.

We have joked about this in the years since life with grandpa, and the phrase, "it's like talking to grandpa," has been used as a type of conversational salve to take the sting out of family disputes and teenage parenting. When the war of words begins to pile up bodies on both sides, this phrase can help to suspend the final death stroke, and block attack dogs of debate from going for the throat. "It's like talking to grandpa," you might say as you turn to walk away, counting to ten under your breath.

The teenage cry, "It's not fair that...(fill in teen angst phrase here)" is disarmed,
The pouty husband's lament, "But she won't listen to me, no matter what I say," is neutralized,
The friend searching for an ally with, "He's just *wrong*, don't you *get* that? Are you on my side?" meets the immovable force.

This magical phrase can also be followed with the punctuating phrase so often avoided in times of distress, "I love you," thusly,

"It's like talking to grandpa (Unspoken thought: how you can't see it my way because of your thick-headedness and stubborn will to do something so stupid, reckless, and ill-conceived). I love you."

Go ahead. Take your best shot. Upset me, go ballistic, freak out, get defensive, lose your cool. No matter what you say, I won't crack and I won't give up on you because despite what's playing in my mind I can just say, "It's like talking to grandpa."

27

LIFE'S OASES

Because of a few isolated experiences in my life I have come to know more about something that others in the world experience regularly, what it means to thirst and then to be quenched. It's a simple physiological reaction to going without liquid for an extended time, often at a time when the body is crying out for relief, which, once provided, produces refreshment and rejuvenation.

When I was a young Cub Scout, I went to summer camp in the mountains above my home, where the Den Leader took us on a day hike through the trees to a lookout point perhaps three thousand feet above our point of origin at the scout base camp. Our little party consisted of six or seven boys, and each of us carried a canteen or water pouch for the hike. We were told to fill them at the faucet in camp because it was the only water we would get all day.

I don't remember much about the hike, except that it seemed endless. It was probably no more than five or six miles total, although I'm sure upon our return that number climbed to ten or fifteen miles as young boys are often tend to exaggerate such things. We stopped for lunch at midday before reaching the lookout point, and then, after reaching our destination, we spent the rest of the afternoon returning to our base. Our water supplies ran dry in the early part of the afternoon, and we had to endure only a few hours of thirst.

In my mind I could only think about the faucet we had left earlier that morning. I could just simply turn it, and sweet mountain spring water would gush out. Around each bend, my eyes searched for that faucet, and as the time wore on, I wondered if we would arrive in time or if we would all drop dead from the lack of water. This too was an exaggeration of my youthful mind, but it felt so real, that when we did finally reach the faucet, we drenched ourselves in its coolness, sucking and slurping from our hands as we reached through the other sets of hands searching for the stream. The faucet we had almost disregarded in the morning we might well have worshipped in the late afternoon.

Several years later, on another campout, we began our hike before dawn from the south rim of the Grand Canyon, leaving our scoutmaster's truck on the plateau and descending into the canyon. Our destination was Havasu Falls, a picturesque blue waterfall cascading from the painted red rock walls of the canyon, a sight that we were certain would not live up to the photos shown us by our leader. It was a hard hike for us, although not one that was terribly long, only about ten miles. What made it more difficult were the switchbacks and the sand.

Getting to the floor of the canyon involved walking down a series of switchbacks, where the trail traverses downward in a steady slope, then turns, or switches back, to continue the descent. Carrying enough gear for five days on our backs, our forward-leaning momentum made it less of a walk and more of a test of our ability to apply our own braking power as we rounded each switchback, fighting against our own inertia to continue in a straight line off a cliff.

Once on the canyon floor, after a brief stop for lunch, we continued our march to Havasu Falls, but we were hampered at every step by the sandy soil. Walking through dry river beds is a little like running on the sand at the beach – you feel like you expend twice the energy to reach your goal as the sand gives way under your driving feet. It made for sore calves and breathless progress in the heat of the summer sun. Had we known that the ten-mile hike was through such parched land, we would have saved more of our water from earlier in the day, but now we were running dry, and no relief was in sight. We couldn't see a drop of water anywhere, and my mind drifted back to the scouter's manual, trying to recall which was the best place to dig for water in a dry river bed. Maybe I could kneel down on our next break and try it. Boy, was it hot!

As we counted the miles we had traveled, we were certain that by late afternoon we would begin to see the sparkling water coming into view in the distance. The only moisture among us was the sweat soaking our shirts and hats. It just couldn't be any farther down the trail. We had to be right on top of it, but we saw nothing. This was barren desert, and we were certain in our parched state that all rivers had dried up, that the falls were a myth, and that we were doomed to wait for rainfall or to go begging for water from the local Supai residents.

Then, from a hundred yards down the trail, our Scoutmaster cried out, "Here we are, boys! This is it!" He was standing among the sagebrush, and there appeared to be a small ridge behind him. There was no water anywhere; but we followed, and, rounding the bend, we beheld our postcard, a hundred-foot waterfall crashing into a pristine pond and running away into a series of natural pools beyond the edge of the pond. We threw off our packs and dove in the water. A few others reached for the giant rope swing and hurled themselves out over the deepest water, dropping into a sun-warmed bath gulping not for air, but for the water around them.

The final thirsty episode occurred in Elat, a small Israeli town at the head of the Gulf of Aqaba, one of the two inlets at the top of the Red Sea, like two fingers forming a sort of peace sign around the Sinai Peninsula in a region where peace is most fragile. Here in the extreme southern regions of Israel, the Negev desert is parched. In many deserts it is possible to see plant life, such as cacti, sagebrush, or juniper brush; but here eyes strained to see whether a shadow on the hillside was a rock or a plant. It was as lifeless as a lunar landscape, with only the road and the dry air to remind us we were terrestrial travelers.

Miles passed behind us without seeing any sign of life, except that from within our sweaty bus as we, a group of about thirty American students bounded over roads rippled with blowing sand. The only water we had was carried in the belly of the bus, and it consisted of water turned red not by Moses' outstretched staff but by the sweet American drink mix we carried with us to make it more palatable. Of course, after driving through the desert for eight hours or more, the red nectar was hot, like being at room temperature in hell. Hot or not, drinking it brought life back to the group, turning lethargy to energy almost instantly. We rationed what we could drink, to make sure we had enough for the return trip the next day.

That night, a friend and I went exploring. Just beyond our camp farther up the beach we saw a few lights and what looked like small shelters, and so we went to see if we might find a faucet or a hose, something to satisfy our thirst in a more substantial way. We came upon footpaths, with ferns at our feet and palms overhead, and just beyond that we saw small bungalows that might have been sleeping accommodations for some seaside resort, although everything appeared abandoned. We saw no one else and heard no voices or sounds of any kind. Then we came upon a shack atop a flight of stairs, nestled among the palm trees and ferns, and light was streaming from the windows above the door. We knocked and entered.

In an instant, we were transported from the memories of a sweaty bus to an air-conditioned room, a bar, complete with tables, neon signs signaling the local beers available on tap, and clean tables and chairs. We were the only ones in the place, except for a large man standing behind the bar. It was like a scene from the Twilight Zone. Had we traveled through some porthole into another dimension? On the other side of the door a few hundred yards away our exhausted fellow travelers rested on the beach, dreaming of hot red punch for breakfast, while we seated ourselves at the nearest table.

"You would like something to drink?" asked the man.

We saw what looked like a large red cooler in the corner labeled Coca Cola, so we shot back, "Do you have Coke?"

His answer was melodious and sweet to our parched throats. "Certainly," he said, and followed with, "Would you care for ice?" We declined, anxious to wrap our lips around the open Coke bottles as soon as possible, without offending our host.

In ten minutes, we had ten empty bottles resting on our table. The Cokes we guzzled down were icy cold, like the kind you see in the commercials where the beads of condensation drip down the sides of the bottle in glistening rivulets. We contemplated marching back down the beach to invite our comrades to join us in this oasis, but it was something to consider carefully. What if there weren't enough drinks for everyone? Would their not knowing be better than knowing and not having? It took another ten Cokes to consider this question with adequate gravity, and finally the secret was discovered when two friends walked in the door. We saw the looks on their faces, surprised at their surroundings, eyes fixed on our empty bottles. They had just come through the porthole. "Here. Have a Coke," we smiled casually.

Our lives take us through many different kinds of deserts, some of them as real as dusty trails or as barren as the Negev hills. We thirst for something just beyond our reach, searching the horizon for a sign of relief, a sight or sound to break the torment and give reassurance that hope is just ahead, a light just up the beach. What is this thirst? Some thirst for knowledge, some for money or status. Others thirst for friendship, closeness or conversation. Often the venues we call oases, the local bar or coffee house, satiate some need other than thirst, or merely mock our thirst as we drown in the drink but remain parched, as if swinging wide on the rope-swing and plunging into the crystal pool finding it muddied and fetid.

Maybe if we search deeper, we might find other oases to soothe our parched lives, other methods to quench what drink alone cannot. Call a friend, make a new acquaintance, visit your local church, read a classic novel, take in a museum tour, or write to an aging parent. Let the icy coolness soothe your parched throat, and pause in gratitude for all things. Here. Have a Coke.

28

THE WRESTLING MEET AND GLORY DAYS

Throughout my life, whenever the topic of school sports comes up, someone might ask, "So what sports did you play in high school?" to which they always supply a multiple choice response before I have a chance to answer, as if they want *me* to guess what it was:

"Did you play football? Hockey? Rugby?"
"No, tennis," I respond.

None of the above. Of course, I couldn't blame them, since no one would have guessed from my size that I was a tennis player any more than they would guess that chess champ Bobby Fischer was a lineman for the Dallas Cowboys.

I had actually been in a perfectly well matched sport up until my sophomore year in high school – wrestling – but I eventually couldn't come to terms with several key factors:

First, the coach was an egomaniac. He was also the English teacher; so he used to give a test, promising to the person who aced it, a bona fide "A" for the rest of the year. The test consisted of questions about himself – his favorite color, favorite movies, and questions about his family. He made sure that the best wrestlers knew the right answers, of course. If I was going to get killed in the wrestling ring, I at least wanted the excuse that I had more *brains* than they did. I didn't really care that they were cheating – cheaters eventually, and remorsefully, meet up with their own ignorance.

Second, I got tired of being around disgusting guys in the locker room. Maybe I was just developing prissiness in my middle teens, but there was something about the spitting into towels before weigh-ins – not to mention the other unspeakable acts known to reduce one's body weight before a match. I couldn't think what this would do for my future, since I didn't foresee a time when eliminating body fluids would be a necessary part of my day.

Third – and I know it sounds crazy – but I didn't like wrestling with fat, sweaty guys. I was big for my age, and had grown beyond the top weight class by about fifteen pounds, so I wrestled in the heavyweight class. This meant that I could either lose the extra pounds and "wrestle down" a weight class, the most acceptable strategy to my coach, or I could stay in my class and use speed and craftiness to overcome the size disadvantage. The guy in the weight class just below heavyweight was state champion in his junior year, and I was no match, so it didn't really matter where I went. I was still going to *practice* with fat, sweaty guys and get twisted around by the state champion.

However, in my junior high days, the coach was a nice guy, the other wrestlers were disgusting but not revolting, and although I was in the heavyweight class, I didn't have anyone else in my weight class, so I practiced with the weight class down, or with the coach. None of this prepared me for the ultimate test that year against the superior team, the Bulldogs.

It was my ninth grade year, and I was the big man on campus. Ninth graders in many schools are the freshmen; but in my junior high school, they constituted the senior class. I had a crush on Joanne Pendleton, whose Farrah Fawcett feathered hair fell luxuriantly over her shoulders, and she used to flip her head so that her hair would swirl around her face like the Breck girl in the shampoo ads – and the whole world seemed to move in slow motion.

As if the manliness of wrestling and the feathered hair flipping weren't enough of a complement to my growing ego, a wrestling movie called "Take Down" was in theaters, and it highlighted a reluctant wrestler who joins the team and overcomes all kinds of hardship to help the team win a big match. I could imagine myself in a big match, with everything on the line, and Joanne in the stands cheering me on to a glorious victory in front of the whole student body.

Well, there they were, the Bulldogs. In their shimmering golden sweat suits, arranged from lightweight to heavyweight, they looked kind of like a stop-motion photograph of the rising sun, and the full eclipse at the end of the line was a guy weighing in at two hundred thirty-five pounds. I knew what he weighed, of course, because we all had to weigh in before the match.

For the heavyweights, they just set the scale at the minimum weight for the class, a hundred and eighty-five pounds, and by standing on the scale, you had to make the right end of the scale lift off its resting position and hit the top position, suggesting that you were *over* the weight limit. When I stepped on the scale, the end of the scale slowly rose to the top, and stayed there. Ahh, I was overweight, the ironic relief of the heavyweight class wrestler. It was quite a contrast to my poor teammates who were in the back room beginning their make-your-weight rituals. Then the solar eclipse stepped on the scale, the Bulldog who actually *resembled* a bulldog, and the end of the scale jumped to the top with a *clang*. He was safe. I wondered if, in the spirit of "making my weight", I should go out and eat something so that we would be more equally matched.

The first few matches went to my team, the home team, and the crowd of students cheered half-heartedly, content to be sitting in the bleachers rather than the final class period of the day, a standard practice for home games. Unlike the dominating displays of the early matches, the middleweight matches were close, and the Bulldogs had pulled to a tie with one match to go, the heavyweight match. Victory in the this match meant not only a personal win, but the crown of glory that comes with winning the whole meet for the school.

Joanne in the stands, the pep squad cheering in rhythm, I stepped to the line opposite the last Bulldog of the day. He looked confident and even a little cocky as he faced me, staring me down, ready to bury me. I worried a little that if he got on top of me, his folds of sunshine fat would smother me like the white cells that engulfed the submarine in the final scenes of the *Fantastic Voyage* movie. The word in the locker room was that he wasn't just big, he was a good wrestler. I was neither.

My coach said to strike early, and catch him off guard. I jumped in and out, not letting him lock up with me. We pranced like two hippos around the ring, each of us taking a shot to grab the other one's leg and failing, rising back to the face-off position. Then, I did it. I leaped through his hands and grabbed a leg, a great white piece of birch tree trunk that tumbled backwards as the Bulldog landed with a solid thump. I held onto that leg and drove with my head into his gut, not releasing until I had tried to deflate as much girth as possible. I had scored a take down, netting two points, and made it to the second period. I was able to escape from him in the second, picking up another point, and avoided a take down. Then came the third period – and the Bulldog was mad. From the starting position, he on his hands and knees and me wrapped over the top of him like a bull rider waiting for the gate to open, he jerked his head back and caught me in the chin; but I kept my composure and drove him forward, landing him on his stomach.

With a minute to go, I just had to keep him away from me. The sedentary crowd had come to life, and the bleachers were rumbling as students were on their feet cheering. The referee was hovering in front of me and said I had better get to work or he was going to give me a warning for stalling on top – he should have given me a medal for even *being* on top, I thought. With his arms tucked in tight against his body, the Bulldog had gone tortoise, and I couldn't extract him from his shell, so I just stayed where I was and kept pushing him around the ring, like a kind of human sponge mop.

Just as the referee caught my eyes and was about to issue a warning, the buzzer sounded the end of the final period. I was alive. The Bulldog was red-faced and full of protests as we stepped to the victory line. The referee raised my arm, and I looked out at the crowd. I had the victory, and the school won the meet.

The crowd poured out of the bleachers and surrounded the giant blue mat as I turned to see the Bulldogs skulk back to the locker room. Then my eyes met Joanne's at the other end of the blue mat, the crowd parting as if to let the children of Israel through the Red Sea – and there she was. She ran to me, and we embraced in a sweaty silky display for the entire student body. It was Hollywood, and I had just won the Oscar.

I think back on the drama of that day, and laugh a little. The scales would rise to the top a lot more quickly now, and the Bulldog's size wouldn't seem quite so intimidating. I have faced bigger opponents in the intervening years, and most of them didn't stare back from across the other side of any ring, but from the mirror in my bathroom. Joanne married a good man and had four kids. I married a woman who loved me, and we had three boys. I can't remember a time since then when I have stood in the middle of a crowd cheering me on, but I have felt joy many times over – on my wedding day, at the birth of my boys, and in the thousand memories I have of simple pleasures and a contented mind – and it is quite enough.

I would like to think that the greatest victory is the one just ahead, the one you haven't faced but have been preparing a whole life to meet. For some this opponent is self doubt, for others it is addiction, or depression. Still others face debilitating diseases or tragic family losses. At such times, think back to the victories you have piled up in the past as you face this new opponent. Forget the chatter in the locker room about this tough new Bulldog. This is your day.

29

ON BEING GIFTED

I'm gifted. Not in the Christmas or birthday way, but in the chosen, elected, hand-picked way. How do I know? I know, because in fourth grade I was selected from among my peers to be a participant in a new gifted program that met in the library once a week for gifted time. I don't think I ever told my parents about this fact, so they were never able to enjoy going to dinner parties and gushing, "Oh, our son is in a *gifted* program at school and he's *soooo* brilliant, *way* ahead for his years. He's going to be *president* one day."

Despite this omission, it was great. Along with half a dozen other gifted students, we were given the run of the library, and no one else could come in while we were in session. I think the administration realized that the intellectual capacities of our humble elementary school were being unjustly inflated by this handful of students, and so to make things fair for the rest of them, and allow them to progress without looking off our papers, we were extracted as a favor.

We didn't do much intellectual ruminating in the gifted program. Our mental capacities must have been too far advanced for our teachers to feel themselves worthy of our instruction. Instead, we were allowed to use the school's video recording equipment to create movies from our vastly gifted imaginations. Over a matter of a few weeks, we wrote, acted, and produced films on several short subjects. The black and white camera we were forced to use was clearly incapable of capturing the proper lighting and shadow, marring the nuances of the film noir genre we were attempting; but, being gifted meant improvising with what you are given, and let's face it, in a world of average people, it takes an incredible amount of sacrifice to produce excellence.

I normally don't like labels, but being "gifted" made me something truly special. I was *more* creative than average people. My artwork signaled true hidden talent. Any attempts I made at music, art, or prose were automatically worthy of hanging on the teacher's wall because they were made by my gifted mind. Average students looked on jealously as I moved freely about the school – no hall pass required – in order to get to the library for gifted class.

School administrators knew me by my first name, and often commented to other teachers that I was a member of the gifted program. I was, in fact, guaranteed a leg up in the grading system, because, being gifted, I was incapable of average work. If teachers unfamiliar with the special needs of the gifted failed to understand me, they were nonetheless obligated to acknowledge my giftedness by starting at the "B" grade and working up.

Alas, my friends were not gifted. Danny played the accordion in a very average way. Jeff's parents grew vegetables in their backyard, tied to the land – how *agrarian*. Mike had no musical or artistic ability, and being average, appeared not to mind. Drifting into this realm of the non-gifted made me appreciate my special status even more, and I knew I owed it to *them* to continue our associations. Maybe it was my first attempt to give back to the people, remembering where I came from, or appreciating my roots. Of course, I was only nine, but I'm sure that even at that young age, my giftedness would not have allowed me to be selfish.

As a gifted one, I believe my children have also inherited my giftedness. My oldest son vomited frequently as an infant because he was gifted – didn't you know that about gifted children? My youngest son screamed and threw tantrums when he would get upset, and it was actually melodious, as if he was actually composing operatic verse. If only we had recognized, and digitally recorded it, earlier! My middle son sat at the piano and played by ear, and he actually composed music while he sat there, a kind of new age, post-modern music that had dissonance and a certain youthful innocence, truly a Mozart reincarnate.

Since your children are not gifted – and I'm sorry for that – let me explain what you can do to make up the difference. It's not going to be easy, so take notes.

It starts very young. You must devote more time to *in utero* education, reading only the classics to your growing baby. I'm sure if you know the right people, you can get connected to someone teaching Contemporary British Literature For Baby's Second Trimester or Quantum Mathematical Theories for the Fetal Mind. Stop watching TV, unless it is something educational, like Discovery or National Geographic. Then you need to start thinking about schools. Where will your baby go to be exposed to other kids who are clearly gifted? You must start saving money now, so that your gift-less child can have a chance.

You must nurture the child's mind by involving him or her in every possible extracurricular activity at school, remembering to blend the arts and sports, the creative and kinesthetic, the right and left brain stimuli that gifted children don't need. Although your dismally average child may wilt under the workload or sway under the schedule, just keep it up – you're building for *their* future here, and there's no time to lose. You might consider buying him or her a smart phone right now, and teaching your young one to use a blue tooth device in order to learn the importance of networking and connectivity in a digital world. There's no room for analog thinking when your child's not gifted.

Government support for the gifted is something I can whole-heartedly support. If we can understand the ways of diagnosing giftedness at an earlier age, we might reduce the overall burden placed on society by needlessly nurturing the merely mediocre. I don't want to sound callous about it, but if we are going to compete in the global economy, our gifted children must begin learning Mandarin Chinese right now. Can't you see the logic of it?

Oh, and about those so-called music programs at your school? We should eradicate the banal blowing of brass or the soulless sighing of strings by the non-gifted masses. Let them listen to the gifted performance and share in the collective praise rightfully owed to those of the gifted class by those who have only minds big enough to dream of such accomplishments. Remove the brushes, pastels, and clay from the sluggish hands of those who have no capacity for creativity. Pampering the prodigious will pay big dividends in the future, not only for your average kids, who will have the opportunity of appreciating all that is profound, moving and artful, but also to society at large by relieving the masses of their frustrating inability to inspire anyone other than the rube, the neophyte and the dullard.

In the end, when society has paid its price for my giftedness, I will rest well, knowing that it was all worth it. No price was too high to pay; no parental sacrifice was too great; no petty playground sport with average comrades was worth conceding; no creative opportunity was denied for the simple lack of government funding.

After all, I'm gifted.

30

CIRCUSES AND PRISONS

Like most kids – or like most kids who get sent to the principal's office – I had a rebellious streak in me when I was in school. At first it was due to sheer boredom, and later it was due to what I saw as violations of the unwritten rules between students, teachers and administrators. If they taught us something worthwhile, or at least interesting, we would go along. If not, the battle was on.

Rebellion takes at least two forms: the overt rebel and the subversive rebel. The O.R. reeks of pot smoke and fires rhetorical questions at inopportune times during the lecture, such as, "Hey, wouldn't it be cool to hang out with Hitler?" No one really expects the teacher to answer and no kid is going to disagree with a psycho pothead, but there is that tension in the moment before the teacher snaps where you think to yourself, this could get ugly. The O.R. doesn't mean much harm; he just wants to damage the teacher's reputation in hopes that he can once again solidify his bad reputation for being a psycho pothead O.R.

The subversive rebel works more quietly, and crosses gender, race, and intellectual boundaries. These S.R.s write notes in class taking shots at the teacher behind his or her back, silently infecting a portion of the classroom while somewhere else another S.R. is plotting a game of mind control with the teacher. This S.R. might comment, "But Miss Jones, you said we could work on that assignment *today*. I didn't do the assignment because I knew I had an extra day." Miss Jones, knowing the S.R. student to be compliant and hardworking at other times, changes the class assignment, thus giving a day off to her students.

I was more of an S.R.

In seventh grade, my teacher, Ms. Shelton – we called her Ms. Skeleton because she was a gaunt, aging woman with pronounced eye sockets and a sunken nose – was lecturing on the history of the Indian tribes in our part of the country. This was a time before we used the term "Native American" and long before we really knew that Indian people came from India. As she droned on about the anthropology of these tribes, the background noise in the classroom rose from *pianissimo* to a decidedly *mezzo forte* disruption. Her voice could still be heard just above the chatter, but any sentient being could simply look around and see that ninety percent of the room was neither watching nor listening. Ms. Skeleton just went on, louder this time, as if pulling out her trombone to respond to the surging of the string section.

I was sitting in the back row, and as I surveyed this performance of Ms. Skeleton's Symphony on a Native American Theme, I chuckled to myself wondering where it would end. It was that moment before the snap, and I knew it was just around the corner. Wait for it…here it comes…

"That's it!" the bony-faced teacher cried, slamming her book on the desk and finally looking out at the disarray for the first time. "It's like a circus in here!"

From the back row, an S.R. saw the opening, and in a voice just loud enough to be recognizable, but soft-enough to be sub-O.R., I sang the first few notes of the Barnum and Bailey Circus theme, "Deet deet deetle deetle deet deet deet deet." Like two laser drills burning through metal, Ms. Skeleton's eyes caught mine. I looked to my left to see Sullivan, the pothead, smiling at me as if to say, "Welcome to O.R. land, man. Here's a reefer."

I was sent to the vice-principal's office, and had to repeat the whole story for him, which seemed to infuriate him, officially speaking, while also amusing him, strictly off-the-record. I don't think the school knew what to do with S.R.s. We were pretty good most of the time, and we were usually "A" students, so we could be shamed into going along with things. Bring a note from home, sign this form, promise not to sing circus themes again, and the warden would let us off with a warning. At times, S.R. behavior was inward and individual, a mutinous monologue, like in Accelerated Math class.

Accelerated Math was just not my thing, but I had been so proud of myself for being invited to pull into the fast lane that I couldn't refuse. I found myself struggling with the logic of math. What was with the constant canceling out on either side of the equal sign? Did it mean that, in the end, all things are equal? The one thing my parents and teachers had taught me about math was that it would teach me practical knowledge that I would need the rest of my life. But story problems seemed to be just the opposite of real life. If you were in an auditorium and needed to count the seats using a mathematical equation that was going to take you an hour to figure out, why use the formula – just count 'em, I thought; and once they were counted, someone should just write it down and pass it on so we don't have to do it again.

This was my problem. Story problems were little vignettes of life that had no real bearing on life. My S.R. nature really got worked up about this, and my story problem illiteracy culminated when I had to take the mid-term final. The mid-term final consisted of twenty story problems. I read through a few of them, arguing to myself why anyone would write such drivel. The characters, plot, and setting were void of any creativity at all. That's when I came across the swimming pool short story:

Question: If you were filling a swimming pool of xy dimensions from a hose, at z rate, how long would it take to fill the pool?

I decided to write in the missing parts of the story, so I wrote something like this:

In this story problem, the question of filling time is unknown, so let me explain. If I had a swimming pool, and was asked by my dad to fill it up, I would probably turn on the hose full blast, make sure it was inside the swimming pool, and then go in the house to watch Gilligan's Island (the after school show of choice). *After about an hour, I would go back to the swimming pool, make sure the hose was still in it, and see how far it had filled up. If it wasn't that far, I would go back in, make myself a sandwich, and watch* The Brady Bunch (a second-rate after school choice, but certainly better than watching a pool fill up with water). *I would continue checking back on the swimming pool until it was getting pretty close to the top, and then I'd turn the hose off.*

Math teachers I have met have not had much of a sense of humor, and neither did this one. When I got my paper back, a very red, very large "F" stared back at me. He had not commented on my creative writing skills *at all.* I soon found myself demoted from Accelerated Math, giddy that my S.R. plot had succeeded. No more solitary confinement.

Occasionally, my S.R. traits were expressed outside of the classroom. One of the unwritten rules between students and The Man (administration) was around lunchtime, and by the time we arrived in high school, lunch rituals were well understood. We were certainly willing to stand in line for such delicacies as Gangrenous Salisbury Steak, Pressed Turkey Parts, or Fried Mangled Mexicali Delight; but once we got down to eating, we expected the teachers to stay away. Good referees are never seen on camera, and that's how we wanted our overseers of the cafeteria. I ate lunch with my band buddies, and Mark – another S.R. – had a very special ritual of stuffing everything that he didn't eat into his empty milk carton. It was a little compact tribute to waste management. Apparently the vice principal did not agree, or perhaps he was just tired of dealing with O.R.s, and so he felt it was time to stir things up with the S.R. ranks. Bad move.

Doctor Amundson, a lanky Lincoln-esque character who wore the same tweed jacket every day, stepped up to our cafeteria table, and it seemed that the top of the table was about even with his knees. He leered at the overstuffed milk carton, with Essence of Horse-Meat Burger oozing from the opening, and inquired, "What's wrong with that?" I had all kinds of great retorts to that one, just dying to get out:

"What's *right* about horse-meat burgers?"
"Its round shape doesn't fit very well into the square milk carton without some modifications, and in this case Mark has succeeded very well."
"Nothing really, want a bite?"

Instead, I just watched my buddy explain that he just wasn't hungry. I could see in Dr. Amundson's eyes that it wasn't over, and in that moment, he pushed the tray back at my friend and went on a rant about how he was wasting food and being disrespectful toward those who prepared it. It just seemed a little over the top. This was my friend's lunch – he paid for it – and now it was being shoved back in his face by The Man overstepping his bounds. As Dr. Amundson grabbed my buddy's arm to escort him to the office, I stood up and faced Dr. Amundson.

"Hey, he's just eating his lunch. What's your problem?! You're *way* out of line!" I shouted.

Again, my volume betrayed my S.R. roots, and I was hauled down to the office like some O.R. kid. After sitting outside the office "on ice" for an hour while Mark was being interrogated, I was asked in to Dr. Amundson's office. He asked Mark to excuse us, and I was left alone to deal with The

Man. I was expecting suspension or at least a strong scolding, and so I was surprised at the softer tone adopted by Dr. Amundson. We had a rational discussion about the lunchroom fracas, and it was clear that I was getting amnesty this time. I thought that he was probably intimidated by the number of S.R. students I represented in these negotiations, knowing that if he lost my faction, the S.R.s and O.R.s could form an evil alliance against the administration. This thought alone might have given the doctor pause. It was more likely, however, that his conciliatory air was due to the realization that he might face repercussions if this incident was more widely known. We each expressed our points of view, and as we shook hands and I walked out of his office, it felt like we were letting each other off with a warning.

In life, there is a delicate balance between S.R.s and O.R.s. Those of us who are given to mischief, horseplay, and practical jokes don't really understand the risks taken by the O.R.s. After all, it's better to live in a school prison where the guards let you go to P.E. or band class than it is to sit in a stale detention classroom. Learning to cope with the wardens, guards, and fellow inmates we encounter in whatever prisons we find ourselves is not only a part of life, it can become a creative exercise of free will. So next time you get a lecture from the police about the dangers of driving without a seatbelt, the next time your garbageman rails at your poor placement of the garbage can or the home association president tells you to mow your lawn, just watch for your opening, listen for the pause, and let it out: "Deet deet deetle deetle deet deet deet deet."

31

LIFE, WORTH LIVING

Look around and you will find abundant evidence of the cheapening of life, a cut rate, bargain basement, liquidation of the soul.

Enter the world of any boy, age seven to seventeen, and you will find that the price of life is about fifty bucks, or the price of a video game. For that price, you can become a first-person assassin, a cruel brute, a galactic monster, a locked-and-loaded killing force mowing down everything from mutants to mothers. You can save up "lives" as you acquire more power so that when you "die" you can use up a saved life and continue on – a sort of feline view of life (although I object to most cat analogies – see Cat Hatred) that allows you to throw your lives away in pursuit of taking more lives. But these are just games.

Of mortal consequence is the red tag sale on life in the inner cities where the wrong fashion choice or the wrong friends might equate life to the cost of a mere bullet; or where the pre-teen pusher is bought for a pair of shoes, a hit, or simply the promise of protection. A depreciating life here is not worth saving, not worth the investment. It will return only chaos and yield dividends of death.

On a global scale, we see regional conflicts where brutality and retaliation continue in an endless cycle. Like dead stalks of corn, the dead lie shriveled, hollow, rigid, the golden fruit beneath hidden permanently by the harvesters. Lifelessness, empty shelves of cities wasted, fertile lands spoiled, can be purchased cheap on a massive scale for those who wage destruction for the masses. High price, high return, in this twenty-four-seven clearance sale.

As we look out our windows at this cheapening of our greatest commodity, it might be easy to see why some of us lose hope. "Why bring a child into *this* kind of world?" some couples say as they contemplate parenthood. Still others, faced with the financial costs, social stigma, or the burden of parental responsibility extinguish the spark of life once conceived in a rejection of the most precious of God's gifts. What kind of world *is* this, where brutality replaces innocence; where integrity is sold for the price of a golf game or a new car; where virtue and drugs are bartered side by side to the highest bidder?

Some of us turn inward, turn away from windows on the world, retracting from it, like tortoises into comforting shells. For us, the immaterial summation of life's balance sheet – on the one side, assets of hope, love and companionship, and on the other liabilities of loneliness, tragedy and despair – results in a deficit, a depression. Life flickers low like the last reaches of a candle's flame in the smothering dark. "No light, but rather darkness visible[1]," was John Milton's characterization of that destination of the fallen. Depression's crushing waves on the sandy shores of life erode hope until, at last, the beach closes, shutting out family and friends in a rigor mortis of the soul.

I get the blues, have cloudy days, mope when things don't go my way; but these weather changes in mood pale when contrasted with the climactic shifts of depression. Others find relief in writing about it, cathartic cleansing of tormented minds, while others seek to play upon our sympathies, claiming to be the noble victim of circumstances beyond their control. "I am depressed," when spoken aloud betrays this pitiable yearning, since to admit it is to desire to move beyond it – action unthinkable to the depressed mind.

I am not a clinician, and do not claim to have expertise in recognizing depressive states; however, I have my own experience from which to draw, in the spirit of neither catharsis nor sympathetic appeal. It is a simple story of a gift from a friend who taught me the way to hope, the way to move beyond today's sorrow. She was not a trained psychiatrist, just a high school friend.

In my senior year of high school, I went into a depressive spiral that began sometime in autumn and continued through winter. I will not expound on the potential causes of this condition in part because it is indefinite and indefinable; and knowing was not the source of ultimate deliverance. Having moved deeper into the cave, the entry was a distant thing, hidden from view, impossible to discern. That I had descended was clear to me then, and now.

Some see depression from the outside as a struggle between two states, one euphoric and one despairing; but for me it was a suspended state of absence. A vacuum of *emotionlessness* was all that was left, a void, where my joy, sorrow, anger, and hope had atrophied. Voices at the cave's entrance, from friends and family, inquired where I had gone, what was wrong, and why had I withdrawn. I retreated further, unable to explain, unwilling to engage.

In William Styron's memoir to his descent in *Darkness Visible*, he expounds perfectly the life behind a life; an invisible participation in the mundane: "…the sufferer from depression…finds himself, like a walking casualty of war, thrust into the most intolerable social and family situations. There he must, despite the anguish devouring his brain, present a face approximating the one that is associated with ordinary events and companionship. He must try to utter small talk, and be responsive to questions, and knowingly nod and frown and, God help him, even smile[2]."

Then, someone entered my cave. I was in the family-less room looking at the TV when Allison entered. We had worked together as leaders of a student group and had known each other for nearly a year, and although we cared about each other, we had never dated or taken a romantic interest in each other. And here she was. Was this going to be another unsuccessful attempt to draw me out? Who had sent her? *How long would this attempt last?*

She said, "I want you to come with me. I'd like to go for a drive."
"Okay," I said, wondering where we would go, what inspiring site she had selected for the backdrop of our empty conversation.

We got in her car and she drove, saying nothing, and pulled into the parking lot of a fast food restaurant about five miles from my house. Families were filing in, enjoying themselves inside, the definition of normalcy outside my bubble. She turned off the car, and fixed her eyes on me. She hesitated, and then said in a firm but compassionate tone, "Life is a *choice*. You can wake up tomorrow morning and *choose* to have a good day. You can decide what you want life to be." She was not upset, and no tears welled up in her eyes. These were words well-planned, intended to push, not to pacify. "The choice is yours," she said, staring into my eyes, and she turned back to her steering wheel, starting the car.

I didn't say anything. I couldn't say anything. She drove me home in silence while I absorbed the message left hanging in the air, "The choice is yours." The next day, when I awoke, I chose to leave my cave and walked out into a spring day.

Styron wrote that the task faced by those who try to steer a friend out of a depressive – or even suicidal – cycle may require "an almost religious devotion to persuade the sufferers of life's worth, which is so often in conflict with a sense of their own worthlessness, but such devotion has prevented countless suicides.[3]"

Since this first battle in the war for my soul, I have often asked myself what makes life worth living.

I have decided that one reason is life's memories. If we close our eyes, the photo album of our mind opens to reveal the sights, sounds, and smells of a life worth living: a fireworks show on the Fourth of July that lit up the sky with wondrous sparkles; a golden sunset that drew our extended gaze; a piece of music that stirred us to excitement, hope, or sadness; the scent of a campfire and the warmth in darkness; the quenching sweetness of lemonade on a hot summer day; or the touch of a hand or a warm embrace. It is not the absence of these things now, but the abiding memories in our minds, on our lips, and in our ears that reminds us of a life rich in experiences – treasures of the mind.

Among our precious assets are the memories of loved ones and friends whose influence made us who we are. From the physical features we wear to remind us of our parents to the sage advice of grandparents whose words still whisper in our ears, each intersection with another's life creates a stopping point, a place to reflect, a juncture to which our minds might return once more if we retrace our steps. Perhaps a teacher inspired you with a story – remember how your imagination soared? Did your heart leap nearly out of your chest with your first crush? Was it your older brother who stood up for you and kept you safe, or became your best friend? Did your cousins dress up on Halloween and trick or treat with you? What kind of pet did you have growing up, and how well did he/she know you? Who was it that stayed with you when you were ill, wrote you a card, called to say hi – they were there once, and they will be again.

This brings me to the final reason why life is worth living. It is the promise of a brighter future. I'm a sucker for Coppola's "It's a Wonderful Life", and every Christmas when my channel-surfing hand catches this wave, I ride it to shore. I have always been fascinated with the notion that one life can contribute to so many others in unknown ways. A compassionate word at the right moment could prevent tragedy; a small kindness could multiply in reverberating acts of good will. It could begin with you.

Whether the past is a nostalgic comforting blanket to you or a burden of regret, pain and fear, your future is unwritten. No life can become fulfilled *in absentia.* Heroism, artistry, wisdom, generosity, and success are all impossible for you if you choose to leave before the end of the movie. Are you a late bloomer? Who would know if you depart before the spring?

Would you rob your posterity of the gift of life? Their absence from life's stage will undoubtedly leave holes in the unfolding script of humanity. Whose lives might they have saved, what service might they have done in your name, and what beauty might have flourished in their gardens that would brighten one corner of the world? To the questioning couple wondering what dread this world might bring upon their unborn child, I might ask, "What good is your child capable of *bringing* to this world?" or "How might this suffering world heal from your child's hands?"

Life is worth living because of the life that waits beyond. Over the horizon of today's valley of sorrow is another valley where you might drink from cool clear streams and bask in the warmth of sunny skies. A thousand memories await in the valley beyond, but you won't find it crouched inside your cave. Come out. Live.

NOTES
1. "Paradise Lost", John Milton, in John Milton Complete Poems and Prose, Merritt Y. Huges, Ed. Bobbs-Merrill Educational Publishing: Indianapolis.
2. Darkness Visible: A Memoir of Madness, William Styron (1990). Vintage Books: New York, pp. 62-63.
3. Ibid, p. 76.

32

ARE YOU GAY? AND OTHER SIMPLE QUESTIONS

Donald and Mike were not friends of mine, but we walked home together occasionally because they liked to cut through my backyard to get home faster. One day, as we were walking home, they started kidding around about something that was obviously an inside joke to them.

"Ask him," said Donald to Mike.
"No, you ask him," said Mike to Donald.
"What?" I coaxed.
"*Make* him answer," sneered Donald, as he and Mike tackled me.

This was a position that we found ourselves in quite frequently. One boy would be on his back, and another would be kneeling on top of him, pinning his arms with his knees, hands free. This allowed the person on top to tease the boy on his back by tapping on his chest with a knuckle, or to administer other means of torture like face slapping or pretending to drool down on the face of the pinned one, but sucking up the spittle at the last minute. Disgusting? Sure. Welcome to boyhood.

In this case, torture was not the goal, but extracting information. It's strange how honest we were at times like this. The threat of torture was enough to force any confession, and so I wondered what question they would put to me, and whether I would have to answer honestly. Here it came.

"Alright, alright," said Donald, "I'll ask, but you *have* to tell the truth."

"Okay," I said, looking up at Donald's ugly grin, checking to make sure a loogie wasn't descending. No, I was safe for the moment. Then, as if asking the location of some hidden treasure, he said in a quieter tone, "Are you *gay*?"

Mike snickered and looked my direction.

That was it? That's the question? What's the big deal, I thought. After pausing to think about it for a few seconds, I said gladly, "Ya, I guess so. I'm pretty happy."

They went crazy with laughter. Donald fell off me, curling over in laughter. Mike looked at me with wide eyes, "You said it. You're gay!" They descended into another fit of cackling laughter, like hyenas on laughing gas. Now I was uncomfortable.

Being gay, in my formative years, meant that you were happy. Remember the lyrics we used to sing, like,

I feel pretty,
Oh so pretty,
I feel pretty and witty and gay!

Well, I didn't sing a lot of West Side Story at that age, but I was aware of the tune. Or what about,

Don we now our gay apparel, fa la la la la la la la la.

At what point did gay mean *gay*? Judging from the hysterics my answer had caused Donald and Mike, it must have been around that time. And no, they weren't gay.

Our language has seen some significant changes because of social movements, immigration, or increased sensitivity.

My brother and I used to play cowboys and Indians. We knew what that was, and we knew that the Indians would always win. Although the little western outfits are still sold at the local drug store, and little plastic toys of cowboys and Indians are still packaged together, what is it called now – cowboys and *Native Americans*?

I remember when we were growing up we had black rubber galoshes that we stuck our shoes in, and these things zipped up over our shoes to keep out the snow and slush. It was not unusual for Mom to say, "Don't go out without your *rubbers!*" Horrors!

Growing up, we all wore *thongs*. Showing your thongs was not considered in bad taste because their gay colors (ha!) flossed the toes rather than the posterior.

In grammar school, we learned that the proper pronoun to fill the spaces in such phrases as *everyone had ___ own ticket to the show* or *each of us was sitting in ___ seat when the bell rang* was *his*. Now we circumlocute this usage with awkward substitutions or we try to phrase it another way to convey one common acceptable androgyny.

We used to speak of *mankind* without regard for womankind and *cavemen* without cavewomen.

What is it like to be *woman*handled?

Certainly much of our language has changed for the better, particularly racially divisive words, although some organizations would find it hard to take on new names, like the National Association for the Advancement of African-American People or the United African-American College Fund. Just get back to us on that one, please.

When you are going to enjoy a nice seafood smorgasbord with friends, it's a bit awkward to shout, "Who's got the *crabs*?!"

Why is it okay to rail against the indecency of pulling into a *handicapped* spot or using a handicapped stall in the restroom, but we somehow cringe at that term when applied to something other that parking spaces or restroom stalls. Maybe we should tell each other to stay out of physically challenged spots or not to use the differently-abled stalls. We need a ruling on the field for that one too, please.

I really don't fret much about politically incorrect language. We have learned to swap out words over time, and that will continue to be the pattern as long as we have political correctness. But do we have to call it *political correctness*? When have you ever seen a politician who is correct?

I would like to propose a few new terms to replace political correctness while preserving the connotations of the term. How are these substitutions?

Offensive equality – to ensure that all groups are equally offended, we can adopt this term and use it after every slur.

Don't like that one? How about,

Consensorship – the state of being where enough of us agree that repeated use of the word offends enough of us that we add it to the banned column.

Or what about,

Neutral extremism – preaching a doctrine of neutral language so that no group is unduly denigrated or praised.

Labelous – an adjective describing one's need to attach descriptive terms to anything.

Perhaps we could just adopt *Correction Officers* and *Word-ens* as chief vocabulary enforcers. Anyone caught using a word on the disapproved list would report to redaction camps where the words would be forcibly erased from their memories.

We can only hope that it doesn't come to that. We would have to change many of the classic works of literature to remove words that are no longer acceptable to our enlightened age. Our kids certainly should not be allowed to read these offensive words or understand the historical derivations of such terms. Teachers should not have to face the difficult moral questions inevitably raised by the presence of colorful language. In fact, it might be faster if we adopted a more expeditious route to linguistic parity – let's just burn the books and get on with it. Oh, I guess that's been done. That word was called *fascism*.

33

THE ROCKWELL PAINTING I HATED

Norman Rockwell's art captured Americana on the cover of the Saturday Evening Post for almost five decades, and the images haunt us with sentiments nostalgic and wistful, like walking through an antique store longing for a return to times that are now merely rusted, yellowed and obsolete. But there is one painting that is glued to my memory, unable to be pried free.

In the decade of turquoise, avocado and mustard known as the seventies, I had occasion to visit the doctor's office for regular examinations by the general practitioner who had delivered all of my five siblings. Dr. Howard's office was a stand-alone brick building wedged between the dry cleaners and the drug store, and it had one feature that I had never seen in a building of that time nor since – the doorknobs were all at adult eye level. At the time, I sensed the sinister nature of the doorknobs, certain that it was a secret plot conceived by doctors and nurses to put the means of escape as far out of the way of our reaching hands. Of course, I was gifted, so I easily understood this (see, On Being Gifted).

Although I was a large boy, and could have easily escaped the torture room behind the big turquoise door, I felt a certain obligation to remain inside, under the watchful eye of my mother, Dr. Howard, and Nurse Hazel. It was like stepping into a type of conditional imprisonment, knowing that if one submitted to all devices and manipulations, release for good behavior was possible.

Stepping through the fun house door and onto the tile floor, I was immediately greeted with the punishing Essence of Rubbing Alcohol that hung in the air like the cheap cologne worn by ID-bracelet-wearing sales executives. But this scent, unlike the intentionally oppressive sales approach that follows the bad cologne wearing execs, was followed by something more dreadful. We'll get to that.

Inside the waiting room, poorly lit, were a few colorful plastic chairs strewn with aged Reader's Digests and Highlights magazines. Stubby transom windows at the top of the outer wall made it clear that if you gave up on the doorknobs and attempted to make it out by this alternative route, you would fall far enough once free to fracture some appendage. Escape meant certain return. It was like the cooler in *The Great Escape*, but without the mitt and baseball.

The Commandant, Dr. Howard, wore a white medical smock with a stethoscope sticking out of one pocket. His beaming face and warm smile seemed to me to be a cover for what I was certain had to be a gleefully twisted mind, and he seemed to have a spring in his step as we walked down the long hallway toward the chamber, the rubbing alcohol scent nearly suffocating me. It wasn't long now. I must be strong.

"Just take a seat there on the paper, and I'll be right in," the evil doctor grinned, his face disappearing behind the doorknob.

There it was.

Sitting on the butcher paper atop the steel examination table like a piece of ground beef being weighed at the meat counter, I looked at the painting on the opposite wall. There, a boy is bent over, posterior exposed, while the white-coated doctor, back to him, prepares a hypodermic. As the minutes glacially inched along inside the examination room, I studied every detail of that print, comparing it to my surroundings and finding it eerily similar, right down to the youthful victim about to be skewered.

Enter Nurse Hazel. In this sanitized stalag, Nurse Hazel's white dress and nurses cap, nestled atop her dark thorny hair, were a perfect compliment to the doctor's smock, fascist fashions that lent a certain air of uniformed precision to the unfolding interrogation. In rapid order, Nurse Hazel moved me to the scales, noting my weight and height, peering over the clipboard, emotionless and steely-eyed; and then, she reached for the dreaded alcohol rub.

"Lie on your stomach, and undo your belt," she said. She didn't add, "…or you know vhat vill hahpen to you," but it was sort of implied.

Staring up at the shot of penicillin she was preparing, I felt very much like the boy in the painting, except that I could see what was coming. The sensation of the chill air of the examination room on my exposed derriere was just registering in my brain when all of a sudden Nurse Hazel struck from behind, jamming the needle into my fleshy hindquarters so firmly that I wondered if she was trying to push through to the examination table. That would certainly limit my possibilities of escape.

And she waited.

During this period of the shot, my mind reflected again on the Rockwell art, and I wondered if this is the moment that the painter envisioned in the moments following the boy's dropping of the trousers. The freckled-faced inquisitive boy in the painting peers at the doctor's credentials on the wall awaiting the needle as though he were sitting at a soda fountain waiting for an ice cream. If Norman had drawn not *Before the Shot*, but *During the Shot*, we would have seen the poor child writhing in pain, eyes bulging, teeth clenching, while the needle protruded from his posterior. Would *that* have appeared on the Post?

Still waiting.

After what seemed an eternity, Nurse Hazel extracted the needle, concluding this entr'acte while Dr. Howard took the stage with the next method of torture, the finger prick. Having survived the near-fatal stabbing from Nurse Hazel, no secret government plans were going to spill out of me now that the pain in my punctured rear had heightened my senses. I braced myself for the worst, but the unkind prick of the finger passed so quickly that the doctor was unable to extract anything more than a few drops of blood. No tortured confession this time, Herr Doctor.
"Okay, young man," he said as if acknowledging that I couldn't be broken, "you can put your shirt on, and you're through for the day."

Yes, I had not only survived the interrogation, without fleeing for the high doorknob, but I was about to get the ultimate reward for the conquering hero: a coupon for ice cream at the drug store. Walking out of the cooler into the sunlight, the fresh air filling my sterilized nostrils, I ran to get my ice cream, betraying the penicillin bee-sting in my behind. This scene, the *After the Shot* painting in my mind, shows a boy holding his behind with one hand, melting ice cream in the other, kind druggist in a white coat beaming from behind the counter. Paint *that* one next time please, Mr. Rockwell.

34

DO IT YOURSELFISHNESS

Do-it-yourself projects are opportunities for us to take our handyman (sorry, handy*person*, see Are You Gay, and Other Simple Questions) skills out for a walk, working the creaks out of our backs that have sat for too long hunched over keyboards. Occasionally we venture away from the comfort of QWERTY and keypad only to find ourselves lost in a vast wasteland, the warehouse centers where we seek the right tool for fixing stupidity, or gadgets to undo idiocy. They don't exist.

When my wife and I lived in our first home, a two-bedroom, multi-level tract house out on the fringe of civilization, I decided it was time to add an office to the unfinished area next to the family room. Looking at the exposed two-by-fours and cement floor, I repeated that same deluded creed that many of the innocent do-it-yourselfers have, "Well, whatever I do, it *can't* look worse than this."

Of course, in the backs of our minds, we also briefly consider calling a friend or neighbor who has actually *done* this type of improvement successfully, but we hastily discard the thought knowing that the joy of looking on a completed project is more gratifying when shared with none. Like the runner in a marathon race – who has never run a marathon – we head to the starting line, the local lumber store. There we see the elite, the elders, the *contractors*, and we avert our eyes, ashamed to be in the race next to these sturdy champions, tool belts glistening, testimony to their victories.

My tradesman-tough "truck" was an old Plymouth TC3 two-door sedan, with a louvered sport hatchback that had already circled the earth three times, and now, stuffed with sheetrock and lumber looked like a runner wearing chaps. The little red handkerchief nailed to the farthest protruding point was the do-it-yourselfer's admission that he had neither the conveyance nor good sense to hire a contractor. It might as well have been a white flag of surrender; but wrapped in my self-deception, I was fighting to the death.

Ultimately, the wall I constructed to divide the room was in place, pounded and pried until it finally rested somewhat near the intended point. My father in law came over in the middle of the project, and my wife threw open the family room door revealing what I had hoped to keep from view, especially from this wood-shop veteran. As he walked up to the wall, he questioned whether I had placed the studs on fourteen or sixteen inch centers. This was like my wife asking me whether I liked the black shoes with the silver buckles or the black shoes with the silver buckles. "Uh...," I stammered, revealing that which he so clearly saw.

Let me just pause here to say that as long as the wall has wood in it, and the sheetrock can be nailed or screwed upon it, thus hiding the gaffs made in its construction, I don't think it should matter particularly. After all, the house was standing *before* I built the wall, and it would still be standing after the final coat of paint was applied. Of course, this kind of layman's logic had also led to my expulsion from advanced math (see On Circuses and Prisons). Reagan's words lingered in the air, "Tear down this wall," but unlike my German brothers, I just applied the sheetrock to it.

The project continued, and I learned that walls built to standards other than a ninety-degree square just look a little silly. "That's okay, we'll put the desk there," I rationalized to my wife. This is the second grand delusion: if it can be covered up with art, furniture or wallpaper, it's fine. Of course, this is a progression of the mind sinking into insanity, but, having invested so much of ourselves into the project, we are hell-bent on seeing it through to its hideous conclusion, the finish work.

In those days, the texturing applied to walls before the paint was a popular thing, and our house had what I referred to as the spittle-upon-the-wall texturing, as if a thousand obnoxious bullies loaded up mouthfuls of mud and sprayed the walls. Not having access to a thousand obnoxious bullies, I resorted to a special tool for this, a sort of pump-action mud spitter that left my unfinished walls looking more like a very blustery-breathed bully and a wimpy-winded weakling got in a fight in my new office. Large clumps and small pinpoints shared the same space. "We'll hang pictures," I reasoned, my wife's eyes rolling back in her head.

We eventually sold the house – sight unseen – to a real estate broker whose client, I'm certain, would cheerfully look at my wall and say to himself, "Well, whatever I do, it can't look worse than this."

On another occasion, my brothers-in-law and I were called upon to help with a roofing job. My father in law's five-year-old, leakless shingles were just too dingy looking, and he had decided to pile on some fresh-looking asphalt roof shingles. Yes, this was before he had gazed on my home improvement skills in the prior incident.

I love my father in law. Truly. He was a principled and passionate administrator and Dean of Business at a local community college, expanding the offerings and propelling the school to university status during his tenure. I once heard him give a speech to a group of faculty, when I was a lowly student newspaper reporter, in which he actually said, "We are here for the students. *They* pay our salaries." He had guts, and as the author behind a series of statistics texts, he had brains too.

His only fault was an I-can-do-it-cheaper-myself delusion that differed from my it-can't-look-worse-than-this reasoning. So there we were, the three of us, my father in law, my brother in law, and me. The third brother in law hadn't arrived, and would be a couple of hours behind us. Although he represented only twenty-five percent of the total roofers on this job, statistically speaking, he also represented one hundred percent of the total experienced roofers, creating a deficit of
    a)   25 percent roofing experience.
    b)   50 percent roofing experience.
    c)   75 percent roofing experience.
    d)   100 percent roofing experience.

Correct, the answer was "d." I knew this, and so did my roof dwelling brother in law, but we had a clear foreman on the job, and undeterred and unphased, my father in law was cooking up a story problem in his brain. He was on a ladder at the bottom of the roofline, looking up at the geometric patterns in front of him. While I sat astride my bag of shingles halfway up the roof, I thoughtfully listened to his powers of reason dissect the roof.

"Now let's see. If you're nailing on shingles there, you're exactly fifteen rows above where I'm nailing. Of course, we have to preserve the off-set look of the shingles, so that would mean that every other row would have to start in the same place; but then you have the shingle really divided into thirds, so…what do you think, Robbie?"

"Ya," I replied, unfamiliar with the proper methods of shingling, convinced that a reasoned, mathematical approach had to trump what I was thinking. "I guess that's going to work," less sure of this statement than any story problem I had ever tried to solve. If the house had been going at the rate of sixty miles per hour, and another house leaving Cleveland was passing it going one hundred miles per hour, it would have been a more likely scenario than the one I found myself in now, trying to understand how the roofing tiles were going to meet in a perfect pattern halfway up the roof.

After a few more ruminations of the Dean, and a few adjustments from my perch, we began nailing down shingles. The pattern we were creating was sort of a modified control chart, and from a purely statistical viewpoint, the lines traversing the roof askew of the existing shingles clearly demonstrated that my work was out of the acceptable tolerance range.

It was around this time, just as my father in law's brow was doubled over in correlations and variances, the other twenty-five percent of our team arrived. Our old statistical friend, Vilfredo Pareto, once theorized that eighty percent of the land was owned by twenty percent of the people. This eighty/twenty rule came to be known as the Pareto Principle, and it was now roughly applied to the roofing problem. In this case, twenty-five percent of the team held the answers to the problem, and through a series of logical questions, my brother-in-law solved the equation, a Socratic solution to the mind numbing statistical soiree:

"Why are you starting halfway up the roof?"
"How old is this roof, anyway?"
"Why are your bags of shingles at different places on the roof?"
"Who's working on the *other* side of the roof?"

Like finding the end of repeating pi, our statistical story problem ended in an instant. First, you don't start halfway up the roof, just like you don't start mowing the lawn in the middle. Second, you don't need to re-shingle for about ten years or unless your roof has leaks, you might create a worse problem. Third, you place your bags at the peak of the roofline, where you are supposed to end up, and where they are within reach as you work along the roof. And finally, roofing can be done from opposite sides of the house, since the proper work ends at the peak.

The clarity of an experienced mind can, in a matter of moments, undo the worst fumblings of the deluded do-it-yourselfer. So next time I go out to build a wall, shingle a roof, install a toilet, or pour a cement patio, I remember this experience. And I hire a contractor.

35

QUESTIONS THAT TELL

When my son was a junior in high school, he came home and proudly announced that he was invited to join a classroom debate representing the minority view. When I asked what the topic was for the verbal sparring match, he enthusiastically replied that they would be debating whether imperialism was a good thing.

I think he could sense from my blank stare that I did not share his enthusiasm for the topic, and I asked, "Is it your position that imperialism is good?"

"You bet," he said eagerly.

"Do you know that you've already lost the debate?" I queried.

My son's blank stare in return was a signal that this game of catch we once shared with baseballs and mitts had graduated to questions about questions.

I went on to explain to him that the teacher had effectively created a forum for expressing the *teacher's* point of view, and this was not a debate at all, as I demonstrated by asking a few follow-up questions.

"Has your teacher ever described the United States as an imperialist nation?" I asked.

"Yes," he said without hesitation.

"What is imperialism?" I followed up.

"It's what we're doing in the wars we're fighting."

In my offspring's defense, he had either forgotten or never really experienced the truth that all students come to learn, whether in their twelve-year sentences served in public schools (see On Circuses and Prisons) or in extortive undergrad indoctrination camps: teachers have agendas, and their agendas are always right. In the debate for ideas, the person who shapes the questions wins the debate.

Some questions have a way of hiding Mack trucks in fogbanks. Answer them, and you enter the mists with only one possible outcome.

"Do you know how fast you were going?" is a mine in the water.
"Does this dress make me look fat?" is a hand grenade tossed lovingly in your direction.

Other questions are meant to merely frustrate and annoy us, knowing that we have no other choice but to entertain the question as though it really needed an answer.

"Do you really wish to delete the file?" is a rhetorical mosquito buzzing in your ears, and yet we have to pay attention to it.
"Do you wish to speak to a representative?" is a splinter in your brain, daring us to consider whether we are certain that a live person is preferable to the digital droning of the computer voice.

Some questions go to our moral core, such as answering in a jury selection process, "No, I have never committed – or entertained thoughts of committing – murder in the first degree," or when filling out the new patient information for a doctor, "No, I have not used illegal drugs or consumed alcohol during pregnancy."

No, while these questions can be annoying, embarrassing, or harbor certain ill consequences, the real insidious inquiries are those used by pollsters, pundits, and politicians to lead public opinion like huckster lawyers leading a witness.

To express distaste for traditional marriage, they might shape questions such as, "Do you think an abused spouse should remain in a failed marriage?" or "What is the number one reason cited for wanting to leave your spouse?" We rarely hear polls reporting answers to, "What do you like most about your spouse?" or "What are the factors that lead to long-lasting relationships?"

If these publishers and press corps members hold the view that religious people are misguided and unintelligent, or that religion is the "opiate of the masses", then they reason that it is in the public's interest whenever they fan the flames of religious intolerance. They might ask, "Do you feel people not of your faith are doomed to hell?" or "Would you prefer a greater blurring of the line between church and state such as proposals to increase values-based education?" Each question ironically paints the religious as intolerant and impious. "To what extent do you agree that religious extremism incites violence in our society?" places terrorists and clergymen on the same end of a secular continuum.

To suppress debate on global warming as a man-made condition, the question monger can simply ask questions that state what he or she believes to be obvious truths, "What are the top ways you can reduce your carbon footprint?" With this question, we can learn to accept and adopt this term and the consensus obligation we must feel about reducing these dirty footprints. Rather than asking for empirical evidence, those asphyxiating greenhouse gas goblins might also ask a group of city workers laying asphalt in the July sun, "Does it feel warmer to you now than it did ten years ago?" Of course, they might not have been engaged in sweltering hot road improvements ten years prior, but they know that it sure is hot now.

Sometimes polling questions begin as small lessons, such as, "Trans-fats are the major cause of obesity in youth ages 12-18. To what extent would you favor a law governing the use of trans-fats in school lunch programs?" They might as well tell us, "Since you are too uninformed to know the difference, we'll bring you the packaged facts and solutions and you can tell us how right we are." *Oh, the humanity*.

My humble recommendation is that we challenge the questions before we give our answers. Next time you are asked a question by a "tell-er" just respond with a question. For example, when a politician asks a rhetorical question about increasing taxes such as, "Wouldn't you admit that paying slightly higher taxes to benefit the poor and needy is part of being a good citizen?" just reply, "Are you saying that the food I put on the table for my family should go to feed the mouths of someone else's child?" Better still, "Wouldn't you agree, Senator, that the poor deserve better aid than can be given by the government, and that laundering my potential charitable contributions through taxation is actually less efficient?" Watch him squirm.

You might also try to insert your own statement-question, "Since it is true that paying taxes is part of being a good citizen, and one use of taxes is to protect and defend our nation – a benefit realized by all citizens – then shouldn't we expect that all our citizens pay into the funds allocated for this. Or are you recommending, Senator, that only those of a certain income group should be entitled to the protections afforded all citizens?" By this time, the politician would have developed severe and sudden hearing loss, and the phone pollster would have reached a bad connection.

Is the way in which a question is asked a conscious choice on the part of the speaker to control the debate? Perhaps I should ask my imperialist son.

Tell me your question, and I'll tell you mine. Together, let's uncover your agenda, expose the assumptions behind your telling question, and explore the depths of your world view. Now that you have prepared the banquet table with the china settings and cutlery to suit *your* meal, I would like the chance to change the menu. I promise that the meal we share will be as savory as the one you had planned, and the conversation will fill us both.

36

TO DIE FOR

In our over-reactive, hyper-sensitive, ultra-neurotic society, we often hear the superficial rants of the masses:

"I would *die* without my (fill in the electronic gadget)!"
"I'm so tired, I may just fall over and *die* right here!"
"I couldn't believe it when I walked in the room; I *nearly died* to see her wearing the same dress as me!"
"Those shoes are *to die for*!"

Of course, we don't really mean that we would expire because of these relatively trivial things – at least I don't think that the *majority* of us feel that way. To hit the reset button on our collective tendency for hyperbole, it might be worth considering the serious question, "What *is* worth dying for?"

First, we have to consider the question (for more on this, see Questions That Tell). By asking the question, I assume that for each of us there is something we consider so valuable, so priceless, so irreplaceably precious, that we would trade our life to preserve it. Maybe there are some of us unwilling to make that ultimate sacrifice, no matter what. However, we have plenty of evidence to the contrary, beginning with the military men and women, the firefighters and police officers who run into life-threatening places from which the rest of us have fled.

So what is worth dying for? Let me recommend a short list.

First, *self-preservation*. In other words, when threatened, fight back, defend, and attack if needed in order to survive. After all, being a martyr is great, but since you only have one life to give, keep it with tenacity so that your accumulative perpetuation of good works becomes an undeniable testament to your cause. Some may argue that self-preservation is selfish or somehow less noble than giving up for the sake of a cause greater than one's self (see Stumping Teacher for further thoughts on survival). If so, then let us selfishly cling to life as long as we can draw breath or ponder a thought that the cause may go forward.

In this case, self-preservation does not extend to the preservation of your acquired goods – these are replaceable, and you are not. Would you give your life to preserve your big screen television or your new car, computer, or a pair of shoes? Some have risked their lives running back into the flames for a precious heirloom ignorant of the fact that the most precious heirloom is life itself, and the memories we collect in our minds along the way (see Life, Worth Living).

Second, *preservation of your spouse or family* is a worthy trade for your own life. What thought surges through the mind of someone facing impending death? Those who have faced this ultimate test report reflecting on loved ones, wishing to hold them, longing to express their love and mend old wounds. When we, as parents, peer into our children's rooms at night while they are sleeping we are reminded of the sacred duty given us to protect them, nurture them, and help them stand tall in the winds of adversity. Failing in this, we fail utterly.

Why is it that we keep pictures of our loved ones nearby, whether we work in an office or on the front lines? These reminders of home and family give us comfort and reassurance that what we do during the day honors the contract we signed with them when we looked into their eyes for the first time. For some of us, we will return home at the end of our shift and kneel to collect the payment for our day's efforts as a young son or daughter hugs our neck and says, "Hi Daddy." Others of us, faced with the possibility of death during our shift, look on these family photos as inspiration to face our enemies with resolve and unshakable courage, firm in the faith that life with them is worth any personal price we might pay.

Third on this list of people worth preserving are *the innocents*, those among us who need and deserve our protection. Just as we work and fight for the chance to return home to our loved ones, we ought to do the same for those whose loving arms reach out seeking relief. Who can look on a suffering child and coldly turn away? Yes, images of destitute and starving children are often used to serve an activist's agenda or a non-profit's fundraising push, but when we see their eyes first-hand, how can we fail to lend a compassionate hand?

In days past we held inviolate the phrase, "women and children first," and yet our modern movements have called this into question, adding contemporary qualifiers regarding what is woman's worth. Can we acknowledge the capabilities and strength of our women, while still protecting those whose hands cradled us in birth and whose kindness and humanity bring life to us all? Perhaps it is simply an old-fashioned chivalrous creed we no longer believe; but please, women and children, take my place on the life raft or on the first transport out of harm's way. I'll catch the next one, or I'll contentedly stay behind.

Finally, for what principles or beliefs would we offer ourselves as trade to preserve? I would like to suggest two: *freedom* and *faith*.

What is freedom? Words fail to capture fully the depths of the striving soul's search for freedom. To understand freedom requires a cataloging of the costs to preserve it. Visit any national cemetery, and the endless white rows of headstones, like cross-shaped dominos marking the lives of those brave souls at rest beneath, remind us of the human toll defending freedom. Tyrants, taskmasters, and terrorists array their forces in vain attempts to defeat it, as though freedom were a piece of ground, a city, or an army. Their grandest achievements are smoldering cities, blood-soaked shores, and burdened backs; but freedom's light shines through the smoking embers, washes over stained sands, and bears up the load, ever hopeful.

Freedom finds expression in a thousand simple acts that Americans take for granted. We get in our cars and drive across states freely, from one end of the country to the other. No State-run church calls us to worship services or dictates the content of our sermons. The State's red pen does not censor our literature or our press, and we can wander around art museums depicting themes and subjects that can equally demonize or deify our political leaders. The profane and the pleasing can equally share the same stage in our open society. Our educational system, even with its flaws, equips our children with the tools to become independent thinkers, rather than conformist cookie-cut-outs of a party dogma. In most parts of the country, we can own firearms without the threat of confiscation by the local municipality or without the threat of forced enlistment to defend the State.

Last of all on my list is *faith*. It is part of the triad of truths, the other two being hope and charity. Faith has somehow come to mean religion, as in "people of faith" or "faith-based organizations"; but the faith worth dying for is something much deeper. It is not a zealous extremism, as the enemies of faith assert, but a solemn force that sustains the ideals and values upon which our society is based. Many who fled to our shores carried that faith in their hearts, and then maintained it as they struck out into the wilderness to tame the west and establish communities of like-minded citizens.

We have many threats against faith today. Indeed, this f-word strikes fear into the hearts of many in the media. News broadcasts highlight religious fanatics, but somehow spend little time on the armies of faithful volunteers who feed the hungry, give shelter to the poor, and repair the damage of flood, fire, and famine. What makes faith worth dying for? For the millions of faithful, it is simply that without faith, what is worth living for?

So the next time you feel as though there is nothing to live for, consider what is worth dying for. In this we will find a life of meaningful struggle, and hard-fought battles to the death as we protect each other and hold to the ideals that preserve our society. Oh ya, and that freedom thing...it's *to die for*!

37

QUITTING THE BAND

"We should form our own band!"

This enthusiastic proposal, to many teens, is like stepping in line to buy a lottery ticket, self-assured of the positive outcome while failing to notice the bent figure of an elderly man ahead of them who has been trying for twenty years to hit it big. Four friends and I stepped into that line, and we formed a band called Afire – not A Fire, but Afire. It was the first question our potential fans wanted to know.

"A fire? You mean like a campfire?"
"No, afire, like being *on* fire."
"Oh," they said dispassionately, not wanting to ask the obvious next question, "Why?"

We never had to explain why, so the name stuck. We were afire, ablaze with lots of ideas about becoming a band, but fizzling in all aspects of execution.

Our guitar player, Ron, was the one pushing to form the band, and he was the guy with the parental money to pull it off. After all, in the order of rock band formation, first comes funding *and then* flunkies, not the other way around. Ron was a pretty good lead guitarist, and he knew all the standards from Aerosmith to ZZ Top. By sheer will, he was going to see this through, and he gave the rest of us our cassette practice tapes and talked endlessly about landing a first job before we had really agreed to form the band.

My friend, Kyle, was on keyboards, but he was only committed to the idea of the band if we could have back-up singers; and so he went freelancing among his girlfriends to find willing – if not able – vocalists. That brainstorm turned out to be a mere summer shower, since the girls didn't want to sing back-up if we didn't have microphones or a lead singer. As Kyle's plans were unenthusiastically extinguished, Ron was blazing ahead to recruit Dan as our lead singer.

Dan was a tall skinny guy with a Red Sea hairdo, dark black hair parted in the middle, waves rising up in black sea walls, and then pouring down to his shoulders. Dan was a heartthrob, and had won the lead in the school musical. He could carry a tune, and he brought a key branding element to the band: the red jumpsuit. He looked afire leaping around the black coal amplifiers. Don *was* afire.

Chuck, our drummer, matched Ron's and Dan's blazing enthusiasm for the band, but was more mechanic than musician when it came to his instrument. He was a small-framed introvert (not that I have anything against that – see Introverts Unite!) who looked as if he was about to fall asleep as he reached up to beat the tom-toms and crash cymbal. He was more like the unseasoned wood on the fire, smoldering and sputtering rather than igniting.

I played the bass, and matched more the feelings of Kyle when it came to the band. If it was going to be the source of high school fame at the annual talent show, I could go along with it for now. In fairness, I should have told the others that I was more interested in a sort of campfire commitment to the band rather than the extended forest fire type of commitment to Afire. If the band lit up the talent show, and then burned out, that was fine with me.

This ensemble of the highly interested and the merely bored assembled at Ron's house to practice once a week. Our practice sessions consisted of listening to other great bands on Ron's hi-fi, and then attempting to replicate the music with only smoldering success. We found that the fewer chords and solos necessary, the better. Despite Ron's dedication to transcribe Eddie Van Halen solos, the musical equivalent of putting tracing paper over the Mona Lisa, our sound never really came together. Never, that is, until the talent show.

The talent show was kind of a throw away event in the world of high school assemblies. In fact, had the administration canceled the whole event, the student body would only have been slightly disappointed, not because they would miss the parade of dismal performances, but because it was one less occasion to see their friends and poke fun at the principal's pitiful attempts to quiet the crowd. It was a universal truth in those days that principals were twenty to thirty years out of sync with the jargon kids used.

"Okay, youngsters," he would drone, as if we were preschoolers getting ready to work with fingerpaints, "let's just settle down please...."

(No change in crowd volume. Time for him to switch to the veiled threat.)

"Students...," he said, leaning closer to the microphone.
"If you can't quiet down, we will not be able to start the show."

That was the kind of threat we could all live with, and it seemed as though the churning crowd actually got louder.

"Boys and girls...," he adjured, half scolding and half pleading, "...if you don't quiet down, I will cancel this assembly and you can return to your classes for the rest of the day."

(Silence.)

With further ado about concert etiquette and something about how hard the performers had worked for this moment, the principal left, and the first act came out. From just off-stage, the members of Afire watched as a pianist stuttered her way through something classical, with a prolonged pause in the middle while she struggled to find the entrance ramp back to where her mind had exited the composition. From an objective view, she clearly had more talent and determination than we did, but she may have forgotten the other truth about talent show assemblies: they are really less about talent and more about *show*.

A few more acts dragged by – the sawing of a string quartet, the drapery-clad dance trio, a comedian pausing for laughter that never came. One other rock band took the stage, but they had failed to do a sound check earlier in the day, so the straining lead singer never really won the battle with the screaming guitar. The stage, strewn with the dead and dying, now gave way to the final act, Afire.

Rock bands feed off several well-planned elements: a dramatic opening, big amplifiers, and most of all, the crowd. Our opening was perfect. The red velvet curtain rose to a dark stage as Kyle's keyboard set the mood. It was Boston's classic rock song in two acts, "Foreplay" and "Long Time," a perfect talent show number because it started eerily slow, until the bass pulsated it into a chomping rhythm guitar feast, twisting into Ron's well-managed solo licks. Between the red glow of the amplifiers' power buttons, and perfectly timed lighting, we satisfied the first two requirements.

The crowd, dejected, despairing, and dulled by the earlier acts, came to life at just the right moment as the lights went up and our red jumpsuited Dan sprang onto stage. Had the dramatic opening failed, this leaping forth of the red jester might have not only destroyed our chances to win the contest, but would have earned us a permanent place in high school yearbooks as the most embarrassing moment in talent show history. But this was Dan the Beloved, Dan the Magnificent, and he had that one thing that had eluded all prior performers: a fan base. Girls cheered the moment his red sneakers hit the stage, starting a human wave of cheers that rippled through the auditorium as if a rock — Afire's rock — had suddenly broken the surface of a still pond.

As the final chord crashed upon the crowd, the entire auditorium was on its feet. The curtain fell and the cheers rose, as shouts of "encore" stabbed through the curtain. Faced with the looming presence of our principal waiting to re-take the stage from our thundering encore moment, we could only do one thing: we pulled out another classic rock tune as an encore, "Takin' Care of Business." We pushed the assembly into overtime, and the principal didn't even try to reclaim the lost battlefield. It was as though we had defeated the competition, won the crowd, and put The Man in his place. Total rock victory — rocktory.

Of course, after the cheering died, the members of Afire did what all good rock bands do, we broke up. Some might have called it "creative differences" or "personality clashes" but that was just a dramatic way of saying that we just didn't share Ron's enthusiasm. Dan, who had been popular before the talent show, had rocketed into the stratosphere. When he walked down the hall, girls fell like dominoes. Together, he and Ron put together a new band, and they played a few summer swim parties and small dances, but within six months Afire went out.

We never tried to put together a reunion tour, never went into the studio to produce an album, and we never went back to play an encore appearance at the talent show. I have never regretted quitting the band. We were never going to be a serious contender for anything more than a sparking a bored crowd at the talent show. But in a small way, we all won the lottery, not of fortune and fame, but the one in a million victory over our own stratospheric ambitions and inflated egos, priceless memories and lasting lessons.

Many years later, my son, who had banged on a cheap acoustic guitar for a few days came to me and announced, "Some of us are going to start our own band."

"Good for you," I said.

38

STUMPING TEACHER

In recent years, I have noticed that when we sit around the dinner table, and my sons recount their experiences at school, I find myself asking more often than I used to, "Why didn't you challenge the teacher on that point?" From my brief stint as a substitute teacher I am acquainted with the difficulty of gaining and maintaining respect; but some teachers I have encountered over the years are so focused on students respecting them, they opt for stern disciplinary tactics rather than doing the much more difficult job of engaging students in dialogue, coming at a topic through the back door, proceeding from questions to the answer. Earning respect through one's teaching skills is a task worthy of the teaching profession.

I find myself returning to the memory of Mr. Shuman, my English teacher in ninth grade. He was a bulbous figure from his bald head to his expansive waist, which then tapered to tiny feet. He looked more like a reversed hourglass standing there in front of class; but despite the large middle, the flow of sand marking time still seemed to creep along for some. None of my friends really liked Mr. Shuman. His lessons were more intellectual than entertaining, and when he lost control of the classroom – a frequent occurrence – he enforced heads down reading time. This was actually a good thing for me, since I was able to read some masterful novels.

One novel I particularly enjoyed was *Lord of the Flies*, by William Golding. I immediately identified with the social stratification of the British schoolboys marooned on the island, and recognized the characteristics of cruelty shared by the bully class and inflicted on the intellectual sub-stratum in our own school. The book is an allegory much like Orwell's *Animal Farm*, and the underlying themes of life, death, civilization and anarchy are weighty and grave.

Mr. Shuman chose one of these themes to begin our class discussion of the book. He led up to his question with a few references to the savagery on the island, and the complete abandonment of civilization. Then came the question.

"Class…," he began, "the question I want to ask today is…," he paused for dramatic effect, "is *survival* the most important thing?"

I ran over the question in my mind, and it seemed to me that the alternative for survival was death, so I blurted out, "Yes!" and Mr. Shuman invited me to explain that point of view.

"Well, without survival nothing else matters. If you're dead, you're dead. That's it," I reasoned with all the eloquence of my ten years of schooling.

Mr. Shuman looked at me, and I couldn't discern beneath his doughy face whether he was seething or satisfied. He just waited. Nothing.

"Okay…" he haltingly said, turning away from me. "I think we'll have some reading time now."

That was it, the discussion ended. Did I have the right answer? Was I going to the principal's office?

After class, Mr. Shuman pulled me aside and said, "You know, you completely changed my plan for today. I didn't know what to say when you said survival was the most important thing. I was going to talk about the importance of social order, but you stumped me. And you were right – that's why I couldn't say anything else."

Now I was stumped.

How could he acknowledge that I had gotten the best of him and that I was *right*? In the whole history of education, I thought this had to be a first. From that day, Mr. Shuman and I became friends, and a mutual respect developed. We did get back to the class discussion of *Lord of the Flies*, and I reveled in this new freedom to express myself, and Mr. Shuman taught me to contradict or support based on evidence from the novel. Suddenly, I didn't have to agree with the teacher, and that was okay by him.

From that day on, I have grown to love literature. When I went to the little community college in my town, I found another teacher like Mr. Shuman. She taught American Literature, British Literature, and Women in Literature, in addition to several composition courses. I took every course she taught, and I scheduled advisory time with her to discuss assignments and to seek advice about my future college plans. Lessons were full of nourishing give and take, and that mutual respect I had felt with Mr. Shuman grew with Ms. Harrison. She required each of us to buy a paperback dictionary so that we could look up any unfamiliar words, unwilling to *be* the dictionary herself to prop up our lackadaisical appreciation for vocabulary. The dreadfulness of going to school was – for an hour each day – suspended while I went to my English courses. When I graduated, I was awarded the Top English Student, which I'm sure was due more to the number of classes I took rather than any academic achievement.

So to all the teachers out there, can I issue a small appeal? Resist the urge to be unconditionally right. Delay unveiling the correct answer. Invite thoughtful challenges. Teach *learning*, and not just facts. I know our tests require us to give our students a finite set of red-letter dates and formulas; but if on occasion you find a student who stumps you, pull him or her aside and give a little encouragement. You never know, but you might inspire someone to continue learning, and you will have earned that most elusive gift of all, respect.

39

THE GREAT MOVIE PERSONALITY TEST

Going to the movies is still a thrill for me. For about the price of a fast-food meal, you can be transported into the future, thrust into nail-biting terror, shunned by a lover, and make it home in time for dinner. Nearly every weekend, my wife and I try to find a movie at our local theater, and I think back to the great movie-going experiences I've enjoyed.

When I was in elementary school, the local grocery store sponsored summer movies for kids, so my mother and my aunt bought the ten-movie package. On Saturday morning, my brother and I, along with our three cousins, were dropped off at the movie theater, along with hundreds of other kids. This was before the multiplex cinemas, when theaters were worthy of being called theaters. The screens were a mile wide, and the seats terraced up and away in gentle slopes, covered by the balcony seats – always the most coveted by young kids wanting to throw popcorn onto the crowd below, especially when the movie turned out to be rather ordinary.

Summer Saturday movies were always low budget "B" movies, so we had several of the black and white Godzilla movies, and we enjoyed the spectacle of a giant lizard kicking through houses, derailing trains, vaporizing military equipment, and clumsily knocking down electrical towers with his sweeping tail. The theater seethed with kids chattering, sharing candy, and screaming when the monster materialized. It was as if Godzilla was just one lizard-step away from squashing everyone in the theater.

In this Japanese monster genre was another very special summer movie, "War of the Gargantuas." It was the tender story of two furry animals that were contaminated in a radioactive stream, causing them to grow into Godzilla-sized apelike creatures, one orange and one green. The question that occupied our minds the most after this movie was which monster each of us liked best, as if there was some special significance in this trivial choice. Surprisingly, there was a meaning behind the choice. The orange shag carpet monster that started off so ill-tempered, actually turned on the green giant monster who was hell-bent on mayhem and destruction. Therefore, the orange choice was a vote for compassion, while green was the vote for anarchy.

Sometimes the movies were so poorly matched to the audience, in this case five young boys, that we merely mocked them both during and after the screening. This was the case with the seventies version of "Lost Horizon." It was as if a thousand hippies had taken over Shangri-La and turned it into a commune complete with sugary Broadway numbers and psychedelic costumes. Of course, we did approve of one scene in the closing minutes when the main character's girlfriend leaves Shangri-La and instantly ages hundreds of years into a real prune face – great cinema.

Other movies were a dead on fit for young boys, like John Wayne's "The Cowboys" where a group of young boys hires on to help The Duke move several hundred head of cattle, all the while being chased by cattle rustlers. John Wayne was larger than life, and we were certain he could get out of any situation with his six-gun and his swagger. That was until he was shot down like a dog at the end of the film, the first time any of us could think of him dying in a movie. "John Wayne can't *die*," we chorused. We were devastated, unlike the joy of the prune-faced lady.

Our "B" movie tastes received an automatic grade advancement in the summer of '75 when we went to see "Jaws." It was the most terrifying movie we had ever seen, and even in our land-locked hometown, we imagined the worst. Could salt-water sharks survive if someone planted it in a freshwater lake, or – heaven forbid – a swimming pool? Hearing the low pulse of the theme music on the transistor radio was enough to make us check the water in the local pool for any twenty-foot sharks that might have escaped notice.

For teen boys, there was no greater moment in movie openings than the "Star Wars" premiere. We waited in lines that stretched around the block, and we couldn't wait to see it a second or a third time. Our scoutmaster, a young guy who always joked with us about girlfriends we didn't have, offered to take our whole troop to see the movie and he threw in, "and bring any of your girlfriends along." So I asked Mary Bradford, two years older than I was, if she wanted to go see it. She immediately agreed, but was somewhat miffed when a car full of boys showed up to take her to the movie. Apparently no one had girlfriends, and the scoutmaster had really been kidding. Maybe that's why I didn't see much of Mary after that.

Thinking back on those early movie-going experiences, I realize now that part of the thrill was not just in seeing bone-crunching sharks or laser blasting space cowboys, it was the audience. There I was with my friends, and a thousand other like-minded fans sharing something that had brought us to the theater to cheer on our favorite hero or to sample a taste of another universe.

So I thought that if movies could bring together like-minded people, maybe there ought to be a movie personality test, to sort out who is who in this wide movie theater called society. This is not a trivia test about the movies, but rather a personality test on you, the moviegoer. See how you measure up in this non-scientific test.

Just circle "yes" or "no."

Yes	No	1.	Do you talk endlessly about lessons from "The Godfather"?
Yes	No	2.	Did you enjoy the Harry Potter and Lord of the Rings series so much that you decided to buy fan trinkets from either series, say a wand, sword, or an amulet?
Yes	No	3.	Can you appreciate an animated movie now and then?
Yes	No	4.	Do you claim at least one black and white movie among your favorite movies of all time?
Yes	No	5.	Did you swell with pride in our military after seeing "Saving Private Ryan" or "Patton"?
Yes	No	6.	Did you find yourself laughing uncontrollably at "Monty Python and the Holy Grail" or "Airplane"?

Yes   No   7. Did you get teary-eyed at the end of "It's a Wonderful Life" or "Dead Poets Society"?

Yes   No   8. Did you think you could never get enough of "Titanic" or "Somewhere in Time"?

Yes   No   9. When you heard the lines, "And I really hate you, Harry" from "When Harry Met Sally" and "You old poop," from "On Golden Pond" did you understand these to be expressions of love?

Yes   No   10. Are all your favorite movies about comic book heroes?

Yes   No   11. Did you enjoy the quirky romances "My Big Fat Greek Wedding" or "Mama Mia"?

Yes   No   12. Are you always up for seeing another slasher movie?

Yes   No   13. Have you ever watched the epics "Lawrence of Arabia," "Ben Hur," or "The Ten Commandments"?

Yes   No   14. Do you wish you were James Bond?

Yes   No   15. Were you able to solve the mysteries in "The Sting," "The Sixth Sense," or "The Illusionist" before they ended?

Yes   No   16. Did you enjoy "The Sound of Music," "The Music Man," or "The Wizard of Oz"?

Yes   No   17. Did you enjoy "To Kill a Mockingbird" or "The Grapes of Wrath" because you didn't want to read the book?

Yes   No   18. Are you still upset that the government has the Lost Ark of the Covenant back in some warehouse?

Yes   No   19. Do you go out of your way to catch a good independent film in an old art-house theater?

Yes   No   20. Do you stay home and rent movies instead of
                      going to the theater?

Answer Key: If you answered "yes"—

1. You're probably a narcissist.
2. Your appreciation for fantasy escapism has gone too far, you're just a big nerd.
3. Congratulations, you are a child at heart. Of course, this does not apply to the hallucinogenic "Fantasia."
4. You're old fashioned, so what?
5. You could be suffering from unbounded patriotism, take an "Apocalypse Now" and call me in the morning.
6. You may have a worthy sense of humor, or you could be just silly. If you would add "Dumb and Dummer" to the list, you're just silly.
7. You probably find joy in searching for life's deeper meaning.
8. You are probably of one romantic type, the bad obsessive type.
9. You are probably of another romantic type, the lasting likable type.
10. Sorry, you're just shallow and pretentious.
11. Okay, so you're shallow, but at least you're not pretentious.
12. You are probably cruel. Stay away from my dog (see My Dog's Eyes).
13. You are locked into the puritanical notion that you should suffer long to find real worth.
14. You value brains and brawn, but you're a misogynist. Darn.
15. You may be a great problem solver, or think yourself prophetic.
16. You have enough of an appreciation for music that you are willing to tolerate corny sequences like the cuckoo song, shipoopi, and the lollipop guild.
17. You are used to taking the path of least resistance to get what you want.
18. You have what's called incompletion anxiety disorder. Sequels usually cure this, but not in Indiana Jones' case.
19. You take pride in finding your own path rather than following the crowd.
20. You're agoraphobic, but at least you've got the Internet.

Of course, the fact that we can share perspectives on the world by simply going to the movies together still makes this a magical medium. So come on, let's go see a horrible "B" movie, settle in with a buttery bag of popcorn, and prop our feet up on the seat in front of us until the people complain – unless we're at a slasher movie.

40

THE WORST ADVICE

We all have people in our lives that we seek for advice in trivial matters, such as where to take someone for a nice dinner or a suggestion for a favorite book. Others we seek out for more serious decisions, such as which university to attend or what career options we might consider. Knowing whose advice to seek out and whose to adopt is not easy, particularly because advice *givers* are in such abundance and often their presumed wisdom is based on experiences only imagined. Getting the best advice is a lifelong process of observation and listening, constantly evaluating whose advice endures.

Early in life, we went to our playground friends for advice, when they knew as little about life as we did, and when their approval was tantamount to our well-being. Did we seek them out because we were without other – more proven – sources? In my boyhood home the advice was always right in front of us. My parents had a black, wrought iron trivet they kept hanging in the in the kitchen with the Dutch saying, "Ve grow too soon oldt and too late schmardt." I was always intrigued with the trivet, and wondered about its origin and why the words were spelled wrong. But I never asked them for this simple answer, too late schmardt, I suppose.

Having practiced lengthy onslaughts of parental advice on my older siblings and finding them impenetrable fortresses, I think my parents had developed sophisticated and understated advice-giving skills by the time they got to the end of the family train, my brother and me. This technique amounted to a few well-timed phrases. As we were scurrying out the door to go to school, my mother would call after us, "Make a new friend today!" Later, when we started driving and dating, my dad would give us the send off line, "Remember who you oughta be."

Alone, these two pieces of advice had a memorable impact on me. Although I didn't multiply friendships, and I was certainly not an extrovert (see Introverts Unite) my mother's advice made me more sensitive to the taunting my classmates inflicted on new students, the intimidation tactics bullies used to prey on the weak, and the downcast expression of those who were chosen last on playground teams. My father's advice echoed long after the back door had closed behind me, as I tried to remember the high moral standards taught at home. As a result, I stayed behind on those nights when my friends, with single-mindedness, plotted boyish pranks.

Contrasting this simple and sage advice from loving parents whose shared motive was my welfare, I found myself on the receiving end of all kinds of advice that was meant to serve someone else's self-interest. I had a good friend who tried talking me into starting a business with him, but I had never seen him complete anything he had ever set out to accomplish. In the space of a year, he wanted to be a pilot, a musician, and an entrepreneur, but every well-intentioned launch ended in a flameout within a few months. When I thought about a future linked with this friend, I could imagine sitting at a desk trying to run the business while he would be scuba diving in Australia or rebuilding a hot rod. I chose to ignore his advice.

In the post high school transition into life, my friends were full of advice about avoiding marriage. They all thought themselves to be so singularly successful, that they somehow felt it was their duty to persuade me to steer clear of the traps of marriage. At first, their advice about the traps seemed quite logical; but after living this life of solitude, and reflecting on their advice, I found their words full of emptiness.

Trap number one: "You won't be able to do anything with your friends."

When I thought about this, I considered what we did most of the time as friends; most of the time we were thinking about what to do rather than actually *doing* anything. We were not some group of renaissance artists preparing for our next gallery showing; we were not gifted musicians looking for our big break; we were not peace corps volunteers or anti-establishment activists; we were not athletes preparing for the Olympics. We just sat around complaining about the money we didn't make, the girls we didn't date, and the aspirations we didn't attempt. Doing nothing with my friends seemed like a great argument *for* marriage.

Trap number two: "You'll be tied down to one person."

Being tied down made marriage sound like I was being taken prisoner by marauders and forced into a life of servitude. History is full of examples where defeated populations were subjected to lives of enslavement or indentured service. The difference was apparent to me, however. Tying myself to another person, someone who loved me for who I was and what we might become together was a liberating act of free will. I wasn't looking for defeat in battle, but victory in surrender.

Trap number three: "You'll have to get a dumpy apartment in a bad part of town and eat cheap food."

They were right. I would have to move out of my parents' basement, which although financially worrisome, had its own associated liberating lure. Knowing my own flair for decorating, which consisted of movie posters and my hat collection, I reasoned that my wife could certainly make even the dumpiest of apartments into an inviting haven. The cheap food argument was less of a detractor for me, since I was pretty happy on my steady diet of cold cereal, frozen burritos, and peanut butter and jelly sandwiches. It wasn't so much a matter of eating cheap, but finding someone who could endure my same bottom feeding diet long enough for us to find financial footholds.

Having examined my friends' arguments against marriage, I found it to be a much more attractive prospect, so I ignored their bachelor banter and took the plunge, and bathed in the cool water of companionship and soaked in the warmth of a thousand sunny days. Sharing time with a loving partner was joy fulfilled, and far exceeded my rudimentary reasoning skills. Even during our days of trial, facing them together was a meaningful investment in something that would outlive the struggle.

Married life has its own seasons, and graduating from honeymoon to parenthood is one of those early climactic changes that afford many couples the opportunity for friendly advice once more. Just like the nay saying of my bachelor friends prior to my marriage, the number of dual-income-no-kids couples advising against jumping into parenthood was a cynical chorus of cautions.

Caution one: "You should enjoy yourselves for a few years before you settle down with kids. You won't be able to enjoy any time to yourselves."

Implicit in this type of argument was the reasoning that kids and enjoyment were somehow incompatible. In the self-gratifying life of newlyweds, enjoyment could only come from free time, leisure, and entertainment and these superficial pleasures would have to be sacrificed for the added responsibility associated with raising children. My brothers and sisters had children, and I had seen first-hand the joy they experienced as they started their families. I saw the way the fathers cuddled their infants under their chins, and the care taken by mothers bundling up their young ones going out to play. I remember my sister describing a difficult day she was having, and how – after losing her temper with her kids – one of her boys said something that made her burst out laughing, and how the whole family joined in one giant belly laugh. I was sold.

Caution two: "You should finish school before you start a family."

Of course, there are many reasons for delaying life-changing decisions. By this reasoning, I could have waited longer to get married, and I might have had the gift of a thousand more unfulfilling days and nights with my buddies. Using this same logic, my wife and I could have delayed starting a family until school was over; but since I went on to post-graduate work, we would have started our family in our middle age. Although my wife and I struggled to raise our children while I attended school, I will never forget the inspiration that came from returning home after work or school and feeling little hands squeeze my neck welcoming me home. How could I let them down? The thought of giving up never entered my mind when I was with them.

I have noticed that the worst advice usually bears similar traits. First, it comes from an unreliable source: the rebellious son who advises against parental fealty; the agnostic advising against organized religion; the discontent divorcee decrying the pitfalls of marriage; the unemployed laggard espousing work ethics. Second, the worst advice is that which fails to challenge or inspire, seeking only to reinforce with pillowy words your own desires to capitulate, to trade enduring joy for the ease of temporary approval. Third, advice that is too lengthy to recall will leave the recipient with good will towards the friend who is willing to sail endlessly on life's ocean together while regrettably failing to help them find a harbor.

Any advice, even lengthy diatribes that come from others who don't have your best interests in mind, serves as a mirror or a magnifying glass. It shows the values held by others around us, and challenges us to embrace or shun them, and with every word, our own sense of what is right or wrong is brought into greater focus.

41

BIG JOBS FINISHED

Hard work is a relative term, especially in corporate offices, where relatively little physical effort is required during the workday. Putting in a hard day at the office might involve no more physical exertion than attending back to back meetings, occupying a desk for several more hours, or experiencing heightened levels of stress over hitting a key deadline. Often, the work is a repetitive sequence of indiscreet tasks performed by individuals with seemingly disconnected roles, as if each person were gluing tiles in a massive mosaic unaware of the hundreds of others at work on the same objective. For those seeking fulfillment in this sweat-less production line, and especially for leaders who wonder why talented people devolve into lifeless automatons, it might be helpful to recall the joy of big jobs finished.

One summer, as the school inmates were released on a three-month home leave – also known as summer vacation – my father sat down with my brother and me and asked, "What is something you want so much that you would be willing to work all summer to have it?" We were hooked. Would he really follow through on his promise if we named the ultimate prize? He clarified, "If you can think of something that you really want to have, I'll help you make a list of the jobs you can do this summer to earn it." This effectively set the terms of our summer contracts; our potential gain seemed limited only by what we were willing to do. I wanted pigeons. My brother-in-law told me about the rollers and the homing pigeons he had raised as a boy, and I was convinced that life with pigeons was worth a summer of hard work.

My father sat down with me and I acted as scribe while we made a list of all the jobs that needed to be done for me to earn the birds. Among them, I had to read at least a thousand pages over the summer; and then the list of outdoor jobs started. I would have to trim the hedges on both sides of the yard, remove a dead tree, paint a trestle, help plant the family gardens, clean out the shed, and remove the leaves from the storm drain by our basement entrance. But the biggest job was to dig a six-foot deep pit on one end of the yard behind some trees to use as a root cellar. The idea was to store potatoes, carrots, and other vegetables through the winter months.

Digging the root cellar was a little like digging my own grave. I figured it was called a root cellar because I had to dig through so many roots from the surrounding trees. Every day I would shovel more dirt, chop roots with the ax, and haul away the dirt. After chewing through the first three feet, I encountered another villain: clay. Digging through clay is a little like chopping down a tree with a baseball bat – draining not only my physical strength, but my mental will as my shovel blade seemed to bounce off the clay. It was as if some subterranean magnetic force was repelling the penetrating blade. I was convinced that my father didn't really need the root cellar as much as I needed to finish it, which I finally did. Many weeks later, as my father walked the yard with me, checking off the list of jobs, noting where I had exceeded his expectations, I swelled with pride as I considered the whole of what I had accomplished, pleased that my father had noticed. And yes, he kept his promise, and I became the birdman of the block with my two new pigeons, Teeny and Tiny.

After high school, my dad asked for some more help down at the company distribution center. The backroom and attic storage areas needed to be cleaned out in preparation for potentially sub-leasing the space. I cleaned up the main floor, digging into corners and under rusting apparel fixtures, tossing out the equivalent of a dozen garage sales, and then giving a final clean sweep with the broom, making it spotless in a couple of days. Then I went up to the attic. The air was stale, and with no cross-ventilation, it was considerably warmer than the area just twenty stairs down.

I couldn't tell how big the attic was, because it was stuffed to the front with junk: old mannequins, store fixtures, and refrigerator-sized cabinets made of pressed wood with laminated tops. Although the job as described was to clean up the space and make it look presentable for a potential lessee, I couldn't imagine leaving all this junk upstairs. So, I went to work. It was something of a mining operation, because I would create holes in the wall of junk, haul it downstairs, and return to dig, until I could finally reach the ends of the storage area – the mother lode.

After days of working in the stifling storage room, and sweating through my t-shirts, I found myself confronted with the final big decision, what to do with the cabinets. Each one weighed as much as a refrigerator, and there were more than ten…and there was no one else to help (not that I would have asked, see Do-It-Yourselfishness for more on this psychosis). I could have left them in place, and my father would not have thought any less of me. I had already gone far beyond what was asked. But the idea of hauling out these cabinets, the final stumps in the forest I had just cleared, compelled me to search for a solution. I found that by easing each one onto the stairs, and then nudging it ever so gently, I could gradually bear the entire weight from below and slowly back down each step until it touched down on the landing. I did it, and successfully moved all the cabinets out of the attic, completing a job that I had not intended to do. My spent spirit was rejuvenated by the discovery of a will stronger than the exhaustion I felt.

This determination was only strengthened later after my wife and I relocated three times in five years, putting in sweat equity to the newly built homes we were occupying. Sweat equity took many forms, including painting the interior, planting trees and shrubs, and putting down sod. By the time we were in our third home, I had become something of a sod expert, knowing how to stagger the rows, how to get around landscaping, and how to switch directions on hills so that the sod wouldn't wash away; but our backyard was so large that it couldn't be done in one day with the makeshift crew from the neighborhood as we had done at the other houses.

Putting down sod affects the body in several ways: first, the ability to grip is weakened after a full day spent carrying twenty-pound grassy clumps like trays and pulling them into place; second, the knees get sore and rough from kneeling to position the sod; and third, the back strains at hauling the rolls of sod from the truck to the wheelbarrow, and from the wheelbarrow to the ground. After sodding for two days, and finding myself without additional help, I ordered another load of the lawn carpet and began to put it down myself. I worked beyond the point of exhaustion for two more days, motivated by the beauty of what was forming in the backyard and knowing of the days to come when we could enjoy this as a family. As I eased in the final piece of sod, I looked back down the hill to see my family testing the velvet green grass in their bare feet, and my aches momentarily eased.

What is it that motivates us to complete the big jobs, to push ourselves beyond what we consider to be our physical or mental capabilities? For some, it is merely a desire to provide income for life's necessities. For others, it may be the additional responsibility and obligation we feel to sustain our families. But I think there is something else, something more personal about accomplishing large, difficult, and physically demanding jobs. When we exert our energy and tax our determination, we learn important lessons about ourselves. As the mountainous dirt hills give way to our steady strikes, we see first-hand the progress of our work. As we put the finishing touches on a freshly poured concrete patio or apply another coat of paint to a bedroom, we look ahead and see the dividends paid out in the years to come as we enjoy the fruits of our labors.

Whether you lead thousands of workers filling places on production lines or a few clerical workers in a retail store, give them a goal worth striving for, and clear the way for them to exert all their faculties in the pursuit of something great. Notice the extra effort given, forgive the mistakes made while attempting innovation, and seek ideas from those nearest your customers. When we are challenged with big jobs and finish them, we begin to see our own emerging potential and we remove the governors from our own engines of untapped capabilities.

42

LOSING THE ELECTION

Sometimes our greatest defeats can become our greatest opportunities for self-reflection and growth. The presidential election of 1978 – not of any federal or local authority – but of the supreme student body leader for the junior high school, was such an opportunity. Seen through adult eyes, such an office might be viewed as merely a popularity contest, an opportunity for the school administration to set up a puppet regime to win the support of the masses. Fortunately, in a world where popularity was the primary currency of trade, where clothing labels, hair height, and pubescent physique rated one's personal holdings on the PI (or popularity index), a contest for the celebrity presidency seemed both a worthy and weighty thing. No one expected the president to have any real political power, but popular appeal – that was everything.

I was not a popular kid in junior high, but I was noticeable, since Dan Brown was the only kid who could rival my size. Since most of my growth spurts occurred before I reached eighth grade, I had peaked at the right time for the election. My budding popularity in eighth grade grew when I was asked to play a part in a skit that the cheerleaders were putting together for an assembly. That cheerleaders took an interest in me at all was so flattering that they could have asked me to do just about anything and I would have fallen over my own size twelve feet to accommodate the request. This call of duty was delivered not by one, but two cheerleaders, Debbie and Kari, and they cornered me in the hall one day.

"Hi Rob," Debbie crooned.

Looking behind me to see if another Rob had materialized to answer the greeting, I sputtered, "Oh hi, Deb."

"Hey, we're doing a skit next month for the school assembly, and we need you."

"Ya?"

"You're a big strong guy, and we need you to just stand there and let us dance around you and one other guy, Bruce Arnold."

Bruce Arnold was *the* most popular guy in junior high, so sharing a stage with him, while cheerleaders danced around seemed like the kind of initiative I could get behind. Bruce and I donned our tightest white t-shirts and jeans, and we stood stoically on stage, arms crossed and fists under biceps – a timeless guy trick to pump up the biceps – while half a dozen cheerleaders danced around us to the music of "The Leader of the Pack." On the popularity index, my stock had just gone triple A.

I started wearing cheap cologne that smelled like glazed doughnuts, and I walked down the middle of the hall to go to class, confident that no predators ranging the junior high plains remained a threat to my soaring popularity. It was in this delusionary state that I was approached with another proposition to run for student body president. Of course, I was too naïve to recognize that by backing my run for presidency, others were simply trying to secure for themselves a stake in my popularity, but I only saw the potential fawning of devoted fans, so I agreed. Kari volunteered to be my campaign manager.

The primary election was the first real test of my presidential potential. I had to come up with a three-minute speech to persuade the student body to vote for me, and this would be delivered at a school-wide assembly in two weeks. I fretted over this speech, thinking for the first time that instead of winning mass appeal, my speech might simply reveal how dull and uninspiring I truly was.

It was time for a speechwriter, and my older sister said that she would be happy to contact her mother-in-law, Judy, who had a real gift for writing. I was desperate, so I shed my natural shyness to go to Judy's house, where we brainstormed some ideas. Actually, Judy brainstormed, I simply watched her creative squall roll in, and in about thirty minutes, she had a rough outline of the speech. This was not the normal I-promise-to-put-soda-in-the-drinking-fountains kind of political speech so common to student elections of the past; this was a poetic play on words that rose above the banal woodenness of the other candidates' best efforts. Judy came to my house and while we worked out the final details, she coached me on my delivery, ensuring that my timing would ensure the right words were emphasized, slowing down on my name so that even the seventh graders could remember.

When the assembly came, and I stepped to microphone, I heard applause. Kari had been doing her job, and like any good campaign manager had planted cheering shills around the auditorium. Had I stood and read the ingredients off a box of cereal, I was guaranteed the appearance of adulation. I read the speech perfectly, and paused after nearly every couplet to let the applause wash onto the stage, washing away the other candidates. When the primary election was over, I had locked in one of the two run-off spots against Les Gardner, and the leaks from the vote counting committee indicated that I had nearly twice the votes as Les heading into the final election.

The campaign went supersonic. We made posters, flyers, and contemplated the next media blitz. To conclude the campaign season, the school administrators planned a final election assembly, where each finalist for the various student offices would prepare a five-minute skit. I settled on the idea of a slide show, complete with dramatic music, following which I would come to the microphone, crowds cheering, to give a final word of encouragement to my constituents.

For the slide show, I talked my dad into driving me to the school on the weekend for a photo shoot. There I was holding books, giving a thumbs up in front of the school marquee, then grasping the handle to the school's front door, and again posing by the gardens. Unintentionally, but due to the rising landscape in front of the school, the photos all seemed to look up at me from somewhere below, as if signaling to the masses that their leader on high was ready to look down upon them and hear their complaints.

To provide the appropriate dramatic background for the slides, and to build to that instant when I would take the stage, I selected "Thus, Spake Zarathustra," the theme from "2001: A Space Odyssey." It was perfect, regal, like a coronation. "Dah......dah......dah...... duh-dah!" Kari's narration from off stage was full of trite platitudes to match the slides:

"Rob's there for you, taking us to new heights."
"He'll open the door to your future."
"He'll breathe new life into student government."

The larger-than-life slides, shining on the wall of the auditorium would fade to black, and I would appear in the spotlight to give my final words on cue to the final *duh-dah* of Zarathustra's fanfare. Despite the poor history of staging media presentations at the junior high, we had set up the slide projector, tested the volume, and everything went off without any distracting technical difficulties. The music boomed, the final duh-dah sounded, and I took the stage, expecting thunderous applause; but rather than cheers, I strained to hear scattered applause, like a light rain was falling somewhere in the back of the auditorium. In the spotlight, I raised my arms like Rocky reaching the summit of the stairs in front of the Philadelphia Museum of Art, and uttered something about as profound as what would come from the boxer's mouth, like, "Uh, okay, everyone vote for Rob. Thank you!"

In the aftermath of the election assembly, my popularity began to fade. I heard rumors that some students thought I was "stuck-up" – the egomaniacal state one reaches when the little voice inside sounds like a presidential press secretary defending the soundness of one's own bankrupt logic. Obviously, everyone was jealous of my popularity. I wasn't delusional, just misunderstood. My PI stock was falling, and no one was buying.

Les, on the other hand, had waged a serious and practical campaign, putting people in hallways handing out flyers, enlisting friends and supporters to appear on stage with him, and remaining upbeat about his chances. I hated to admit it, but he was a likable nominee, and he knew something of student government having worked with other student leaders on committees and student publications.

I was surrounded by disloyalty in the final days of the campaign. I saw Kari joking around with some of Les's campaign leaders right in front of me! How could it be that my own campaign manager had deserted me? Those who had been closest to me before the primaries had long abandoned me, and our warm greetings and hallway chats had turned to silent passings and vacant glances.

The election was over long before the final votes were cast. In junior high, the popularity grapevine was as accurate as any spot poll by sophisticated research organizations. I knew that I had lost the mandate of the masses, and now simply awaited confirmation of the bitter defeat. Although the write-in candidate, Pete's dog, had finished third, my final vote count had barely outpaced the canine.

I knew why I had lost. It wasn't the slide show, and it wasn't the betrayal of anyone on my campaign. I had simply become too consumed at the prospect of popularity, learning at last how fleeting and fickle a thing it is. I had placed myself above my peers, and I failed to appreciate the efforts of those around me. I had taken myself too seriously, becoming too guarded and inaccessible, withering at the prospect of losing the acclaim I never really had.

Thinking back, I am glad that I lost the election. Les was a good leader, and he truly deserved the win more than I did. In my diminution, I found myself again. There beneath the façade of cheap cologne I found the person who had once been a loyal friend, the one who distrusted false acclaim, and the one who lived outside of the spotlight, content to be in the supporting cast again. Defeat had given me something precious and poignant at a young age, a lesson in accepting myself.

43

MANY UNHAPPY RETURNS

Customer service counters are the piazzas of both the common man and the sophisticate. As we look across counters into the eyes of the clerks, bureaucrats, and customer associates, our internal cooperative recognition software searches for the warm smile, the eased lines in the forehead, or the softened voice that signals a request is about to be granted, or the pursed lips, cocked head, and rolled eyes that say, "You're kidding, right?" Business moguls and the clinically insane queue up at the same Department of Motor Vehicles window, add their names to the same patient list at the emergency room lobby, and petition at the same merchandise exchange counter for assistance.

Among these equal opportunity situations, the product return ritual is a singular example of the delicate balance of power between customer and clerk, the former seeking complete restoration of the purchase price, and the latter searching for flaws that might discount the item's value or drive the customer – product in hand – from the establishment. The customer service matador waves the return slip while the bullish customer strikes hopelessly at the air in this dueling dance.

To return items, one must learn, and then follow, the rules of the return policy:
No returns after 30 days. This means that although the item has been sitting on the store shelf for several months, the customer's month is more abusive to the item, or we might assume that after this additional month, the item will be obsolete, worn out or broken.

<u>Your item must have a receipt.</u> With the possible exception of the man who buys two sweaters because he wants to see how the color looks in the special lighting in his office, or the woman who buys three prom dresses for her daughter so that she doesn't have to try them on in the store, most people who buy an item actually intend to keep it. We don't save the receipt because it is tossed out with the bag or it ends up in the back of a bulging wallet never to be seen again.

<u>Without a receipt, you will be given the current sale price of the item in the form of a store credit.</u> Even if the item purchased was just marked down today, the customer is going to pay the penalty for buying at full price. The store credit provides the infuriated customer with the blessing of some much needed cooling down time.

<u>Your item must be in its original packaging.</u> Of course, if the customer isn't used to hoarding receipts, the likelihood of preserving the original packaging is pretty remote. Original packaging is becoming harder to reassemble, and over the years, manufacturers have devised new techniques to ensure that once the item is torn open, it's out of play. Take the case of the television cables I purchased from my electronics store. These cables were heat-sealed inside a clear plastic sarcophagus with multiple plastic inserts, which made extracting the cables difficult if one was planning to keep the cables, and completely unbeatable if one was hedging that the purchased cables may need to be returned. I have a collection of cables that were beyond my repackaging skills.

<u>Your refund will be in the same form as the original purchase.</u> This means that if the customer charged the item, it is returned on that charge card. But if the item was purchased with that obsolete form of currency – cash – the store is just going to have to mail you a check in a few days. This rule might more accurately read, "Although we may have received cash from you, you're not getting a dime from us."

Some stores are notorious for their stringent return policies, and the store clerks are trained like CIA agents in advanced interrogation methods:

"Okay, let's see here, Ms. Smith. You say that you purchased this iron one week ago, is that correct?"
"Yes."
"And you purchased it from *this* store?"
"Of course, I do all my shopping here."
"Let's just confine ourselves to the iron, shall we m'am? And what is the reason for the return?"

"Uh, reason? Well, I was hoping to get an iron with an automatic shut-off feature."

"Are you saying that this iron is *broken*, m'am?"

"Oh, no, not at all."

"I see. So you are basing this return on the fact that you just want something *different*, is that it – that you are *unhappy* with the features of this perfectly fine, defect free, iron? Is that what you are trying to tell me, m'am?"

"Uh-huh."

"You understand that an iron like that is going to be more expensive, and you – "

"Oh yes, of course, I'm willing to pay – "

"Right…heh heh, you're *willing* to pay…Hey Ruthie, she's *willing* to pay! If I had a dime for every time someone returning an iron like this said she was *willing* to pay…"

One particularly difficult return happened soon after my wife and I had moved into our first home. My neighbor, Terry, and I had agreed to build a wood fence between our yards, a sort of mutual acknowledgement that although we liked each other, we felt that some sort of barrier would better preserve the relationship, a sort of smaller version of the U.S.-Mexico border strife. For my first fence, I was pleased with the overall result. We had taken extra care to use screws to keep the fencing tight against the rails rather than defaulting to the cheaper nails that might pop out later.

The problem with building a fence, or really any do-it-yourself project in which I'm engaged (see Do-It-Yourselfishness), is that I buy more materials that I need, figuring that it is faster to have the materials on hand, rather than running back several times to buy more wood, nails, paint, or putty. Although I could have applied a mathematical solution to the story problem of the fence, I was not about to hand count the hundreds of screws required for this job. Once the borderline fence was finished, I packed up the remaining screws and headed over to my friendly neighborhood lumber store for a refund on my bag of screws.

So there I was at the customer service counter inside lumber store, with my bag of screws, waiting patiently for the person ahead of me to make their appeal, always a signal of things to come. It looked as though the customer ahead of me had prevailed, so I bravely stepped forward.

"Yes, I'd like to return these screws please," I said with an air of satisfaction having just completed a big job (see Big Jobs Finished for more about this feeling).

"Was there something wrong?" the clerk queried.

"No, they're just screws that were leftover after my project was finished, and I'd like to get a refund," I blurted out, not considering the rules that were clearly posted behind the lofty hairdo of the customer service clerk.

"Hmm. Do you have a receipt?"

So it was going to be the old interrogation racket, huh?

"No, I don't have my receipt, but – "

"Oh, well we require – "

"But you have these screws right there in the back, in those red bins where I purchased them a week ago."

I have to pause to give a little history with this lumber store. As anyone who has ever lived in a recently built house knows, especially in the case where a part of the down payment is to be provided in the form of the sweat equity, the home owner's best new friend is the lumber store. I had been a regular fixture in the lumber store nearly every day for the two weeks of fence building, and on numerous occasions prior to that purchasing hand tools, paint, pegboards, hoses, sprinklers, and shovels. When I entered the store, the clerks just gave a knowing nod as if to say, "You're back – what'll it be today?"

As the clerk continued her consideration of my request, I realized the sudden tenuous position I was in. I had unwittingly blurted out my receipt deficiency too early in the trial, and now I found myself to be the hostile witness for the prosecution. Suddenly, my giddiness at completing the fence was replaced with frustration that this final phase was not going as planned; and there it was, the slight eye roll followed by the head tilt. That did it. I just couldn't help myself.

"Wait a minute," I felt my face redden, my voice rising, "Are you saying that although I have come in here day after day and purchased hundreds of dollars worth of supplies from you people that you're not willing to take back a few screws? I don't understand. It's not as if screws wear out, and you can certainly resell them by just tossing them back in the big red bucket there. Look, I'll walk back with you to show you exactly where it is."

"We *know* where it is, sir."

"Okay, fine," I said. "If that's the way it's going to be, here's what I'm going to do. I have two more sides of my yard needing a fence. I am not going to come back here to spend the several hundreds of dollars to complete the rest of my fence."

Madam Prosecutor behind the customer service desk did not even flinch at my oath to disloyalty, and so I was compelled to continue my rant.

"And *more* than that, my job involves training hundreds of people in quality methodologies, and this example is going to be a great one to add to my repertoire. I will make it a point to tell every class this story, and let them know exactly where I purchased these screws, and how difficult you made it for me."

The defense had rested, and I walked out with my screws, and my dignity, I thought. I held true to my promise, and I never went back in the lumber store. I built the rest of my fence with supplies from another store, and I actually did train many employees at my corporation and recounted my tale to dozens of classes. Several of my trainees told me that they had changed their minds about shopping at the lumber store after my experience.

Was I vindicated? No. The lumber store, despite the loss of several customers, continued to thrive and is still in business today. The screws I fought to return are long since rusted. What remains is simply the memory that my joy at completing the fence project had turned to defeat, that I had publicly lost my temper, and then had shown my smallness by refusing to let it pass into a distant memory, instead putting my own injured ego up for public display with each retelling. A bag of screws. I was like the main character in the story by Guy de Maupassant who wears out his lifetime protesting a false accusation, who continues his defense from his deathbed, "A little bit of string – a little bit of string. See, here it is, M'sieu la Maire."[1]

Despite the many unhappy returns in our lives – or the bag of screws we can't seem to forget – it is time to let it go. Bruised egos, like bruised bananas, are best thrown out, or made into banana bread.

NOTES
1. From <u>A Piece of String</u>, in *Short Stories of de Maupassant*. Guy de Maupassant (1941).

44

PALTRY PANIC

Sometimes I wish we could hit the reset button on the world. What if we could go backward in time, just temporarily of course, and see with new eyes the modern conveniences surrounding us? Our expectations for what is possible – and what should be ours by right – have been so inflated, that we periodically fail to appreciate all that we have, the wonder of the times in which we live.

When I see someone at the grocery store complaining about waiting in a long line of people to check out, I want to hit the reset button and go back to a time when our ancestors raised their own food, farmed their fields, and plucked the chickens that we now pick up casually as we speed through the frozen food aisle. When I see someone in the office having an adult tantrum because they can't get enough bars on their mobile device to make an urgent call, I want to hit the reset button and go back to a time when we had to go to the telegram office or sent messages in pony express packs.

We are reminded of our dependence on technology on those occasions when the power goes out, and we scramble to find flashlights and candles while we fret over the fate of our perishables in the lifeless refrigerator. Not a generation or two ago, we would have marveled that we could make our own ice rather than waiting for the local ice man to cometh. We might have also trekked to the outhouse rather than padding across a warm floor to the flushing toilet that today might even come complete with a heated seat. Today our disposal clogs, and we dash to the store for a remedy or dial a plumber to save us from the kitchen waste that our house was unable to digest. In the past, our kids might have complained at the much more disagreeable task of hauling the stinking bucket of kitchen goo outside to slop the family hog.

Press reset.

So taken for granted are these modern appliances and technologies that we fail to see how they have saved us time, discomfort, or personal injury. When my wife shreds a block of cheese in her four thousand RPM auto shredder in about three seconds, I think back on the knuckle skin I lost from the hand-operated grater when I had to shred cheese for my mother. I remember dreading the prospect of hanging Christmas lights as a teenager because the electrical cords were so prone to shorting out that if we weren't careful we would get a shock that numbed our hands and forearms.

In addition to the changes wrought in our homes, we have experienced quantum leaps in this age of information that push our expectations far beyond what was imaginable by our parents and grandparents. We impatiently slam our fists computer keyboards that take several seconds to recall tens of thousands of documents and references on a subject that would have been inaccessible to us had we spent a week in our local library. We rant and curse when our phone runs out of battery life while chatting with a business associate – who might be on another continent – while remaining unimpressed that we have nearly unlimited and instant connectivity to all parts of the inhabited world at our fingertips.

Press reset.

Our stresses are not only bound to the technical advances of our day; many of us are so tightly wound up about ourselves, our children, and our situation in life that even minor setbacks send us to therapy. Little Timmy brings home a "D" on his report card, and we see it as a personal failure, as willful academic neglect by Timmy's teacher, or as a biological anomaly in Little Timmy's brain, rather than recognizing that Little Timmy didn't apply himself, missed some assignments, or simply wasn't as smart as the other kids. The horrifying thought that our Little Timmy might not be as bright, and that he might end up as a professional cleaner of commodes or as a proverbial ditch digger, is so shattering that we will search for any other explanation with parental indignation.

We have become so conditioned to believe that all children are gifted (see On Being Gifted) and possess the same potential for academic, musical, or artistic achievement that some of us have grown intolerant of average performance. That our children are learning scientific theories, mathematical equations and literary criticism, supplemented by musical, athletic, and artistic programs in a curriculum that is the envy of other nations, might fail to enter our heads in our anxiety over Little Timmy's momentary lapse.

In the past, there was no use crying over spilt milk, but now we wring our hands that the milk might contain growth hormone or that the countertop harbors life-threatening bacteria, and we have suddenly worried the human race from the top of the food chain to the bottom. However, in the last century, we have witnessed the eradication of diseases that once claimed millions; we have new treatments for heart disease and cancer, and life-saving procedures that surgically save many others who would have died without the hope of reaching adulthood. Now we crowd the emergency room when we twist an ankle, get a sore throat, or experience a headache.

Many of us struggle with the vicissitudes of a more static, wealthy life than was experienced by our farming and hunting ancestors, such as obesity and addiction. As we pursue the Adonis or Aphrodite body that we know exists in each of us, we jump from one fad diet to another or medicate ourselves with herbal concoctions believing we have found the secret formula that has eluded millions of others. Our daughters fear the bridal gown fitting more than the wedding, and we keep our swollen bodies away from muscle beach rather than enjoying a day in the sun with our kids. I can just see our ancestors chuckling as they watch us like hamsters on stationary bikes, treadmills, and rowing machines going nowhere to get the same compulsory exercise that was part of their daily existence.

We used to joke about our grandparents walking to school through the harshest conditions, intrepid explorers blazing trails through winter storms and over mountain passes. That was when we walked to school. Now we scream at the school administrators if the bus is five minutes late, or if our child has to walk around the corner to the bus stop. The mere threat of inclement weather cancels school, and we huddle at home like frightened sheep, peering out our windows at weather that would have meant a damp day at work in times past.

Rather than hunting for food out on the plains or in the dark forests, we bargain hunt, arising early for after Christmas sales so that we can cover the hunting grounds early. The distress of finding an empty rack or receiving a rain check for a sold out item ruins our day, but at least we can return home to a full pantry, unlike our forebears who had to trade hunger for exhaustion as they went to their beds after an unsuccessful hunt.

Press reset.

Maybe our societal resilience has been weakened by the many advances that have come in our lifetimes. We panic, worry, fret, and fuss over things that matter less than ever before, and our ability to cope with these minor inconveniences and temporary setbacks has been so compromised by the onset of infectious ease, we may have forgotten how to stand on our own, how to fight through the pain to finish the job. We may have become preoccupied by worries of microbial importance when the threats that lie ahead are mountainous and consequential.

Does this mean that we are in an irreversible state of terminal dependence or chronic modern myopia? As in times past, perhaps an act of nature or of man will trigger the reset button for us and restore that which is lost gradually with the passing generations: historical perspective.

So the next time you scream at the traffic as you wait on that six-lane superhighway that covers old buggy paths and the pock-marks of a thousand hoof-prints, the next time you dress down your dry cleaner for taking an extra day to deliver your ten items of pressed laundry, the next time you start to foam at the mouth having missed an appointment in your electronic calendar, just repeat after me:

It's not nuclear holocaust, it's not teen pregnancy, it's not homelessness, terrorism or inoperable cancer. Don't panic.

45

THE BEST WEDDING GIFT

I have never been a good gift giver (see Rejected Gifts, Rejected Love). For some, giving gifts that have special meaning for the receiver is a highly refined science in which the potential gifter reads subtle clues – often months before the gift is presented in its special package. A raised eyebrow on a casual day at the mall, a nearly imperceptible lingering around an item on display, an expressed interest made in passing over lunch; these are the signals that ping back to the giver's radar. My radar screen is dark most days, as if I were navigating in the deepest abyss in the darkest corner of the vast ocean.

Wedding gifts have always presented difficult gift giving decisions for me, as I try to weigh the range of practical gifts, like toasters, irons, and vacuum cleaners, with the more sentimental gifts, like photo frames to remember the occasion, gift certificates for a special evening out, or a set of his and her iPods with the happy couple's wedding song at the top of the playlist. I tend towards the dolefully practical, and have recently reverted to the old unoriginal favorite: cash.

It is from this uninformed and unskilled background that I would like to give my suggestion for the best wedding gift. Get something to write with, invite the neighbors over, wake the kids, and stop the presses; this is the definitive answer to your wedding gift woes.

The best wedding gift is the one that takes more than mere months to find; in fact, it takes the better part of a lifetime. Brides will not register for this gift because no one but you can get it. No gift box with special Styrofoam shapes exists that can contain this gift. It cannot be returned, exchanged, or passed on to another couple. It is the most sentimental, most custom-made, priceless bestowal you can provide, and it will likely outlast the honeymoon, the golden anniversary, and may live on for generations of penguin-suited grooms and shimmering-silken brides.

The gift is *your marriage*.

That's right. Your marriage, the one that has endured the poverty of "for richer or poorer" and the anguish of "in sickness and in health," is the pinnacle, the summit of the wedding gift excursion. The subtle clues have been there from the beginning of the receiver's earliest memory as they looked up and saw loving eyes and felt the warm embrace of mother and father. Their childish eyes peered through peek-a-boo hands to see mommy and daddy kissing in the kitchen or snuggling on the couch. They lingered as you described to your awkward teen how to start up a conversation, etiquette for paying the bill, or holding the door open.

When you raised your voice in anger with your spouse, demeaned him or her at a party, or refused a tender request, they noted the event, anxious about the future prospects of receiving your gift. Dining on daily doses of entertainment poking fun at the old fashioned, obsolete, crumbling institution of marriage, your gift receivers doubted, grew disillusioned, or determined never to accept the pretty silver package and bow. However, something they saw as they meandered through life's market reminded them of your gift, sitting quietly under glass, just out of reach, glowing with tantalizing warmth.

Packaging this best of all wedding gifts is a difficult task, but perhaps your words put down on the finest parchment, handwritten in careful calligraphy would suit the precious nature of your gift. Card companies have tried for years to capture such sentiments, but your words, stripped of poetry or honeyed words, will outlast the finest commercial attempts in the wedding card aisle. Find the words that describe your formula for success.

Giving marriage advice, whether in a whispered conversation in the hallway at a bridal shower or in a well-crafted tome, can be a little intimidating as the espoused principles become the ruler by which your own marriage is measured. Bearing this in mind, I would like to offer a set of rules that my wife and I established at the start of our life together, more as a template for you to insert your own words rather than as a set of universally applicable truths.

Rule 1: No keeping score. We came up with this rule based on a wedding gift we observed in the lives of some close friends, Chuck and Cathy. Whenever we went to their apartment, they were always fighting about whose turn it was to empty the garbage, do the dishes, or turn out the lights in the next room. We could imagine somewhere a ledger in which Chuck and Cathy settled their accounts at the end of the day, achieving an equal tally of tasks below each name, resolving the equality of their partnership by requiring that neither partner invested more than fifty percent in the total marriage account. It occurred to us that, however sentimental, love meant being willing to give more than was required. In a regrettable I-told-you-so, Chuck and Cathy's balance sheet ended up bankrupting their marriage.

Rule 2: Don't go to bed angry. The principle of resolving differences as the sun sets in the west is an effective deadline to impose on a marital blow-up or a simmering spat. This rule served us well for many years, and probably helped us skate over a number of little concerns early on; but the possible downside to this one is that in trading the silence of sleep for the honesty of wakeful conflict we go to our beds passively polite. Perhaps this rule ought to be revised: *Don't go to bed with unresolved anger.*

Rule 3: Don't say the D-word, not even in joking. The D-word is divorce. The prevalence of this little word in talk shows and the celebrity press has removed the stinging stigma once associated with a defunct marriage. With tongue in cheek, some couples threaten to go a-courting in front of a judge to divide up the spoils of an unforgiving, relentless battle of wills. The D-word, said once in jest, twice in spite, the third time becomes the contemptuous poison for which there is no satisfying antidote.

Rule 4: Don't speak negatively about the other person behind his/her back. This ought to be so obvious, but somehow in the rush for the approval of their unmarried or unhappily married comrades, some resort to putting down their spouse when he or she is absent. This verbal flogging of a loved one unable to speak is a betrayal of trust, a false confiding in those who have taken no vow with you, who chortle and whinny like drunks at a funeral, who, with their agreeable debasement of your beloved, befoul the cherished and profane the holy.

Your advice might be summarized in one pithy statement, or be nearly Constitutional in its sweeping scope; but remember that the Maker only needed Ten Commandments and our Bill of Rights in its brevity has sustained a nation for over two centuries. Oh, and when your wedding gift reaches its concluding well wishes, and you have signed your work, and had it notarized by your better half's veritable witness, remember that nobody wants a crummy letter of advice for a wedding present — so slip in a little cash.

46

HEROIC DEEDS TO COME

Who were your heroes when you were young? Were they the movie stars who graced red carpets like royalty or were they sports figures who exhibited the indomitable spirit of the underdog or the excellence of the expert? Did your heroes occupy a higher orbit, unreachable by mere humans, or did they circle closer to your view? Perhaps you met your hero at a shared intersection and he or she set your feet on a new road. Are you one of those heroes yourself? Don't underestimate your heroic qualities.

Heroic acts are reported frequently, and we talk about them excitedly to our friends and co-workers, sanctioning the heroic acts and slandering the mere grand-standers, reserving the title hero for only the bravest, most honorable and selfless acts. Maybe heroism earns such high regard in our marbled halls because it is the antithesis of a million selfish, calculating acts witnessed as we plod through our days. Heroic acts renew our hope in the human race, strengthening our faith that goodness prevails.

Heroes might have training to perform heroic acts as part of their jobs, like the fireman who rushes into a burning house to save a child or a pilot who guides a crippled plane to a safe landing. These are heroic acts, yes, and it is their professional training and cool-headedness in the face of catastrophic dangers that we honor. We see our trained soldiers move with precision as a synchronous force against our enemies, and we see their resolve, determination, and raw courage as they defend freedom and preserve the innocent. Their combined mission is heroic, grander in purpose and scope than any individual accomplishment.

Still, there are heroes who we might categorize as accidental heroes, those who stumble into the limelight after performing some heroic act. A boy saves his friend from drowning, a mother talks a kidnapper out of his evil intention, a bystander rushes in to save an accident victim before professional medical help arrives; all are heroes, and yet rarely did they have training to perform these acts.

Or did they?

Where are heroes grown, and from what seeds do they sprout? If we were to examine these accidental heroes and understand what it was that prepared them for the response that came so naturally to them, what might we find? We may find that they received some informal training, or picked up some bit of knowledge that they were able to utilize when the moment came.

Maybe the boy who saved his friend was simply living out what he had been taught in Boy Scouts, to be prepared, or to do a good turn daily, mottos and creeds that sunk deeper than the patch worn on his uniform. The criminal might have been disarmed by simple motherly kindness and compassion passed from mother to daughter for generations, or by a sermon that entered the listening ear and penetrated the heart now recalled in a critical moment. A bystander rushes in because he or she simply couldn't bear the thought of standing still, of watching a fellow being suffer and do nothing, an emotion born of a lifetime of service, of looking to others' needs, of subduing personal comfort to help someone who needs us *now*.

How do we become heroes? We answer the challenge to be heroic in a thousand ways each day. We heroically stand up for what is right, for truth or for goodness. We stop to give aid to a stranger whose car has broken down, or we help a neighbor carry a heavy piece of furniture upstairs on our way home from work. We contribute to worthy causes, both monetarily and through our own sweat, supplanting our own desires with the needs of others, moving out from behind our comfortable cover to walk among the needy and give aid as best we can at a time of our choosing.

Then comes the test of your heroism-in-training. It's not so much a comprehensive exam yet, not a life or death scenario, just something simple to see if you'll stop along the road. Can you break out of your routine for a minute to make that stop to help a brother – when it is inconvenient or especially difficult for you – or will you continue on, refusing to get involved, retreating into rationalization, certain that another will stop and answer the call? You meet the eyes of the needy and look away, willing yourself not to see what you cannot deny.

This is not meant to be a general rebuke for our lack of compassion, but a reminder that we all possess heroic characteristics, and one of these is bravery. What is bravery? Is it found in the tenuous analysis of pros and cons, weighing the personal cost to safety, comfort, or reputation before deciding to do what is right? No, it is acting *now* without regard for our own needs. How far reaching is our compassion if our arms, atrophied from infrequent service, can no longer reach out, embrace, or lift another? These muscles require regular stretching to remain of use.

Opportunities for everyday heroism are many, and they await our response. Before we experience that ultimate intrepid test of life and death, we ought not to shrink from such interim opportunities at heroism. If you can do nothing more than drop a coin in the red bucket outside your local grocery store during the holidays, let it begin with that. Anonymous gifts are always appreciated – find a neighbor who is out of work, and leave a bag of groceries on the doorstep – it is the grown-up version of doorbell ditch, and might be called "relief ring."

We may hesitate to give, wondering whether our actions will be misread or misinterpreted. One of the first lessons learned in lifesaving techniques is that the drowning victim often flails about wildly seeking a saving hold on someone while potentially injuring the rescuer. We shouldn't be so concerned about the ones we help failing to appreciate the gift and injuring our pride. Life saving is often thankless work and anonymous drudgery, but it is no less heroic as you drag souls to shore, guiding their feet to solid ground.

Hollywood has brought so-called super heroes to the screen, various virile representations of bugs, rodents, and robots, and these cartoonish characters give us one portrayal of heroic hyperbole; but true heroes don't show up swinging on ropes or driving sports cars. No, more often they are found wearing hairnets in a food line or driving old trucks full of secondhand goods to families on the other side of town. They don't wear masks, yet we don't know their names as they pass among us (see The Guy Behind the Scenes). If we inquire, they might reply, "I'm nobody special. I'm just like you."

I suspect that many nameless heroes are among those whose selfless sacrifice is remembered by the survivors of the September 11 attacks.

201

Whether in towers that were certain to crumble beneath their feet or aboard airplanes that were certain to doom all aboard to the same fate, heroes moved among the crowds saving close friends and complete strangers, or staying put to give comfort when hope had run out. Those trained for the job responded in heroic fashion, fulfilling and exceeding the call of duty. Those trained in Scout troops, youth groups, CPR classes, volunteer service, or the military, rose to the challenge. They rushed in – they brought hundreds to shore, often giving their lives in the attempt.

Will you have that type of courage when the time comes? Will you be the hero or the victim? Who knows when the next natural disaster will strike or when the terrorist's evil plan will succeed in a disastrous instant? We cannot know the day or the situation when the alarm sounds for us, and although we may not be able to prepare fully for this type of seismic event, we can nonetheless take steps now to keep ourselves mentally and emotionally fit for duty when the unthinkable occurs.

You are that future hero in training today. Walk tall, head up, alert to the needs of those around you. Comfort a crying child on an airplane, give comfort to a lonely veteran, slip the cashier a twenty to help pay for the young mother's groceries behind you, take a meal to a sick neighbor, shovel snow from the walk of a widow, and help push a stalled car to safety. No, you won't get your picture in the paper, but you may inspire a hundred heroic acts by your example; and maybe one day, when you find yourself looking up from the side of the road, you will look up to see the eyes of the Samaritan helping *you*.

47

QUIET PLACES

"It was late and every one had left the café except an old man who sat in the shadow the leaves of the tree made against the electric light. In the day time the street was dusty, but at night the dew settled the dust and the old man liked to sit late because he was deaf and now at night it was quiet and he felt the difference." – Ernest Hemmingway

Hemingway paints a quiet bar where an old man retires in solace for his nightly brandy, and we reflect on the quiet places in our own lives. What is it about our secret retreats where we seek solitude, rejuvenation, and respite from the clutter of life that soothes us? Is it the "clean, well-lighted place" where we can sit and watch the caged world through shuttered windows, safely concealed? Is it the empty road stretching out into the desert before us as we drive headlong into oblivion?

We each have a way of finding our own retreats. Some prefer a crowded room, seeking retreat from a life of solitude, while others drift away into empty hallways making excuses to retreat from the crush, finding welcome in the darkened library while the party continues on the patio, like a distant radio playing beyond the closed door. Some, unsatisfied with that proximity long for the anonymity of a vacant beach or the isolation of a mountain cabin at the end of a winding dirt road.

I have always found comfort in quiet places, my sanctuaries. As a young boy, I shared a bedroom with my brother, so I ached for a room of my own. One summer, my father had a second-floor room added to our one-level ranch house. It was a large study, with a walk-in closet, accessed behind an unassuming door from the master bedroom. Climbing a winding set of stairs, I could enter the silent room. I used to enjoy sitting in my father's executive chair before he came home from work, drawing myself up to the significant desk. Sometimes I would lie on his closet floor, the smell of cedar shoetrees and woolen sweaters filling my senses like some well-crafted fatherly potpourri. In this room, I created my first fictional story, dictating to my father who tapped out On the Rocky Mountain River on his Smith Corona. From this room our family would also venture onto the rooftop to watch fireworks on holidays. I felt safe there, hidden behind the unassuming bedroom door, and my thoughts – such as they were, for a young boy – were elevated to match my surroundings.

In fourth grade, we moved to a new home with more land, and quiet space enough for me to live out my pigeon raising dreams (see Cat Hatred or Big Job Finished for more about this). The pigeon coup was a plywood box about five feet square on each side, with the front side covered only in chicken wire and a large door from the backside, large enough for easy cleaning. Several times during the year, my dad would bring home a load of fresh sawdust from the woodshop at his work, and I would scrape out the old clumps of sawdust and put down a fresh spongy pine floor for my birds. Then I would climb inside, prop my back against one wall and stretch my legs out toward the other wall, and watch the pigeons. They seemed unconcerned with the intrusion, and allowed me a peaceful seat as payment for their new soft floor. It was enough not to speak, but just to observe, and I too knew that they were watching me. I studied their balancing prowess as they flapped atop the broomstick perch I built; and I wondered how it felt to soar as I cradled them in my hands.

Once I had wheels and an open road, I found new quiet places. I lived near the mountains, and I had a brand new motorcycle, so I became a regular on the canyon roads on most weekends, finding new places to park and paused to breathe the mountain air and listen to the music of the cascading streams. One very special place was a restaurant several miles from the mouth of the canyon. The waterwheel and falls generated from the pumping station at the base of a small bridge was just a façade, contrived and false, but beyond the spotlights of this scene lay a grassy field and several gazebos nearer the tree line.

The grassy areas and gazebos were never lighted, reserved mostly for wedding parties during the day, fading back into the shadows at night. Moonlight would turn the dewy grass clearings into fields of pearls and the moonbeams would send out snowflake patterns from the gazebos' latticed roofs. Deer would occasionally venture from the tree line onto the grass, and then dart back into their forested cover sensing my presence, considering me a fiend in their mountain home. In this still mountain sanctuary, the glare of my adolescent cares from the world below faded into the shadows, and the blare of advice-givers (see The Worst Advice) were temporarily muted by intention-less babbling brooks.

For solitude seekers, finding a quiet place to dine out can often be a challenge. Although the restaurants I have frequented with my family are all abuzz with scurrying servers and chattering diners competing for air space with the so-called background music, and ambiance amounts to a corner booth farther from the bar, it wasn't always so. I think I had better taste as young romantic, when I would save my newly taxed remnants of a paycheck to take a date out to a quiet dinner for two. My favorite spot was a little French restaurant utterly hidden from view, violating the three rules of retail – location, location, location – for something more preciously elusive. We were greeted in the dimly lit restaurant by a throng of servers and hosts who remained beyond the light surrounding the table, serving each dish with quiet deference.

"Your harvest greens, sir."
"Ah yes."
"Your tenderloin, medium-rare, m'am."
"Quite."

This also proved to be an effective test for my female companion, who either would become easily bored by the suffocating silence or would wrap herself in it while cuddling into an engaging conversation that merely tickled the candlelight with breathless words.

Silence broken by whispered tales, shared joys, and consoling expressions is like the melody of Aeolian chimes carried on a breeze awaiting the next warming wind. Such is dining out in a quiet place.

Years later, I found myself alone behind the wheel of a rental truck packed with every material possession on the way to a new home where my wife would join me in several days' time – and there was still room in the truck. The normal drive of six hours turned out to be nine, because the truck had a governor device that kept it from going over fifty-five miles per hour, except when I was driving down the other side of the summit as I traveled the mountain passes. I welcomed the slow pace, and in my hopeful and giddy state, looking forward to my new life, complete with a new job and a new apartment community – complete with outdoor whirlpool – I was overcome with the silly urge to sing. So there I was crawling over the hills in my big orange tortoise truck belting out every campfire song, folk tune, and Sunday hymn in my repertoire. I hope the Lord has since forgiven my blasphemy at making up my own words to fill the lyrical deficiencies in my governor-restricted brain. Sometimes the joy of life's open road demands an end to somber solace.

After several more moves, three kids, and two dogs, my patient partner and I agreed that I should go back to school for a PhD and that we would buy a new home closer to school and work. We were fortunate enough to find a buyer and move out of our old home, but then faced the reality of looking for temporary housing that would take dogs and a short-term lease. Our only solution to the unlucky limbo was to move into a hotel room for three months, with our family of five, accompanied by the yellow Labrador and the golden retriever. I would return home from work, make my way in the door, over the dogs, the fold out couch and three boys watching TV, grab my stack of textbooks, and go to the only quiet space available – the open seating near the evening buffet counter in the lobby. Like the two bartenders in Hemingway's tale, the clerks working the hotel's check-in counter were probably riffing on this strange occurrence at the nighttime buffet.

"Why's he here?"
"Reading."
"No, I mean, what's he like a student?"
"Ya, a really old student."
"Why's he studying here?"
"Room 125."
"Huh?"
"You know…room 125…the dogs…the kids…?"
"Oh, right. What if he blows his brains out right here in the lobby?"
"Ya, what if…"

I'm happy to report that we did survive life in the hotel, and moved into our lovely home, with the private study located next to the kitchen. I had quiet space again, not to be shared with an older brother, three boys, two dogs, or hotel staff. My wife has a permanent pass to this room, but even she lets me seal the entrance to my cave for uninterrupted hours at a time.

The background noise on the other side of the door occasionally calls me out of my cocoon, but we all get along retreating to our respective spaces when we need some alone time. Strangely enough, having found my way back to solitude, I have found myself – on rare occasion – straining for a sound to cling to, some assurance that life exists beyond my four walls, a validation that I am not truly alone. I look ahead and see the time when my last son leaves home, taking that reassuring rumble with him. I won't need to close the door to my office, especially when my wife is baking homemade bread in the adjacent kitchen, and the dogs will always be my welcome guests.

When the game room falls silent and the TV sits for hours with that gray expression, perhaps then I will pine for a cluttered, clamorous, and crowded place. So if you see me slipping into the back of the Denny's for eggs and toast that I could easily prepare at home, don't think twice about saying hello or pouring my juice. I think I will probably welcome the interruption in that well-lighted place.

NOTES
1. A Clean, Well-Lighted Place, in <u>The Complete Short Stories of Ernest Hemingway</u>, the Finca Vigia Edition. Charles Scribner's Sons: New York, 288-291.

48

FIGHTS I DIDN'T START

Boys have a certain genetic code that includes a fight gene, an uncontrollable urge to punch, wrestle, or twist a rival into unquestionable submission. A good fight is one that has a clear winner, as determined by several factors such as blood drawn from the opponent's face, a desperate outcry of "uncle" or "stop" from his bloodied lips, or his cowardly fleeing from the fight ground. In these cases, we have no need for a jury of peers, the verdict is clear. Winner stand here, loser stand there. Retaliation is unnecessary and complaining is unworthy.

I have never been much of a fighter, not because I lacked the fight gene, but because I never had a need for it due to my good fortune of being blessed with an inverted growth curve. Until my last year or two of high school, I was always the biggest kid – or close to it – on campus. I was the playground bouncer, the guy who the weaklings and nerds wanted to hang around merely for the impression of protection, like hanging a Beware of Dog sign on your house. The only potential danger in this approach is when someone calls the bluff and says, "Let's see that dog," or "He doesn't look so mean." No one in school had dared to call that bluff.

Sometimes a person finds himself in fights he didn't start, and in the confusion of the moment he misses one key element of the fight: adrenaline. Without it, a fight is a lopsided bluster, with one person willing to go the distance while the other never really grasps what's coming. Of course, I speak from first-hand experience in this regard. I have been in three fights I never started, and never understood.

The first fight I didn't start was in fifth grade on the playground. Four square was our game of choice during recess, and I was the undisputed heavyweight champion of the four square quadrants, yellow lines painted on the asphalt that designated the social order. When the red rubber playground ball would softly loft into my square with a friendly bounce, I would extend my arm and bat it full force with my forearm into one of my three opponents' squares. This was called the *cowabunga*, and it had become legend in the symmetrical boundaries of our battlefields. The other move perfected, but not originated, by me, was the *full reverse spin*. When the ball would bounce into my square, I would punch it near the bottom, sending it back-spinning into my opponent's square, where it would immediately spin away from him or her like a big rubber boomerang. My obscenely-large hands, dubbed "meaty paws" by my classmates, were well suited for this move.

I am convinced that my domination in four square was the reason why Kevin Jameson hated me. Kevin was a kid I could have stuffed in my pocket. He was small, rabbit-quick, and had a bony face and pencil nose. His hair always had a pronounced cowlick in the front, and he wore a wind breaker in class.

There we were, playing four square, and I was permanently in the first quadrant position where the victor stayed and served the ball as long as he didn't fail. I was not a braggart, and I never made fun of other non-cowabunga or back-spin deficient players. It wasn't my style. Just play the game, I thought. Then, when the bell sounded the end of recess, I gathered the ball and was about to go inside when a little fist came up and over the ball, like a very small moon screaming around the gravitational pull of the red rubber sun. It half-connected, half-glanced off my chin, and little Kevin Jameson scurried away to his rabbit hole. It all happened so fast that I don't know if anyone else saw it, or maybe it was that their attention was in the opposite direction.

I didn't know what to do. I wasn't hurt any more than the sting of a good cowabunga, but why did Kevin hit me? Since he ran away so quickly, I assumed it was the only way he could express his disappointment with himself, and probably didn't have much to do with me. I was okay, and he wasn't, I figured. The sting of indignity at being punched in the face by this scrawny kid took me about two minutes to forget as I walked back inside the school. He never said or did anything to me after that.

The next fight was more of a cheap shot by an angry kid, Pierre. It happened at the end of my sixth grade year. Pierre was an Indian kid (no, not a real Indian from Asia, but a Native American, or a descendant of a Native American, I'm not really sure how many generations have to pass before one is considered native these days) who was quite tall for a sixth grader. The rumor was that he wasn't actually a sixth grader, but a seventh grader who was held back. Pierre was the kid you wanted on your dodge ball team because he was relentless once the balls started flying. He could catch anything, and was usually one of the last to die. I was still bigger than Pierre in height and mass, but he had that fierceness and speed that made him a less obvious, but far more dangerous, threat than me. I think Pierre was kind of like popcorn, when you apply enough heat over a long enough time, eventually it will pop. Popcorn Pierre.

So there we were on the last day of school, a day when homework had already left for summer vacation and when teachers and administrators begin to smile, their sternly creased foreheads receding like an angry tide washing out to sea. A tradition at my elementary school was that on the last day of the year, the sixth graders, who would not be returning to our school – on punishment of death – were allowed to leave first. It was with great ceremony that we crowded onto the stairs outside the school, like rockets on a launching pad ready to soar into the official start of summer, which corresponded to the official end of school. There was my grade school crush, Michelle. Would I ever see her again? Would she look my way as we left? Would I – BAM! – a fist caught the side of my nose and I caught a glimpse of Pierre's face before he turned his red jacketed back to me and ran off for good.

My eyes were watery from the blow to my nose, but there wasn't any blood, and the punch hadn't really landed that well. Again, I was left standing there wondering, quite literally, what hit me. I had never had a disagreement with him, and we often found ourselves on the same side of epic dodge ball battles. Why this final punctuating act on the last day of school, when he knew we would never see each other again? I could not reason it out, and can only assume to this day that, like the cowardly Kevin, who punched and fled, that I represented something that he found objectionable. Maybe it was my unblemished four-square record, maybe I had tagged him good in a dodge ball game, maybe he didn't like the way I buddied up to our teacher, or maybe we shared a crush on Michelle. In any case, there I stood on the launch pad sputtering in utter confusion.

The third fight I didn't start came years later on a warm summer night outside of Roller City, the local skating rink hangout. I don't know if it is true today, but skating rinks were popular for several key reasons. It was the only place you could do the Hokey Pokey – you put your left arm in, you put your left arm out – and feel right at home. Also, the snowball skates, where a couple begins, then splits to skate with a newly-chosen partner, and so on, meant that you would get to hold hands with a cute girl under the shimmering lights of the disco ball for what remained of the song. It was also a place to play video games (see Video Games That Delivered), eat junk food, and make fun of the people doing the Hokey Pokey (I said you could feel at home, not that you were immune to criticism!).

On this particular summer night, my aunt dropped a group of us at Roller City with the promise of picking us up in front of the stereo shop across the street at ten o'clock. Such was the embarrassing life of pre-driving teens, choosing dark drop off and pick up points, like covert operatives, to avoid being seen by other teens, mortified at the prospect of being spotted with their "you-kids-have-fun-tonight" parents. So there we were, my older brother and I, my brother's skinny friend, Brian, and our big cousin Jim, waiting in front of the darkened stereo shop on the corner. Jim was a funny guy, always joking about something, and his laugh was distinctive because his mouth would twist into a snicker and the laugh would somehow go from his belly out through his nose – more of a nasal guffaw than a normal laugh. On this night, Jim was in top form, and he had us busting up as we recalled the scenes of hilarity inside the Roller City rink.

Just then, four tall Brian-sized guys came from around the corner, each one walking toward each one of us without saying a word, like man-on-man coverage at a basketball game, but none of us knew we were in the middle of a rumble. I watched the first guy walk up to big Jim and pop him in the face just as another guy came into my field of vision and I caught a glimpse of his fist right before it connected with my cheek. Stunned, I backed off, as the kid who popped me scampered over near the other boys who were shouting at big Jim. They had overheard him talking about the people in Roller City, and from their vantage point around the corner, thought that *they* were the subject of Jim's skewering sarcasm.

None of us fought back, but Jim and Brian heatedly explained the obvious misunderstanding, with temporary success. Within a minute, our attackers walked on, and our adrenaline kicked in, like a late reflex motion when the doctor taps your knee. No one was hurt, and as the injustice of the corner fight sunk in, we boasted of our vengeful acts should the gang return. Then, our extraction vehicle arrived, and we were once again the Hokey Pokey boys.

211

Three fights I didn't start, and three fights I didn't finish. I suppose if I had been the son of a father who had taught me how to defend with my fists, I might have reacted differently. If my father had demonstrated by his example that might makes right, or that once the first punch is thrown all bets are off, I might have chased after Kevin, Popcorn, or the no-name skater kid to teach them each a lesson. I might not have cared who was right or what I might have done, and devoted myself to a life of revenge upon them and their posterity.

Fortunately, for me and my meaty paws, my father taught me patience, compassion and peacemaking. He was not a timid figure in my early days, and I remember him walking into groups of trouble-making hoodlums on at least two occasions, telling them to straighten up, and threatening to make a citizen's arrest in one case. My older brother was also a good example. We never fought, except once or twice with Sock 'Em Boppers, the inflatable bulbs you would slide your hands into and punch the daylights out of your opponent as if hurling beach balls at him. No one I knew resorted to violence as the ultimate solution.

It takes courage and self-restraint – or just blind confusion in my case – to resist the many threats against us. Unknown bullies prance about us, cowards at heart, blustering with brainless bombast. Immature grown-ups demand respect they are unwilling to show for others. Popcorn Pierres rant at hapless store clerks. Cheeky children mimic their sports heroes' trash-talking examples with their parents and playground rivals alike. You didn't start this fight. So as you stand on the corner, watch out for the blindside, beware the bony fist and the popcorn punch; but even more importantly, be prepared to draw back your fist, hold that curse, calm that rising adrenaline rush, and let the moment pass. Then, when the moment passes and reason returns, you can decide whether *this* is the fight worth fighting; or just pick up your ball and go inside.

49

AN AMERICAN PERSON

I'm tired of it, bored with it, angered by it. Somehow the timeless words, "we the people", have been drained, wrung out, and discarded for the non-inclusive pejorative sounding "the American people." Its usage has become so common in our politics that it slips by our ears almost as easily as it spews from their mouths.

"The American People want reform."
"The American People are looking for us to act on this bill."
"The American People agree with me."
"The American People don't care one way or the other."

Somehow *we* became *them*, the ones on the other side, the ones to be roped in, authoritatively cited, blamed for inaction, excused as too intellectually vacant or apathetic to be worthy of inclusion in *we*. So what? you might dismissively say with a there-you-go-again eye roll; but now that *we* are *them*, and *they* have dismissed *us*, I need to carve out my own place, my own selfish haven, free from the inclusion and intrusion of *them*.

We, the people, created them, the politicians, to raise our representative voices in the halls of the Capitol Building and the White House. However, many of them have developed selective hearing loss in which the lobbyists' voices, the unelected misrepresentation of the collective we, carry through the air to the purchased ear, the frequency somehow registering with the strength of the sender's donation while our votes and voices have become mere static interference.

As a member of the country formerly known as we, I would like to state for myself and no one else, what is important to me. I am only one, but one is enough to throw out your all-inclusive self-serving, bureaucracy-building double talk. You may no longer cite "the American people" as I choose to exclude myself from you who no longer speak for me, an American person. I do not support your saccharin soliloquies dripping with deceit; I wish not to be painted by your broad-brush strokes, sculpted by your sinister spins, nor filtered through your focus group feedback. No, I refuse to be invoked as the reason for or against your muddled and compromised position. I declare my independence from your bureaucratic blather, from your paternalistic preaching, from your co-dependent comradeship.

I, an American person, wish to make my declaration of independence, my departure and succession from your view of our union. I wish to declare a few things that I care about for this nation. If one other agrees with these declarations then *I* will become *we*, and perhaps together *we* will regain our once great pronoun.

I, an American person wish to live in a country...

...WHERE the contribution I make in the form of taxes for the support of our government protects the food I eat, keeps the roads I drive on in fair condition, and defends us from those intent on killing or terrorizing us.

...WHERE the wages I earn are commensurate with my effort, and where my incentive to save, preserve, and build wealth is idealized and rewarded.

...WHERE the schooling for my children focuses on traditional skills, such as reading, writing, arithmetic, science, and history, rather than multicultural tolerance, gender identity confusion, and righteous activism.

...WHERE the government does not inhibit driving without wearing a seatbelt, riding a motorcycle without a helmet, smoking endless packs of cigarettes, making fun of politicians, eating fatty foods, standing too close to the microwave, forgetting to recycle, and even running with scissors.

...WHERE the ideals of traditional family life are upheld through our legislative actions and protected through judicial courage.

...WHERE elected officials are unable to increase wages without a vote of the people and are subject to immediate recall whenever the public feels a politician has violated the public trust.

...WHERE the healthcare I receive is based on my choices and my ability to pay rather than a bureaucrat's determination of my worthiness for treatment.

...WHERE the arts are preserved through the patronage of the public, not through the predilections and predispositions of government-subsidized grants.

...WHERE the marketplace of ideas, as represented by the free press, mass media, and the entertainment industry, is unrestricted, open, and accessible to all, while being subject to individual censorship, rejection, and termination.

...WHERE the lawbreakers are punished with severity equal to their crimes, regardless of money or influence.

...WHERE the utilization of natural resources expands prosperity while protecting pristine streams, golden valleys, and majestic mountains for subsequent generations.

...WHERE the ability of inventors to innovate, for entrepreneurs to experiment, and scientists to stretch imagination should continue unimpeded by excessive regulation.

These are simply a few of my requirements in my union of one. I do not represent the American people, only an American person; but please choose your words carefully before you blurt out that phrase that draws me in to your consenting masses or your contrary critics. I do not give my consent, and my views are not to be sanctioned or discredited by you. I'll have none of that.

Contrary to some, I am not against the institution of government, and I believe it fills a necessary role for the reasons cited above. I do not wish all politicians ill, or revel in the notion that representative government is doomed to sink to the lowest depths that our politicians are willing to go. But, for those of you who intend to go on ignoring us or babbling on about The American People as though we are in your money-lined pockets, you should remember something: we have what you want more than anything, and they are not yours unless you earn them – our votes.

So take a stance for *us*, don't grandstand for yourself. Seek our ideas and listen to our letters rather than listening for the siren song of the influence peddlers. Be willing to lose the election, but preserve our freedom. Recall the core principles upon which our prosperity began rather than giving out I.O.U.s that we can never repay. Stop bribing us with promises of more power and influence if we re-elect you, just do the job we sent you to do today and we'll decide whether you're worthy of a repeat performance. Our votes are right over here - come and get 'em!

50

FAMILY TREES

I'm no tree hugger. In fact, trees and I have had a on and off relationship. They give me splinters, and I burn them as firewood. Their branches blowing in the wind scrape my bedroom window with a foreboding screech, and I chop them back in the fall as payback. But trees have always been near our homes, and some have been so substantial, that they have practically become like another member of the family, a playmate when no one else is available. Like a constant metaphor for growth, change, and death, they mark time parallel with our lives.

The first family tree that I encountered was a skinny palm tree stretching skyward at one end of a giant parking lot near the house where my brother and I lived. We were in New Zealand on my father's church assignment and being the last two trains on the family line, the older kids were off at school and my brother and I stayed at home with our parents. The home was on a sizeable property with trees, a stream, an open grassy area, and even a jungle. Each day was an adventure as we faded into the foliage, returning for lunch or dinner around the same time as the dozen or so young missionaries returned from their labors. One day, for some reason that neither of us can really recall, being no more than five and seven years old, we began to chop down the palm; but finding our preschool toolkits absent of chainsaws, axes, or hatchets – in fact, we had no toolkits – we used what seemed logical at the time, the claw end of a hammer.

Of course, we didn't want my father to find out, although he was *certain* to discover the tree's fate when it eventually came crashing down; so to hide our progress we found an old board and leaned it in front of the scars we inflicted on the trunk. Fortunately, when the tree's shrinking waistline did finally give in to our last blow the hammer, the tree fell away from the parking lot, and we escaped with a stern warning not to do it again, although I thought I also saw in my father's eyes a glimmer of pride in our accomplishment. I wonder if George Washington's father had that same glimmer when confronted with the I-cannot-tell-a-lie confession. Despite our preschool lumberjack prank, we also found trees to befriend.

A much more noble and sturdy tree stood at the other end of the yard, and thanks to the kindness and creativity of the missionaries and my father, we were blessed with a tree house complete with steps, a hatched door, and a second level farther up the tree's thick trunk. The tree was so enormous that it didn't seem to mind the nails or the added weight of a few visitors. I could only get to the main floor and that with the trusted hands of my father supporting my wobbly legs on the makeshift steps, just boards nailed to the trunk. It became a fortress, a castle, and a jungle home for two adventurous boys.

When we returned home to the states, we moved into a home with an overgrown apple tree in the backyard. It was the largest apple tree I had ever seen, a real grandfatherly occupant that split our narrow backyard in two. Every summer, after the tree dropped its fruit to the ground, my father made us a deal of a penny per apple that we picked up. We would fill bucket after bucket with the rotting brown fruit, some that were so eaten through, they should have only counted for half, but my father always leaned in our favor. I have a permanent scar thanks to this tree, reminding me when I had slipped and caught the sharp remnant of a small twig on the inside of my leg. Maybe losing his apples made him cranky – I can't blame a grandfather for that.

A big oak tree down the street at my cousins' home was the scene for another incident. This one was a giant oak tree whose main branches springing from the hefty trunk were like tree trunks in themselves, and where they converged created a kind of meeting space for our cousin clubhouse. Once the five of us could scale the tree to that first landing area, it created a bit of disorder and disharmony. The most upset of all was the oldest one, Scott. He had beaten us to this place in the tree by weeks and months, and he didn't appreciate the invasion creeping up his trunk. A scuffle broke out as his younger brother was standing between the parlor branch and the family room branch, and in an instant we watched the younger one pitch backward, falling the seven or eight feet to the ground. His arm caught the ridgeline of the great tree's root, and the bone gave way to the immovable root. I couldn't stop looking at his misshapen limb, stunned that our horseplay had led to this horrible end. The friendly landing of the oak tree stayed silent for many weeks as Guilt came to visit and found the place to his liking; but eventually we all returned, and each claimed a giant branch as his own.

When my wife and I moved into our first home, a newly built tract house in an underdeveloped part of town, we studied the question of what types of trees to plant to beautify our plain landscape. After some thought, and examining nearby nurseries, we picked out our new addition, a nice little four-foot tall blue spruce. This was going to be planted on one side of the yard, between the driveway and the neighbor's lot line, about a twelve-foot-wide span. Following the instructions for tree planting, I prepared a deep hole, and nestled our pride and joy – for sixty-five dollars, we thought we had spent a fortune – into position. As we were admiring the tree and I was soaking it with the water hose, our neighbor Chris came over.

Chris was a pleasant, but quirky guy. He had this odd habit of answering every minor request with a formal, "As you wish." Since we were new not only to the tree planting game, but also to living with neighbors, we just ignored him most of the time. But on this memorable occasion, he had a real pinecone in his pocket about our blue spruce.

"Hi guys."
"Hi, Chris," I said, while I continued to look at the watering job in front of me.
"Wow, that's really some tree ya got there."
"Thanks, Chris. Yes, we're very proud."
"Ya know," he said placing his hand on his chin – he must have been awed by our little tree, too – "this tree is going to really grow."
"Well, we sure hope so, Chris."
"Well," he feigned hesitation, "the problem I have is…"
"Yes?"
"It's really going to be a problem in a few years."
"What do you mean? What would the problem be?"
"It's going to grow fast, and before you know it, there are going to be needles all over my yard from your tree," he said as if the needles had already committed their crime.

I was dumbfounded. My wife stood silently stunned. This was our yard, our tree, and we liked where it was. What was this guy's right to tell us where to plant a tree? Not committing to a course of action, we said that we would discuss what to do, and where we might consider replanting it, but we expressed how this was the spot we really liked for the tree, despite his objections. He said he was open to the idea of a different kind of tree going in this chosen spot.

"As *you* wish," I mocked in my head.

Ultimately, in the spirit of neighborly harmony, we replanted our evergreen more directly in front of the house and put a catalpa tree in its place by the driveway, assured that it would probably make the bigger mess. I recently returned to our first home to survey the outcome of this decision. Often the need to think ourselves right is worth going out of our way, even if the argument and the antagonist are long departed. There was our little blue spruce, now about ten feet tall, and the lower branches spanned eight to ten feet in width, a lovely green lawn hidden somewhere beneath its spreading wings. On the other side of the yard grew what must have been a tree long ago, but whose trunk was just barely visible beneath the overgrown branches and leaves that stretched nearly to the ground. It must have been fifteen feet tall, and nearly as wide, with large brown pods ready to fall to the ground. The neighborhood of small orderly houses with well-kept yards had become, like the overgrown monstrosity next to the driveway, a disgraceful sight, a distant memory of what it had once been.

Two moves later, we moved into another newly built home with a large backyard. Luckily, we had bought at the right time, just as a new cul-de-sac was opening up, so we had the choice of building sites. We had found a lot with several mature trees, but the centerpiece of the backyard was a large oak reminiscent of my cousins' Tree at Broken Arm. Now, with three young boys, the first order of business once the sod was in place (see Big Jobs Finished), was putting in a swing. The tree had a large branch stretching over the yard, about fifteen feet off the ground. The makeshift swing was a large board with a hole drilled in it large enough to pass the rope through. After making a knot under the seat at the right height, I had about twenty feet of rope left; so rather than cutting it, I kept it for use as a way to swing the boys from below.

Soon our dog, Goldie, got the hang of the rope swing, and she would help tug on the rope, sending one of my little sons higher in the air, waiting to release him on his pendular rush. Later on, the extra rope was cut, and the boys climbed higher, needing less support now, ever higher, and...there – just brushing the leaves of a distant branch, the brass ring of sorts. Several seasons later the swing broke under my second son. The aged knot under the seat that had so easily borne his weight once now failed, sending him to the ground, and to the hospital for x-rays. He was fine, but the swing was never replaced. However, we traded one form of entertainment for another as each autumn, the generous oak would shower its leaves on the grass, and we raked them into a massive pile, throwing leaves, jumping in leaves, and re-raking the pile, until we finally burned the leaves and sucked in the earthy smoke.

These trees made life richer for us, and they became part of us. A good friend I knew left his office job to go into the business of trimming and clearing trees. He said that on several occasions, when he had to cut down a tree, he would first climb it and sit in its arms almost as a silent tribute before starting his work. For him, it was not some quasi-religious experience, just a reverence for living things, for what the trees had given him. As I think of my friend, Jim, cradled by a giant tree, I understand that sentiment. Okay, I'll give the tree a hug – just one. Thanks, big fella.

51

HOW IS YOUR GARDEN?

Small rituals in life often turn allegorical depending on whether we are prepared to see the deeper lessons right in front of us. Gardens are just one example. When we begin the careful process of sowing a garden, we do all we can to help the seed germinate and take root in the spring; yet by early winter we do all we can to uproot the dying plant whose fruit has long since been harvested and either consumed or stored.

As a boy we kept a family garden where we grew fresh vegetables such as peas, beans, carrots, potatoes and zucchini – lots of zucchini. This tradition continues with my own family, although the garden is smaller and the variety not so impressive. Gardening is one of those rare times in my life when I get very close to the soil, and something primal awakens as I experience once again the cycle of preparation, planting, harvesting, and clearing.

The tiller is a marvelous invention, an eating machine that churns through the grayish layer of dry soil and brings to the surface the slumbering dark, rich soil hidden beneath. Of course, some gardeners use the old-fashioned shovel and rake method, but my primitive urges for soil preparation don't prohibit me from a few modern conveniences. The tiller proceeds to chew through ground in a balance of competing forces, the tines propelled forward by the engine, and the restraining force of the drag bar that the operator sinks deep in the soil to keep the tines from chewing through the neighborhood like some sort of ravenous wild boar.

As my tiller and I tear up the ground in a controlled frenzy, I think of the dualistic nature of the passion that drives us forward, and the reasoning force and values that anchor us in deep soil, guiding us as we lurch forward through new ground. Perhaps you've known a few soil-eaters in your life, those who chew up everything in front of them, skimming over the surface of life without really breaking the surface or digging deeper where the life-giving nutrients lie buried. On the other hand, you may have observed the rock solid diligence of the person who sinks the shovel deep, but whose reach never extends from the current furrow, instead continually scraping the sides of the same hole, never letting go to test the soil beyond.

Planting a garden by hand, next to the miracle of childbirth, is probably the closest thing to divine design that we get to experience. We consider the wide swath of rich earth and design beds for various seeds, considering whether we have more shady parts of the garden or those that are likely to wither in the heat of the day. Some plants require seeds cast into a furrow where they might spring up close together; others must be placed in mounds where they individually flourish until their vines grow together at the bottom of the hill; still others require regularly spacing at certain depths in order for the seedlings to sprout, burst through the soil, and begin collecting the sun's rays directly rather than through the secondary warmth of the ground where they have slumbered.

Like seeds cast along in a common furrow, we too grow up with a myriad of friends growing close to us on whom we depend for our social identity and our strength through challenging adolescent trials. Through society's great thinning process, our numbers are reduced by the premature attrition caused by other pursuits, vocational or educational, or by personal triumphs or tragedies, while life in the furrow continues its ripening effect on the rest, awaiting the time when they too will be plucked from the burgeoning harvest. Far from our furrow, we see others atop their prepared mounds, planted in their privileged places isolated, distant, and untouchable. Here in their isolation they will certainly wither in the sun or flourish to join the intertwining networks of vines from other high places. Others of us simply grow where we are planted, dropping our roots to find what nutrients might be gleaned deep within and stretching our leaves heavenward searching for life-giving energy.

In many societies, the harvest days constitute days of celebration, of ritual gratitude for the gifts springing from the earth. As I go to my garden, I wonder at the colors peeking from beneath their leafy cover, bright red tomatoes, yellowing crookneck squash and purple beets. As reward for a season of toil, the garden reveals its secrets both above ground and beneath. Shovelfuls of hearty potatoes and handfuls of tightly packed pea pods make their way to our table.

A boyhood friend of mine used to sell vegetables from his red wagon as he walked the neighborhood. He always carried a small saltshaker in his pocket during harvest time, and after washing the vegetable in the water from a nearby hose, we would dine on raw red potatoes and green peppers, fresh tomatoes and cucumbers. Discovering the essence of a thing in its natural state was to find hidden sweetness and bitterness.

What about our harvest days? When do we stop to celebrate life's bounties, the goodness of all that we find on our table, whether in the edible sense or in the abstract? Does Thanksgiving for us happen but once a year, or do we avail ourselves daily of the richness life has to offer, whether in the sweetness of buttered corn on the cob or in the comfort of quiet conversation? Perhaps looking at the fullness of all that is ours will cause us to give with greater charity and compassion, as gratitude crowds out selfishness and greed.

After we have gorged ourselves on the last summer squash and licked the salt from our lips, sharing the bounty of life's goodness, we face the final stage of our seasonal cultivation, clearing the garden and putting it to rest for a season. At my house we would gather the corn stalks, dead vines, empty roots, and all that was rotten and dying in one pile and burn it, purging the once thriving space from its unworthy remnants.

When we harvest all that was rich, ripe, and flourishing in our lives, it seems that all that remains is to give away the withered trappings of a life of materialism, clearing the garden, purifying the ground, and returning to the essence of life. This final preparation before our slumber is when we root out the unworthy remnants of bitterness, unresolved grudges, intolerance for past wrongs, and withheld forgiveness. It is then that we turn to the new seeds we have dropped for the coming season and give up the ground to those who follow. How is your garden? Mind the season, tend your garden, eat heartily, and prepare your garden for those who will follow. Your little garden will then endlessly brighten the world and give nourishment to the neighborhood long after the harvest.

52

PARADISES LOST AND FOUND

Spirituality is a subject that tends to cause some of us discomfort. We feel the yearning to know what lies beyond this life, or we marvel at the vastness of space and how we came to be on this infinitesimal blue speck. At times we feel that something more than coincidence has reached down and touched us in some mysterious and profound way. Others of us worry about the inevitability of returning to dust and ashes, perplexed by all that we are becoming lost in the sand.

We are spiritual beings.

I like to think that in some deeper part within us we feel all feel a similar kinship, that brotherhood of man or perhaps the humanity of all humankind. The spiritual identity we share could best be described through our original ancestry – we were once brothers, sisters, cousins, in-laws, and the family grew to extension upon extension, until our links in the pedigree became lost or a distant memory. If this is the case, then we must retain not only the genetic markers that define us as human rather than insect, but something deeper – there below the surface – that makes us bearers of human characteristics such as compassion, service, sacrifice, devotion, or faith rather than merely instinctive beings driven by hunger, thirst, security, or the sex drive, for example.

While some of our distant family members might spend a larger portion of their time seeking to gratify those instincts, we have evidence before us that many still carry this spiritual marker. We see individuals of our kind running in to give aid in a crisis, rushing to the rescue, carrying another's burden, and we must acknowledge that somewhere there exists among us deeper connective tissue that links us spirit to spirit.

So often we are exposed to anti-religious rhetoric that we forget this deeper bond. We are told that religion is to blame for man's problems, that organized religion is incapable of surpassing individual spiritual feelings, and that human guilt is a malady of old-fashioned moral baggage of a bygone prudish tradition. Let's calmly explore these notions and consider our lost and fallen state together, while also acknowledging the goodness and brightness of hope within our grasp.

Religion is to blame for man's problems. If we accept this as truth, we are likely to fall into the same camp as the secular zealots who cite religion as the cause of war and point out the disharmony that exists between religious groups as the basis for the eradication of organized religion. If we accept that religion is the root of all evil, then we must also accept that unencumbered irreligious man is necessarily a far preferable building block for Utopia. If we accept that religion is to blame, then we must be consistent in our belief that worship services, charitable acts and educational aims are all in the service of some sinister plot to undermine the good society. I fail to see the inherent evil in placing food in the outstretched hand, standing shoulder to shoulder hauling sand bags while the flood surges, or giving of one's own goods to clothe another. Blame them if you will, I cannot.

Organized religion is incapable of surpassing individual spiritual feelings. Here we have a simple case of confusion over the aims and objectives of so-called organized religion, as if disorganized irreligion was in some way a recognized alternative. When have the individual spiritual feelings of individuals ever been in conflict with the churches, other than in the mind of the individual expressing such feelings?

Would anyone argue that a monk living in solitude is any less spiritually minded because he does not worship in a church? And yet a monk is part of a collective whole, a servant to the body, an integral part of the whole realizing its mission to serve the poor, rescue the downcast or educate the illiterate. If religion were merely about instilling spiritual feelings in its members with no cost or obligation, why would it necessarily be a religion? One could simply enjoy the fresh mountain air, meditate, or learn yoga. No, organized religion is about fulfilling a humanitarian mission, a mission of saving lives and feeding souls. It is service, work, sweat, and toil in behalf of a greater whole. It grows, enlists members, draws funds and organizes in order to affect a noble result.

Finally, the malady of guilt, the lamentable state of the religiously infected mind, is an affliction that would not exist were it not for religious sermonizing. If this is true, then it must also hold true that the irreligious feel no equivocation about reigning in desires such as greed, lust, or selfishness, or that the society has a sufficiency of law enforcement or State controls to force compliance and order – wardens policing hallways in the national penitentiary. Perhaps the irreligious society has some philosophical underpinning so powerful that it is able to replace that connection with the divine; and yet, how does one have unshakable trust in man and his philosophies, when man is not omniscient or omnipotent. Is there a worthy substitute?

While we create a logical construct within which we debate the relative value of various belief systems and their governance structures, we miss the larger point. In the debate over the souls of the human family, why don't we entertain another construct, that good and evil are locked in a battle, and in this eternal struggle mankind chooses sides based on what he or she perceives to be truth. Spirituality then becomes a search for those truths to which we will align ourselves on the battlefront of our lives. We will search the moral systems, organizations, and teachings in order to uncover goodness and eschew evil. We will seek to realize the missions to which we were born.

If religion is the creation of man, and not the creation of God, then truly it is flawed and has always been so; otherwise an opposition must exist. However, if the embodiment of an evil and opposite force does not exist, then against what does God fight, if not himself? Is it divine logic that pits the Eternal Force against itself? Surely not. Then good and evil must on occasion occupy the same sphere, with mankind acting taking the part of saint or sinner, grasping tools fashioned to slay or save, annihilate or exalt.

The seventeenth century poet, John Milton, sought to "justify the ways of God to men" in his treatise *Paradise Lost* and its epilogue, *Paradise Found*, in which he expounds the great Argument of good and evil, of divine salvation and devilish ambition. Contrasting the Tyranny of Heaven and the Apostate Angel, Milton reveals that which makes devils of men and saints of sinners.

If we accept as equally true the possibility of absolute righteousness in the nature of God and utter rebelliousness in his satanic offspring, then we must discern what is the mission of one operating in hopeless opposition to the Divine Being. Once discerned, we can flee those who espouse his ideals and his justification for enmity. Of this war that begin in the world of the gods, our Nemesis cries,

> *Too well I see and rue the dire event,*
> *That with sad overthrow and foul defeat*
> *Hath lost us Heav'n, and all this mighty Host*
> *In horrible destruction laid this low.*

He continues his lament,

> *To do aught good never will be our task,*
> *But ever to do ill our sole delight,*
> *As being the contrary to his high will*
> *Whom we resist. If then his Providence*
> *Out of our evil seek to bring forth good,*
> *Our labor must be to pervert that end,*
> *And out of good still to find means of evil;*

If then, this contrary being were to make war, it would be not as an absence of religion, but as a *perversion* of it, according to Milton. His mission would not be redemptive, but single-minded resistance, a dogma of twisted religiosity and manipulation of his human enemy. Revealing the opposition's motive, Milton describes the rationalization that drives our enemy,

> *Here at last*
> *We shall be free; th' Almighty hath not built*
> *Here for his envy, will not drive us hence;*
> *Here we may reign secure, and in my choice*
> *To reign is worth ambition though in Hell;*
> *Better to reign in Hell, than serve in Heav'n.*

And so we see the space we occupy threatened by those who are opposed, and who are comfortable in their consigned state to reign in the outer regions, the periphery of what was once holy ground, outcasts of the Eternal family. Hell's version of freedom where one reigns under a despotic and despairing being, whether in flames or not, must truly define the ultimate perversion of that which is God's free gift to act, and not to be acted upon. This was free man as embodied in Adam and the enemy force arrayed against him,

> *I have made him just and right,*

Sufficient to have stood, though free to fall.
Such I created all th' Ethereal Powers
And Spirits, both them who stood and them who fail'd;
Freely they stood who stood, and fell who fell.

To the battle, the Divine Deliverer sends the anointed King, the Son,

As my Eternal purpose hath decreed:
Man shall not quite be lost, but sav'd who will,
Yet not of will in him, but grace in me

Upheld by me, yet once more he shall stand
On even ground against his mortal foe,
By me upheld, that he may know how frail
His fall'n condition is, and to me owe
All his deliv'rance, and to none but me.

This is the great promise of deliverance, and the Eternal purpose that unites all who claim reverence rather than rebellion. It is through grace and humble submission to His will that we find our salvation and deliverance. As the Father of all holds the beacon out to mankind, he reminds us that within each of his children he has implanted that divine marker,

And I will place within them as a guide
My Umpire, Conscience, whom if they will hear,
Light after light well us'd they shall attain,
And to the end persisting, safe arrive,

Is this the religion that divides man, sets families at opposition, straps bombs to young men and women, and sets the world on fire? Is this the mission that we have allowed to define we who are religious? Certainly what has been lost must be found, and religion must once again reassert its place through the good works and moral lives of those professing fealty to a benevolent and merciful being. Worship must renew in our hearts our own frailty and dependence on His grace; and finding within us that conscience of the heart, we shall follow the light to that safe harbor and battle no more.

NOTES
1. <u>John Milton Complete Poems and Prose</u>. Hughes, M. (1957). Bobbs-Merrill Educational Press: Indianapolis. 215-263.

53

MOTORCYCLE LOVE

We're not supposed to love...things. We ought to have more willpower than to look at the one hundred inch big screen TV with lustful thoughts. We must avert our wandering eyes from the leather jacket that seems to beckon us as the salesperson unchains it from the rack, and we feel as though a good friend has been pardoned and released into our worthy keeping. They are just things after all, and not people. That relationship you had with the expensive purse will soon fade, and it too will be replaced one day in a fickle flip flop as your eyes fall on another more worthy companion into whom you will pour your life's contents.

I too loved another. A thing.

It was my Yamaha 250cc Enduro motorcycle with the red gas tank. I won't bore you with the technical specifications of this particular bike, but it was a head turner. Its previous cousins were utilitarian and soulless, but this beauty was built to play in the dirt and then jump back on the road for an evening cruise around town. It had made a brief appearance in one of the James Bond movies, so it had a sort of gutsy elegance, like a tuxedo wrapped around a Tommy gun.

It was my main transportation during my junior and senior years of high school, and I was always throwing a buddy on the back to give him a ride home. When I was running late for school, I would pop the key in the ignition, and in one motion push off and straddle the tank, like a cowboy putting a leg over his trusted mount, and then coast to the bottom of the driveway where I popped the clutch and it would spring to life. Speed bumps melted under its rear mono-shock system, and curbs, potholes, and casually-placed dirt piles beckoned me and my throaty red friend to stay and play hooky.

Nearly every night I would go out riding. I had a regular circuit around the neighborhood. I would head south onto Wander Lane, a road that twisted alongside a small creek for several miles. I never wore a helmet on those rides , and I never felt guilty for not wearing one; no, I was convinced of my own superior riding skills and my ability to get over or around any obstacle. I knew every inch of that road, and I grew accustomed to the chill when I would go through a gully where the cold air settled; I would hit the gutters just fast enough to absorb the shock without losing speed; and I would slow down to navigate a hairpin turn before opening up into a straight-away, the wind whipping my tears straight back through my hair and over my ears. On a motorcycle it wasn't so much about where you went; it was how you got there that mattered, and faster was good, but creativity in the route was better.

As I grew older, my circuit also grew. I expanded my knowledge of every backstreet and great riding challenge in ever widening circles. Some nights I would ride downtown through alleys and parking garages, rarely stopping. It wasn't unusual to put fifty or sixty miles under my knobby tires in a night. Riding a motorcycle, particularly one that doesn't come with its own windshield and stereo, is a completely different experience from the protected anonymity of a car. The rider is exposed, out there on the bike, hearing the sounds of the road, the conversations between passengers in passing cars or waiting pedestrians as they move about the city. I would smell the rain before it arrived, feel the change in temperature, and calculate the time of several alternative routes home before the first drop fell.

As my ever-widening concentric circles grew, I began finding new destinations where I would dismount and park for a time. The close-in haven of choice was a nearby canyon just a few miles from my house, and about five miles up the canyon was a restaurant with a man-made waterfall, waterwheel, and a grassy area nearby. Most nights I pulled into a vacant parking lot there in the mountains. It seemed the restaurant preferred wedding breakfasts and daytime pictures rather than nightfall. It was here that I would rest my bike and retire to a gazebo near the tree line, where I could close my eyes and listen to the rhythmic sounds of the water spilling from the waterwheel and quietly contemplate my place in the universe as I looked up at the stars through the crisp Alpine air. I'm no Thoreau, and although I enjoyed the simplicity of my surroundings and the peaceful escape, I found the snaking roads of the canyon to my liking, and my thundering red friend agreed. We became more skilled with each circuit at ascending and descending the canyon at ever faster speeds, learning which corners had enough of a built-in bank that we could accelerate, and which ones were susceptible to gravel from the mountainside making conditions too dangerous for high speed maneuvering.

The farther-out destination of choice was the hot tub at the lodge in one of the ski resort hotels about thirty miles from my house. I would don my swimsuit under my jeans, and ascend the canyon, the big brother to the waterwheel canyon nearer my house because of the wider roads and the steeper drops that kept my thrill-seeking in check. Once inside the ski resort, I would park my bike and walk ten minutes to the lodge where I would step inside for a soak in the hot tub. After the ride, it was the perfect way to relax and enjoy the mountain air. Of course, heading back down the long canyon in a wet swimsuit was just tempting fate too much, and knowing that one slip on that road would mean either a long aerial thrill to the canyon floor or a short sliding body rub, also known as road rash, I determined to spend more time closer to home. As a student, my personal finances were also a factor in how far I could venture from home, and more than once I had to coast down the canyons until I could get to a gas station to invest my pocket change in a sip of fuel for my thirsty friend.

Occasionally I would share these night rides with my girlfriend at the time. I'm not sure if her tightened grip around my waist was due to her fondness for me or a reaction to the peril that she faced when we went out. Of course, I owned a helmet, and I insisted that she wear it on our rides, so perhaps she never fully appreciated the same unencumbered feelings for the ride as I did, helmeted as she was behind me. She did get to see the waterwheel, and Wander Lane, but I kept the long rides through town and into Big Brother Canyon strictly to myself – hoarding the joy for fear of its diminishment in the sharing.

The bike embraced my thrill seeking, nurtured my contemplative retreats, and with a twist of the throttle revved my rebelliousness. It became an extension of me, and I suppose that if it had a soul, I was an extension of it, merely riding where it chose to take me.

As with toys from our youngest memories, I eventually parted with the motorcycle, selling it to pay for more grown-up ventures that were beyond its ability to satisfy merely with 250cc and its throaty bluster. The expanding ripples of my life carried me far beyond the alleyways and canyons that once wrapped around me; but I never forgot that bike. One evening when my oldest son was surfing the net, I told him of my good friend, the red bike with the white fenders, and together we set about searching.

"Is it this one, Dad?"

"No, that's dull and orange, and see how low it sits to the ground? No, mine was more aggressive looking and it was a monoshock, not like that one with the shocks by the rear tire."

"Maybe this is it?"

"No, it's not cherry red, and – wait – oh, maybe that's it."

There it was, the Yamaha 250cc Enduro with the red tank, white fenders, and the monoshock system, with big knobby tires and pinstriping on the tank. If I had been fumbling through an old high school yearbook for a long, lost love, I couldn't have been more thrilled than I was to have finally found a picture of my old friend on the internet.

"That's the one."

"Sweet ride."

"Ya."

54

THE PERFECT PRACTICE

Practice makes perfect, so it's said, and we pursue the dream of perfection with the assurance that if we toil and sweat we will achieve that breakthrough moment, the poignant predicate to our dedicated striving. Growing up I learned the value of practice, and learned that sometimes perfection could be achieved in the practicing, that the very nature of our earnest seeking could be the essence of perfection. The means – in fact – become the end when we achieve the perfect practice.

Growing up, we had a tennis court in our backyard, and my dad had built a practice wall from some plywood and green paint. We painted a white line across it at the same height as the net, and this became our form of tennis solitaire for that summer. I remember my dad challenging us to go hit the practice wall and keep the ball in play for at least fifty hits above the net. When we met for dinner he would ask about our progress on the practice wall, and we would proudly respond that our numbers were climbing, from twenty to thirty, and from thirty to forty.

I hit the court nearly every day, and tested my skills against the practice wall, finding that its solid surface was steady, consistent, and unlike its human competitor, it never missed a shot, never sent a ball lofting over the fence; it simply returned what it was given. From our kitchen, it was easy to hear the rhythmic crack of the tennis ball striking the wall, and I silently counted while my brother practiced, quietly rejoicing when I heard the rhythm pause and begin again. He hadn't made it yet.

Finally, after the summer had nearly run out, the mark was hit. My brother made it first, and he declared his victory over the stubborn wall. I went back to the wall for several more days until finally I had coasted through the twenties, recovered from two drop shots in the mid-thirties that almost handed my wooden opponent the game, set and match, but there I was, so close now...47...48...49...and 50! When my father came home that night I proudly declared that I had beaten the wall and achieved the mark for which I had practiced all summer.

Perfect.

Like many other kids in my neighborhood, I took music lessons. My parents had arranged with the principal bassist of a local symphony to take me on as one of three students in her group lessons. Each week, I would wedge my oversized violin into the back of my mother's mini station wagon, and she drove me to the university for my lessons. Walking the halls to get to the dimly-lit classroom, I heard the arpeggios of sopranos warming up with their piano accompanists, prelude for my lesson at the end of the hall.

I always seemed to rise to the occasion when I was performing, and bass lessons were just another example. I didn't really practice much during the week, but when I made it to the lesson, I was able to pass the tests. That worked for a while, but I'll never forget the week that Geoff upstaged me completely on a difficult etude we had been studying. He won the prize for that lesson, a one-pound Hershey chocolate bar. But it wasn't the loss of the candy that caused the pit in my stomach; it was the realization that my talent had met its limits. I could not go from one lesson to another, expecting to improve my skills. Practice was the inevitable and dreary answer.

I kept thinking about Geoff and the candy bar. I resolved that I would not lose to him again; or more accurately, I would not let myself down again. I practiced every day that week, sawing away at my strings. I set the egg timer and vowed not to set down my bass until the time was up. When I had finished practicing the etudes, I went back to scales and bowing. Then I repeated the whole routine again.

The following week I was ready. I eagerly strolled down hall, noting the arpeggios again in my head, thinking about how my fingers would perform the arpeggio, and how my bow would draw the sound from the strings. My senses were stirred, and I was fully inside the music, where technique gives way to expression. I took first place in all the challenges that week, and walked away with the prize; but I didn't eat the chocolate bar right away. I savored it from afar as it sat on my nightstand reminding me of the victory, not over Geoff or Daniel, but over myself. I had conquered complacency that week.

Perfect.

I started playing racquetball at the age of fourteen or fifteen, and enjoyed hitting the ball inside the closed court, not having to constantly chase after the ball as in tennis. I thought I was learning the game well, since my brothers and I were able to sustain rallies of some length, and I was getting hit by the ball less frequently, and hitting myself less frequently with the racquet. One evening after another friendly and injury-free game, I stared down into the court watching a young man near my own age hitting the ball, practicing by himself. It was as if he could hit it wherever he wanted it to go, forehand or backhand. He was anticipating where it would land and he would be right there to smash it into the front wall again with the snap of his wrist.

I wanted to hit the ball like that. I went to the library and I rented a video of a guy hitting a ball in slow motion, twenty times with the forehand, and then twenty times with the backhand. I noted the way his weight shifted, and the speed he was able to generate by turning his whole body and letting the racquet trail behind in a final snap. From that time, I began practicing on my own when I wasn't able to pick up a game, and then just for the practice.

I was improving, but I still didn't have the effortless control I had seen on the court years earlier. In college I took a few group lessons, and I learned a great principle in the art of practicing. One of the goals in racquetball is to hit the ball off the front wall as close to the ground as possible, creating a "roll-out" – where the ball hugs the ground, making a return stroke impossible for your opponent. During this lesson, the teacher placed a racquetball on the ground against the front wall and challenged us to hit it from deep in the court with another ball. It was like asking us to hit a golf ball on a wide fairway with another golf ball from back on the tee – it was impossible, we thought.

Then he said, "You may think it's impossible, but you see, it's not about actually hitting the ball – it's about coming close. If you can come close to hitting the ball every shot, and roll out twenty in a row, you will advance your game." With this new insight into practicing, I went to work week after week trying to hit the ball. I would position myself ten feet from the front wall and take fifty shots, then move back to fifteen feet, and then near the back wall, and then I would repeat with the backhand. This went on for months, and I saw improvement. I was beginning to feel the sweet spot in my racquet every time I made contact with the ball.

And then, one day, I hit the ball. That little blue ball that was so tiny all those months suddenly moved. I set it back in place, and a few days later, I hit it again. Then I hit it on the backhand side. After months of practicing, and after years of pursuing this same practice regimen, I realized that I had developed the control, the snap, and the confidence I had seen in another player many years earlier.

Perfect.

Of course, I had not achieved perfection as a tennis player, bassist, or racquetball player. No, I found that other pursuits were of more importance than dedicating myself to the game or the instrument with the same kind of tenacity as those weeks or years of practice. But the lessons I learned in practice have remained with me.

We might look at life as a series of practice sessions. We bake a loaf of bread, and the yeast fails; so we practice again. We attempt a do-it-yourself project and we resort to hiring a contractor to rescue our failed efforts. But we keep practicing. A toddler throws a temper tantrum in the grocery store, and we practice the art of unflinching public mortification. Later we practice a speech to a rebellious child, certain of failure, certain we are not getting it right. We face loss, and we cope with defeat every day. And we keep practicing convinced that one day we will get it right.

I don't know when we earn our status as a perfect parent, perfect teacher, perfect boss, perfect cook, or perfect community leader. I suspect that it is only in the lives of others that we see the perfection of those years of practice. A friend says, "Your son/daughter is a great kid," or a student sends a note: "Thank you for being a great teacher – I learned a lot from you." An adult son or daughter says, "You made the difference in my life." Then you realize that you actually hit that little golf ball on the wide fairway. Yes, for one moment you were perfect. So keep practicing – you may be closer than you think.

55

SUMMER MOUNTAIN MUSIC

There he was again, the deliberative bass voice of Earl Nightingale, from somewhere deep in the speakers of my mother's mini station wagon with the fake wood paneling, welcoming us to another installment of his grandfatherly wisdom as we made our way up the winding canyon road. It was early summer in the mountains, and the sun that had poked through the trees near the bottom of the canyon was now completely obscured as we cut our way through the crisp morning air silently hoping that we could hear the rest of the radio monologue before the high mountain slopes brought intrusive static to the velveteen voice of our host.

Occasionally my mother and I would simply listen, and then continue on our way silently through the tree-lined road, alternatively careening too fast around corners and crawling too slow for an impatient tailgater. Sometimes, my mother would comment on the advice from the radio show, reinforcing the themes of success through hard work and optimism in the face of doubt. It was certainly timely wisdom as we completed our journey, arriving at the open mountain valley of the nearly abandoned ski resort. This particular summer the main lodge was home to nearly thirty bassists who were students of Emily Wood, gathering to prepare for a recital. Several of us also sat in as members of the National Youth Symphony, a sort of summer camp for teenage musicians working under the baton of a well-known maestro.

While I went off to a variety of rehearsals and clinics, my mother took a course in concert piano performance. A truly gifted pianist, she maintained

238

a full schedule of students for nearly fifty years, and she had composed and arranged a number of published church pieces. I had always known her musical abilities were something special, a gift in the truest sense, but I had never been able to speak with her about this shared passion until we spent the summer together in the mountains.

The day would begin with a bass clinic for all students, and then we would find a quiet corner of the ski lodge to practice. Long cement hallways would echo with the sounds of students at various levels practicing their recital pieces. Although in distant parts of the same building, we could hear each other's successes and failures as if the building were one giant jukebox playing records that skipped and halted aimlessly; never quite making a complete tune. Later, I would meet up with my fellow section mates and we would join the symphony rehearsal.

Warming up was like watching athletes at a track meet, stretching and sprinting in front of each other, sizing up the competition. There was the pre-teen cellist who could nearly make his strings glow red with his aggressive bowing. Farther back was the oboist playing scales that hovered somewhere near the ceiling. Enter the maestro. Unlike other orchestras and youth symphonies, where the conductor had to practically cajole a melody out of the most skilled players, this group was made up of the best performers from all those other lesser groups; and the conductor assumed we all had the technical capabilities from the beginning. We rehearsed on the outdoor deck of the main lodge near the gondolas; the mountain faces serving as a natural amphitheater to hikers, bikers, and the improvisational dance troupe that practiced on the adjacent walkway leading to the hiking trails.

Rehearsals were punctuated by drills that were the maestro's version of follow the leader as we would venture up and down scales and arpeggios in time with his baton; and then he would pause to enlighten us about the piece of music we were going to perform. He had a way of putting the composer right there with us so that we couldn't dream of offending them by playing below our abilities. As bassists, we were the low rumbling background that rarely received any notice except in absentia; so from my back of the balcony view, I was able to take it all in – the mountain music, the cool afternoon breeze, the oil painters out on the hiking trails, and the occasional wafting scent of grilled burgers on the top deck.

At the end of the day, I would meet my mother at the car and we would spend the ride down the canyon retelling the events of the day. It was there that I saw my mother's eyes light up as she talked about her experiences and pushing beyond her comfort level, living the concert pianist dream that had so long been sacrificed for unappreciative students and amateur ears. She always said how difficult it was for her, and how it reminded her of earlier times when she was studying in college. She talked of her days not with regret for what could have been, but with a deeper appreciation for music and – I sensed – for the mother she was, for the choices she had made, and for the gifts she had been given through music. She reminisced of musical groups she had accompanied as a young woman, and of the performances she had prepared for, certain that she was meant for service behind the soloists.

As we prepared separately for our performances an opportunity came up for my mother to help accompany some of the other bassists who would be performing at the upcoming recital. She stepped in that very day, working with several of the better bassists. I remember a compliment from Joe, one of the veteran performers, a man in his thirties who was near the end of the recital, where the real talent would perform after the audience survived the sawing sounds of a dozen mediocrities. As we were completing the final dress rehearsal he said, "I want you to know that I have worked with many other accompanists in my life, but Mrs. Kjar is the best I have ever had. " He went on to talk about her technical abilities as an accompanist, and she beamed beneath her averted eyes, not wanting to stay in the spotlight quite as long as Joe was offering it. I was able to see for the first time how talented she was. That's my mom, I thought proudly.

The summer in the mountains was full of other glorious moments. One of the most memorable was the sight of thirty bassists taking the stage with a professional symphony behind us and performing in unison a section of Prokoviev's Lieutenant Kije Suite. Another was the thrill of performing in two concerts with the National Youth Symphony, where I had the unique pleasure of watching real talent shine and where I learned the difference a gifted conductor could make. It was a thrill I will never forget.

It wasn't until years later that I realized how much I had learned that summer. I was at the top of my musical abilities, and I began to mull over the idea of becoming a professional. It was a chance to see the commitment required to do this as a career, not only as I watched the track stars sprint and the maestro drill, but as I sat in the car with my mom, listening to the repeated tales of the blissful memories of a thousand amateur performances. Was she sad about not becoming the concert pianist, the soloist with top billing? Far from it. She was happy, contented, assured of her place in the musical constellation, and of the contribution she would continue to make. How many lives had been enriched by her gift, whether as students, audiences, performers, or family and friends?

To have a gift and to share it with others is the essence of performance. I learned that summer that I could be happiest remaining forever an amateur. I had brushed up against paid musicians and realized that it was not the life I wanted to have. I learned to appreciate in a new way all that my mother had sacrificed to provide an income during hard times, to develop her talents so that others could shine, trading concert halls for multi-purpose rooms. I think back to the drive up the canyon on those early mornings and I'm certain that if Mr. Nightingale had met my mom, he might have proclaimed her success story in worthy low tones like Zeus from Mount Olympus.

He might have talked about the reputation she had gained as an accompanist, or the compositions bearing her name that were performed by world renowned artists, or perhaps the hundreds of students whose minds were enlightened by their teacher-guide. However, had he done so, he would have missed the real story of her success beyond the music, the successes she saw of the six children she raised and the hardships faced through the years. After all, music was simply her part-time job.

56

FRESHWATER SHARKS

The summer of 1975 changed the way that many of us went to water. That was the year of "Jaws," the year that the low pulsating musical thunder summoned the great white monster from the deep and sent chills down our spines. That was if we were on land. In the water, it was like coming face to face with our own irrationality staring up from the shallows of swimming pools and freshwater lakes.

Our family had a motorboat, and several times during the summer we would venture to a nearby lake and put in for an afternoon of fruitless attempts learning to slalom water-ski. We would practice getting up on two skis, then dropping a ski as our free foot searched for the back of our remaining ski, discovering that our wavering faith and our own mortality kept us from walking upon the water as we merely skimmed – then sank – into its mysterious waves. In previous years, the water was a friendly blue bed we were content to snuggle into if we fell, ski-less. We would joke at the frogman impression from our failed attempts to get up on skis. The frogman-skier, unable to cope with personal defeat, would reluctantly drag at the end of the rope for a hundred yards before surrendering water-logged. Even when we were able to emerge from the water and put on a show worthy of Cypress Gardens, the entertainment wasn't complete until the skier staged an over-the-top wipe-out. The welcome water would cushion the fall, sending up shimmering spray, drawing cheers from the boat-bound fans.

Somehow that summer, our pre-Jaws innocence was replaced with fear about what laid waiting below the water. Freshwater or not, every nibble from a passing bass, every brush with algae, reminded us that the water had changed. Was it possible for pranksters to put a twenty-foot shark in a freshwater lake, and how long would it survive? I often asked myself, waiting anxiously for the motorboat to make the turn to pluck me from the water. Entering the boat, I imagined the rows of teeth just missing my leg at the last second as I stepped from the water into the safety of the boat and my mother's towel-draped arms.

I remember my sister waiting in the water as the ski rope was being coiled for a toss out to her orange-gloved hands. "Love Will Keep Us Together" bubbled gleefully from the transistor radio onboard, and then, what was it? That low rumble started from somewhere behind the radio's speaker, as if rising from the water, stirring our pulses as the theme from Jaws was set to strike. My oldest brother turned up the volume, and this action had the desired effect on our sibling shark chum on the water, and she nearly sprang from the lake and shed her life vest, content somehow back in the boat. It must have escaped her that if Big Mr. J had devoured mouthfuls of tourists, the little Kitner boy, Robert Shaw and most of his sizable troller, he probably didn't have much of an appetite left for an after-dinner fromage – our small fiberglass motorboat. John Williams' theme song and Spielberg's monster generated a Pavlovian repulsion from the water, as macho boaters became sissified land-lubbers for the duration of the '75 summer.

Later that summer I was enjoying a swim in an Olympic-sized outdoor pool with my cousins when I thought I saw a shadow in the water. This is when I knew that my fears of the Great White shark had finally crossed over from a mere remote possibility, that a shark could live in freshwater lakes near my house, to an uncertain irrationality, that although I knew a shark could not live in chlorinated swimming pool water, I wasn't one-hundred percent positive that the shadow was from something other than the grey toothy torpedo lurking beyond the eight-foot depth. Yet kids continued to swim, unconcerned, and boys catapulted from the high dive as if it were impossible that a twenty foot monster was waiting to meet them below the surface. I knew better.

The final straw that year, before the onset of a welcome autumn and winter free of water sports, was a trip to a larger and much clearer lake several hours from home. While most lakes immediately around our house were comparatively shallow and warm, causing plants to grow and silt to stir obscuring a view of the lake bottom, this particular lake was large, deep and clear. Floating on the water and looking below, it was possible to imagine swimming in three dimensions to a diagonally deeper point in the lake. This freedom of movement must be what attracts snorkelers and scuba divers – who have not seen "Jaws" – to the coral lair of the beast.

As I was enjoying this moment of anti-gravity, my eyes settled on a darker spot in the lake. It may have just been a passing cloud causing the blemish, or maybe some deeper valley below my feet; but there it was again, the theme song before the attack. Since I had somewhat accepted that sharks did not occupy the public outdoor pool, it was now nearly likely that they were here: bigger lake, deeper water. Oh ya, they were here. I watched my white feet below the surface, appearing whiter against the dark lakebed, almost like the soft underbelly of a fish, wondering if they looked tasty wriggling against the bright sky above. Fortunately, the lake was cold, and I was able to gracefully end my slalom attempts on account of numbness rather than a fear of freshwater sharks.

Although I have entered many bodies of water since then – and have enjoyed a snorkeling adventure on several occasions in sharkly waters – I have never forgotten the summer of my hydrophobia, or more accurately, my galeophobia. I was not particularly comforted by the statistics quoted by shark-loving researchers about the numbers of shark attacks each year, nor even reassured by the reports that death by shark was "unlikely or rare." No, what got me back in the water was the sheer enjoyment of being in the water and fearing what I might miss if I stayed on land.

My wife and I took two of our boys on a cruise years ago, and for one sunny afternoon I bobbed in the warm waters of Puerto Vallarta with my boys. Time stopped, fears washed away like sandcastles on the beach, and I floated carelessly. What keeps a person from going in the water? Well, I know about that. But what keeps a person from staying on land? That's sometimes a tougher one to answer.

What imagined fears limit our ability to see past the uncertainty to the richness of life in three dimensions? What are the freshwater sharks we avoid? I can think of a few.

"It's a dangerous world out there." True, but we are better equipped to handle it than ever before. We have seat-belts, flashlights, safety-harnesses, steel-toed boots, and Kevlar gloves. If you stay in because of what might lurk outside your door, you are a prisoner just like the man in the shark cage. Study self-defense, not for the rational need to use it, but to combat the irrationality that you might. Meditate on the world beyond, and let the attraction of moving in three-D pull you outside, let the smell of mountain air or salty beaches tempt you into the deeper water.

"If I take time off, I might get fired or my boss won't like it." That may also be true, but how do you know? Have you ever asked for time away to be with your kids – to bob in the water at the beach or to share a bike ride to nowhere? Is your boss the freshwater shark that doesn't exist except in your mind? Go ask. Go ask now before your kids grow up and you're left wondering what that day together might have done for both of you. The clock is ticking, and it's not the time clock you just punched.

"I'm not a kid anymore." You may not need to go bungee-jumping, skydiving, or river rafting to prove to yourself that you are alive and vital. Walk in the park near a boyhood home, drop in on a friend you knew in high school, visit a place you read about once but never went because there was the sneaking feeling that a freshwater shark might be there. Youth is fine, but so is age, wisdom, and a life of experiences to refresh and recalibrate on a new world. You don't have to be a kid – you need only curiosity.

"I won't fit in." You may find yourself in deep water with your ugly white legs dangling below you, like bait for the unfriendly predator lurking below, but don't leave the water yet. Dive deeper. Strike up a conversation with a complete stranger. Join a book club and find common ground in the literary discoveries beyond the eight foot marker. Find something you like to do, and then find a group that meets about it or a team that plays for it – take the high dive, there's nothing below but cool water.

You can never be sure about shadows in the water. Your safety is not a hundred percent guaranteed whether in life's oceans or public pools. It's possible, although "rare and unlikely" that you will die from facing your fears; and death from stepping outside your comfort zone may look as inevitable as a dorsal fin cutting the water in front of you. If so, just remember the frogman, dragging behind the boat refusing to let go; or the skier who sends up a victorious spray from a well-designed spill. And go swim with the sharks.

57

BORDER DISPUTES AND ILLEGAL ALIENS

To some, borders are imaginary lines that exist only on maps or in the minds of two cultures. Others prefer to mark borders so that they are impossible to miss, with signs, fences, or sentries standing guard. Patrols canvass the territories along the line, hover overhead, or watch harbors from sea-borne stations. Here is land one, and here is land two. Cross over there and you are in enemy territory, an alien, an intruder. One side of this line has its own language and culture; the people fly their flag proudly from the highest masts, while always watching for incursions from the other side, looking for traces that signal the border has been breached.

I shared a bedroom with my older brother growing up. We didn't consider ourselves less fortunate, it was just the result of too many siblings and too few rooms, so we bunked together. At first our border was the sea of carpet that divided the two continents – our twin beds. We prided ourselves in being able to leap from one bed to the next, spanning the great divide in one giant, Gulliverian step. Things over there were pretty much the same, and we were so overjoyed by our undocumented passage that we would jump up and down upon reaching the new land until our governor father would intercede.

We soon found ourselves in a new room, a basement bedroom much larger than the first, and soon our tiny empires began to grow. We began to have property. At first it was somewhat loosely defined. My brother possessed the two top drawers of a shared bureau while I took the lower two – but they were mine. These drawers had a unique design that allowed a colored piece of paper to be inserted in a slot that showed through the wood pattern on the front of the drawer. Thus, the colors of the top drawers and the colors of the lower drawers were clearly marked. Our twin beds were on opposite sides of the room, and additional markings grew up around these continents that had drifted somewhat since the first bedroom.

We collected stickers from the local ice cream shop, green football shaped stickers for every lime scoop we ordered. Soon the walls surrounding our beds were covered with green stickers like the back of a college football all star's helmet. Other monuments divided the land between us. My side of the room had a clock whose boxy base held two children on a teeter totter rising up and down in a perpetual scene of playful bliss. The scene had a light, and on quiet nights the people of my half of the world were warmed by the two children rising and falling, rising and falling, one click up and two clicks down, comforting the citizens in the dark. The other side had a closet light, and it wasn't nearly so impressive. Still, regular incursions across the sea − literally a blue carpet − were tolerated since the bureau and the closet were shared colonies and the thought of being entirely cut off from these lands would have amounted to violations of treaty. Besides, we still had a common foe, our sisters. The beads in the doorway had been mounted to mark the porous border from the world of boys and the hinterland of the girls.

Transitioning from our blue coral world of the basement, our family prepared for a move farther out in the county to a larger home, and our mother invited us to imagine what kind of bedroom would be our ideal, and we set to drafting. Neither of us drew a room without the other − shared territory was implied having been so long together − so I sketched a whimsical built in bed with a skylight opening to the stars. I drew built in bureaus that would belong only to me, no longer to be shared, with separate closets to secure the treasury that had gradually amassed in the home country.

My wish came true, in part, when we moved into the new home. We shared a room, but the boundaries were certain and indisputable. Two double-doored closets took up one side of the room, with an equal number of windows opposite. Each closet included a built in set of drawers and space for clothes. Within a season, the room had been remodeled and new blue carpet marked the return of a definite coastline under our beds and bureaus. The walls behind our beds were made of special cork-like material, so we could pin up whatever suited our tastes. Blessedly, the new paneling on the walls and closet doors allowed us to clearly count the number of panels on one side of the room and ascertain what was the absolute center line dividing east from west.

This was the peak of the border wars. It started again with stickers. This time the stickers were the profane parodies of products we obtained in our bubble gum packages. The inside of our closet doors were covered with such dubious brands as Crust toothpaste, Minute Lice, Quacker Oats, Blecch Shampoo, and Plastered Peanuts. Cork-boards soon became billboards for what was right about our side of the world. My side had a nice poster of Jimmy the Microbe, a drawing I had done in school of which I was particularly proud, and a crudely rendered sketch of Snoopy, who was my alter ego of sorts, and the mascot of the west side world.

The east side was poorly kept – a shambles. The people on the east side would often sleep late, making all variety of slovenly sounds in their sleep. The east side had a built in desk, with a lamp, but rarely was it used. Those east siders were lazy. To better keep ourselves from the taint of the other side we agreed to actually create a borderline of masking tape on the floor. Before the border, there was a type of international waters agreement that broadly defined the middle of the room; but following the installation of the line, disputes seemed to escalate. Stepping over the line was now a sort of game, a taunt, and each side reveled in the sport. Spending time on the other side of the line, even daring to sit on the bed or use the mostly neglected study lamp were feats of daring and were often met with anger, and occasional border violence.

I remember that during this time, the border issue became so severe that my mother actually packed my brother and I in the car and we went to a furniture store to investigate what types of more permanent barriers could be erected between us to prevent illegal crossings. At the top of the list were shelving units that could be assembled and installed down the center line of the room; however this solution, while solving the border crossing problem, created new concerns since shelf space would have to be shared and each territory had to give up at least six to eight inches of space to make room for the large wall. Until then, the supreme ruler, dad, had largely stayed out of these petty disputes; and he had only become involved in the early days – when joyful jumping on the beds became too raucous. Those bright days had been replaced by darkness and shadows, and no one ventured across the vast expanse of the deep unguarded. Dad intervened again and decreed a cease fire throughout east and west lands.

Before long, sisters married and moved out, and girlish territory was abandoned to the new settlers. My brother took the room down the hall, and immediately he put up a wallpaper mural on one wall, a vast fall forest scene that was puzzling during the other three seasons of the year. Perpetual autumn in the land of the farther west regions, I supposed. Up the hall, I was only too happy to expand my domain to include both closets. The masking tape border came up and a general amnesty was declared to any who remained in the east. Stickers that had marked a competition between two states suddenly became seized property.

The year the last shot was fired across the border was both a time of triumph and a time of solitude. I stretched my possessions into two closets, intentionally leaving no empty drawers simply to declare that they were mine. Posters, pictures, certificates, and stickers increased on the walls, making mine a defined culture. It had become the land of the Bass Player, the Sea of the High Fidelity Eight-Track Stereo, and the only Foreigner allowed was the band playing "Juke-Box Hero" and "Cold as Ice."

The next few years saw my brother move farther away, first to a basement, carpet-lined room, and then he and his family set up home out west, and we relocated to the Great Lakes. All intentional barriers have been long removed. The bureau is all mine. No seesaw children play in the night, and no stickers adorn the space behind my closet door. But I still think of those continents adrift on the blue carpet ocean, and the masking tape line that for a time fenced us in. No borders remain, and no unwanted strangers sneak through. Those trappings that define me – books on shelves, degrees on walls, and clothes in my closet – remain undisturbed. But I do miss those skirmishes.

58

INNOVATION IN TAXATION

Bemoaning taxes is so universal it's merely a cliché, and yet in recent years a new variety of taxes breathes life into the boring taxation systems of yesterday. Income tax was so twentieth century. Property tax – oh please, how unimaginative do you have to be to tax land? Snooze.

Examine some of the great innovations in taxation over the years, and we can see where the future might take us. A generation ago, we flourished through our ability to invent things, new products finding new markets. Now that we have squandered the wealth of a once great nation, we are led to the inevitable conclusion that without new ways of taxing, we just won't be able to sustain our level of spending. And since spending is more important than saving – everyone knows this – we must tax faster, sooner, and create ways to increase those taxes with as little effort as possible.

First, the lovely and ubiquitous death tax. It's got a lovely ring to it. When you die, there's the taxman – sorry, tax*person* – grieving beside you, but willing to push aside that anguish to find a nice resting place for your deceased's spare change. If Ned Taxmore could actually climb in the casket and rifle through the pockets, it might seem a bit intrusive, so instead we reserve the right to tax his assets in absentia. Of course, your loved one paid taxes already on that inheritance, but never mind that. Death is a great opportunity to tax. It's a transaction of the most permanent kind. Birth is so lasting, but death – well that's over and done with, so you're not really able to put up a fight. Your surviving spouse or children really won't miss that inheritance, after all; and what really gives them the right to sit on that pile of cash? It's not going to do the dead any good, so let the living part not only with their beloved, but also with their greed.

Nearly as elegant as the death tax is the sales tax. It's great. Tax the sale of goods. Why? Did someone in the Department of Commerce help Sid the small business owner stock the shelves? No. Advertise the product? No. Pay the lease? No. So why sales tax? Right, because it's a good way to raise money. Oh, right. But taxing a sale is so late in the game, why not get in there earlier? Enter the Value Added Tax. This is great! You can actually *add* value to an item by taxing it earlier in the production and distribution chain? No, you're not adding value, you're taxing – you really don't get this, do you? By taxing the transactions before it gets to the consumer, you are really able to multiply your tax options. The VAT tax, now that has cache. Acronyms are great too, keep that in mind. And the good thing is, since these taxes are supported by such a broad population, raising them just a quarter or half percent each year can go practically unnoticed for several years.

The carbon tax, what a beautiful thing. Let's tax everything that is carbon based – now *that's* broad. I love it. Actually, it's a guilt tax, and that's even better. You have been polluting this planet for generations, and so we'll forgive your retroactive tax burden if you'll promise to seek forgiveness for your existence on planet earth. Every breath you take, every drive you take, you're killing poor mother earth. Admit it. You're not green. You're an eco-sadist. Sicko!

These are all very nice taxes, but they don't fully demonstrate the artistry of the tax system, so let's explore some future possible taxes that might really have the brand power to take taxation to a new horizon.

VAT sounded great, but what about a fat tax? After all, fat people take up more space, so it's only fair. Their clothes contain more fabric, they occupy more real estate on public walkways, and they burden others who have to look around them. It's easy to implement, and we already have the actuarial tables and ideal weight charts, so tax everyone progressively according to their weight. Of course, they do buy a lot of food, so sales taxes might drop if we over-tax the chronically obese. Maybe a smaller tax on a larger population? No, that's too obvious…hmm. I've got it, let's tax every transaction that could contribute to obesity and call it the He Ain't Heavy, He's My Brother Tax Relief Act. The relief comes in being able to name the tax, of course. We'll tax the fast food advertisers, products containing transfats, sofa manufacturers, big screen TV dealers, cable TV providers – wait we already have that one – taxi services (why shouldn't people be encouraged to walk?), elevator manufacturers (why shouldn't they take the stairs?), boat dealers (why shouldn't they swim?). I love it – ha ,ha! What a great tax.

Think, what else?

I know, a thinking tax. We don't want any religious fanatics because they don't really think rationally like the rest of us. Let's tax the pews, tax the hymnals, tax the Eucharist. Tax those satin choir robes – they really weren't thinking about fashion when they designed those! Of course, they can keep their tax exempt status – after all, churches do a wonderful service for the weak-minded in society. Let's just call these little corrections Religious Fundamental Reform Fees. For the very orthodox religious communities we'll apply a Mental Health Multiplier, since undoing all the religious indoctrination is going to take multiple sessions to the already burdened social services.

As long as we're on the subject of fanatics, we don't really care much for sports fanatics. They really are quite loud, and after games they crowd the streets and make it difficult for safe passage for average citizens. We don't want to upset the heavy user fees associated with liquor licensing and the sale of booze at sporting events – in fact, we can probably increase those fees a bit – no one's complaining yet. But let's get back to the noise. Touchdowns tend to incite crowd noise, so let's tax the team a flat Stadium Noise Reduction Tax, or SNoRT, for every touchdown scored by the home team. But then, real sports fans on the opposing team will of course react negatively to the touchdown, so each team should pay its fair share. We then have to think about the public's safety when crowds empty onto the streets after a game. It seems only fair that fans should pay a Safe Streets and Crowd Violence Reduction Fee. We'll add it to the parking fees, just a dollar to start, and then we'll increase it if the team has a winning season – the fans will be so happy they won't miss a doubling of the tax.

We really aren't going big though. Carbon, now that's something. Air. Water. That's it! We'll tax every form of water. Just imagine the possibilities! With every rainfall we'll charge a Rainfall Collection Tax in the regions where rainfall is heaviest, and we'll charge a Rainwater Scarcity Fee in the deserts for every day without moisture. Tax the sprinkler systems that water lawns, golf courses, and corporate offices and call it a Water Evaporation and Exchange Plan (WEEP), and we can guilt the rich into paying so that they can have green spaces. Ice cubes will have to bear the Frozen Liquids Distribution Stamp, and dry ice will have to be packed in special state issued ice packs – we'll just charge a unit cost for those. Dew on the grass will be taxed on Wednesdays, and every water fountain will be coin operated. We'll make a killing in water.

You know, humans have been paying taxes for so long, but animals really take up a lot of space, and they have had a free ride for so many years – it's time they paid their fair share too. People like dogs, and dogs are bigger than cats, so it only makes sense that dogs should pay twice the rate of cats. Exotic birds, snakes, arachnids, and fish will also pay a premium – they're exotic after all. You shouldn't really have them, so you pay a triple rate penalty – we'll call it the Mysterious and Exotic Animal Naturalization (MEAN) Tax. Dog food, dog collars, dog treats, dog houses – they all get taxed. Dog shows for acting dogs and dog tracks for racing must unionize their dogs and provide special working conditions for their animals and, in turn, they will be granted the Federal Racing and Acting for Unionized Dogs (FRAUD) license. It's very prestigious. Cats, while nice, are less dependable in the living form; so we will create a Cat Disposal and Recovery Fee that requires all cat owners to turn in their deceased feline friends so that their pelts can be harvested and resold as fine luxury items such as coats and purses.

Wait, wait, we're not done yet. Words are often to blame for discontent among the masses. We have to think about insurrections and rabble-rousing among the public by malcontents bent on exposing our tax schemes. We'll tax their words so that no defamatory texts will escape the tax master's watchful eye. This public agency will have to exact a heavy tax burden for proper oversight, so perhaps all written works, prior to publication, should go to the Department for the Interpretation of All Public Extracts and Rights (DIAPER) for adjudication. Works determined to be detrimental to the state's interest will be subject to a transfer fee to be paid for a second review by the governing committee, which grants rights for the work to be published in the special Library of the Interior for a small additional licensing charge. Of course, entry to the library will be subject to a heavy user fee.

59

A DISCLAIMER FOR DISCLAIMERS

Warning: Before you read this, be sure that you are sitting in a comfortable seat and that it is adjusted to the correct height for your age and weight. Failure to do so may result in serious injury or even death.

Disclaimers, don't you just love them? Let's just do a little poll. Out of the hundreds of disclaimers you see in a month, how many have you actually sat down and read? If they actually made a difference to our well-being and safety, we would want to read all that fine print regularly, or face our own peril, right? So if we don't believe that we are seriously harmed by failing to read the cautions, warnings, and notices placed on our products, why is it?

A better question might be, if nearly everything meant for consumer use has some kind of disclaimer or warning on it, and the consumer doesn't feel compelled to get out the reading glasses, then for whom is the disclaimer written? The answer, of course, is – everyone? Lawyers, that's right.

Disclaimers are really just advertising for lawyers, a constant reminder that anyone can – and should – bring a lawsuit at any time and for any reason. If truth in advertising were something other than an oxymoronic tease, disclaimers might read something like this:

Disclaimer: To better service your legal needs regarding this product, since you would like to bring a lawsuit, please note that your request should reflect the date of the alleged grievance, as well as the original receipt and names of two witnesses not affiliated with the place of purchase. Select from the following most common grievances for which you and we, can win big,

- The packaging was offensive, and I suffered as a result.
- I thought I bought something else, but I bought this instead, and I suffered as a result.
- I tried eating the packaging (or some other consumer antic not listed here), and I suffered as a result.
- Remember, whether through your own neglect or our client's, we get paid big, so let's start this long fee-for-service adventure as soon as possible. Pick up that phone right now and call the lawsuit hotline at 1-800-SUE-QUIK.

Well, we can always hope for such honesty; but before continuing to verse two of the anti-lawyer battle hymn, let's just reflect for a moment on the leaders of organizations who have taken the advice of counsel for so long, they have forgotten that they are in the business of providing products to consumers rather than building legal walls to insulate themselves from risk. Of course, they don't really believe that their disclaimers protect from lawsuits, they merely want to shift the blame to us so that we will feel guilty about bringing a lawsuit.

Imagine this defense in a courtroom. General Counsel of MCG, Inc., sits at the defendant table, flanked by external counsel of the law firm of at least four last names, and the attorney selected to make the opening statement rises:

"Your honor, on behalf of the defendant, Mega Consumer Goods, Inc., we feel that the grounds for this case were completely fabricated to cast a negative light on one of the finest institutions in this great country. The fact that the plaintiff failed to read what millions – no billions – of other consumers have read and understood for years on the packaging signals not only a willful neglect for personal safety, but also an abdication of the responsibilities we collectively share whenever we open a bottle or break the seal on a life-saving product. Your honor, it clearly states in bold letters on the label that failure to use this product in accordance with enclosed safety instructions constitutes a risk to the consumer and absolves MCG ,Inc. of any responsibility at all. Let me emphasize those last two words, AT ALL, because I want it to be clearly understood by the plaintiff, who failed to read those two words when she willfully ignored them prior to using the product. At all. That's spelled capital A – t, and then a – l and l. At. All. Your witness."

But wait, this doesn't appear to be the same company that always pictures the family around the kitchen table, sunlight streaming in, mother with a warm glow, father with a dopey grin, gifted children ready for a quick quip about how great this new product is, while the music rises and mom delivers the money line, "That's why our family sticks with…"? Yes, that's the one that now puts Mom on the stand to learn how to spell.

I suppose lawyers are so blindingly literal that they picture each of us carefully reading their labels as a normal part of life:

"Hey honey, did you see where I put that credit card statement? They just reissued the privacy rules, and I really wanted to review them before I go Christmas shopping."

"Okay, I'm all dressed, let's hit the slopes!"

"Wait, Jill, did you read that statement that we signed last night when we checked into the hotel? It clearly stated that any injuries resulting from our ski outing are strictly at our own risk, and the hotel's proximity to the slopes does not imply any sanctioning of skiing as an appropriate winter activity."

"Kyle, it's your turn to feed the dog. Kyle? Kyle?!"

"Ya, right here, Dad. I was just reading the warning on my game system. Did you know that flashing lights could cause epileptic seizures and that prolonged exposure to images of death and gore could cause episodes of rage and acts of violence in high stress environments? Fascinating!"

Enough. It's time to demand more from ourselves, or demand less from the lawyers.

First, an appeal to you leaders of organizations.

Stand by your product. That's it. Mr. CEO, tear down this wall – the one you're hiding behind that your lawyers built for you. If your product injures me or one of my family members because your engineers were incompetent or your testing was incomplete, I'm going to sue you for a lot of money. So get it right. Don't short-change safety because you're too cheap. Fire a few lawyers and hire a few more inspectors, or run a few more focus groups with real people.

In exchange, we promise that if you make products that could potentially harm us, like ultra-sharp kitchen knives, hot coffee, or high-powered rifles, we won't sue if we injure ourselves or use them for something other than their intended use. If we do sue out of greed or grief, take that suit, go to court, and defend the product not only for yourselves, but for the rest of us who know what we're doing and understand the risks. Don't take the easy way out and settle because you're afraid of the negative publicity. Go public. We're with you!

I know it's naïve to expect a return to corporate responsibility and public civility, and removing a gang of metastasized lawyers from the organs of our institutions is probably hoping beyond hope; but what if you were a leader who took the risk? I recently heard a commercial on the radio for a bank, and at its conclusion, where you would normally hear a string of disclaimers and provisions about maintaining a certain balance or that some services are subject to additional unspecified fees, there was only a statement – and I'm paraphrasing: "That's it, no disclaimers. Put us to the test to see if we deliver what we promise." I nearly drove off the road. I noticed.

Business has always been about distinguishing yourself from the other guy through higher quality, superior customer service before and after the sale, delivering before the competition gets out of the gates, or lowering the price point. In the age of direct to consumer advertising, how about a direct to consumer appeal based on relentless integrity – not the hang-on-the-wall mission statement about how much integrity to intend to have, but a real-life, evidence-based proof that you stand behind your product?

Remember the Tylenol recall of 1982? Could Johnson and Johnson be blamed for the tampered products that made it into the hands of seven consumers who died as a result? They could have argued that point, but instead, they advised the public to stop using any of their products, used the media to get out the warning, set up toll-free lines for the public, and the CEO went on television to talk. In the end, the public viewed the reaction by J&J executives as a lesson in responsiveness and responsibility, and J&J led the way in new tamper-resistant product packaging.

When a crisis occurs, don't cower behind your lawyers. Don't point to the fine print.

Finally, to you writers of disclaimers, might I recommend a universal disclaimer to be included on all consumer goods so that you don't have to keep trying to parse paragraphs and craft defensible deceits? Here goes.

Claim: In providing this product to you, we claim that we did everything we could to ensure the safety of this product. We also claim that it will do what we say it will do. Further, if you don't know how to use it, call us first at 1-800-ASK-HELP and we'll be happy to answer any questions you have. If you are injured as a result of using this product, please call 1-800-IT-HURTS; we want to know about it right away so that we can prevent further injury to others and also compensate you for any medical damages caused by our product. Finally, if you feel we have mistreated you in any way, please seek legal advice. If you have difficulties finding legal advice, we can recommend a few out of work lawyers who used to stand between you and us. Thanks for your continued trust and patronage.

60

SELLING FRIENDSHIP

Think of your best friend, and then ask yourself, what is that friendship worth? For many of us, we might pause and then answer, "Nothing, it's priceless." However, some foolishly think that as long as you're hanging around, they might take the opportunity to sell you something, failing to realize that the taint of money, once injected to a priceless friendship cheapens it like a red tag sale in a museum. I learned this lesson many years ago when my best friend decided I was in the right place at the right time to make me an offer I couldn't refuse.

Over the last two decades I have seen the soft sell and the hard sell, and know how to recognize both. I offer a brief explanation as a public service.

The hard sell it easy, and you probably recognize this obvious approach before it even fully arrives. A seller makes eye contact, senses that there are no nearby exits, and proceeds with a business card introduction, a 30-second explanation of who they are and what organization they represent, followed by a direct appeal, usually in the form of a no-lose question, such as, "If I could tell you today how you could (save money, increase productivity, take your pick) by (a percentage they make up), wouldn't that be worth a few minutes of your time?" The hook is in the water, poorly baited, and the fish just swims away, "I'm sorry, I've got something right now, but I've got your card, and I'll be in touch."

I suppose somewhere there is a Land of the Hard Sell, where shorter-than-average men who wear lots of jewelry and cheap after-shave buy and sell regularly using this approach because it is still so frequently used. It's just so hard for me to imagine.

"Oh, you mean in just a few minutes of my time I could save millions – well, of course I would be interested, who wouldn't! Explain on, I'm all ears!" Really? Well, that's the hard sell.

The soft sell usually takes place over a series of meetings. The first meeting is merely to exchange business cards, to introduce the seller (if they are selling something pricey, they will never have "sales" in their title, it will be "senior account leader" or "regional partner" or "business development executive" or some such nonsense) and to leave behind some "literature." It's not like they're leaving behind a Joseph Conrad novel or a Shakespearean play – it's just some colorful two-fold with graphs that have little bars on the left and very high bars on the right showing why you should buy this product.

The second meeting is to return to the potential buyer and invite questions about the non-literature. Of course, they don't expect you to have read it, and you can freely admit that you didn't, but like the boyfriend who leaves his prized sunglasses at his potential girlfriend's house so that he can have an excuse to return, so does the business development executive with non-literature. This second meeting is an opportunity to become more familiar, and the huckster might try to use your first name, or – horrors! – something like "Sport" or "Guy" to show that you have moved beyond mere acquaintances. It never really works.

The third meeting wouldn't happen at all, but the faux salesman sets it up as a lunch date at a nice restaurant near your place of business. You eat, and therefore you accept the appointment, willing to tolerate the indigestive properties of the post-meal "sell" because the apricot glazed scallops are too hard to resist. At this point in the soft sell, you have the opportunity to graciously decline any further contact, since you have tolerated three meetings, providing plenty of opportunities to be sold. Of course, it might mean letting a few follow-up phone calls roll to your voicemail or using your administrative assistant to make up a few excuses about why you are so busy, but those scallops were worth it.

If I would have only known the soft sell in my college years, I might have seen it coming and not lost my best friend to a multi-level marketing pitch.

I had a good friend in high school, Carl, who, after graduating, went to work in Pocatello, Idaho. I use the word work very loosely because Carl never really worked in the traditional sense. He worked for his dad when he needed money, and then went through various self-delusionary periods: the I-Think-I-Could-Be-A-Songwriter period that ended when he realized that his inability to read music could hinder his high hopes; the I-Think-I-Want-To-Be-A-Commercial-Airline-Pilot period that ended after he got his pilot's license and realized it was going to take a long time to become a commercial airline pilot; and the I-Think-I-Could-Be-An-Inventor period that ended after several unproductive brainstorming sessions failed to produce a million dollar idea.

Carl was never a finisher. Our friendship had endured the trials of high school, a foreign study program we did together, several bad girlfriends, his auto accident, and a couple of years when we had been apart pursuing our careers. He finally met a woman to marry, and they had settled in Idaho where she worked, in the traditional sense. I was dating my future wife at the time, and Carl invited us to come up for a visit.

I didn't realize that we had already exchanged business cards and literature, and this was the invitation for apricot-glazed scallops. We had a delightful time with Carl and Jane, and we spent much of the day in and out of his old army Jeep, four-wheeling through the snow banks of rural — well, it was all rural — Pocatello. We laughed and reminisced about the great old times with the implied promise that there would be many more to come.

"Remind me to tell you about this new business I'm starting when we get back!" yelled Carl as we were about to roll the Jeep.

"Sure!" I called back, not knowing that I had just eaten my last scallop.

Later that night we were all relaxing after dinner around Carl and Jane's cozy kitchen table when the pitch came. I had already agreed to listen to Carl's business idea, and had some idea where this might go. I had been exposed to various forms of multi-level marketing in the past, so I knew all the buzz-words. The script was somewhat familiar, although I was so surprised at finding myself across the table from my best friend in the middle of a business deal that I sat in absolute silence for nearly two hours while the sales banner unfurled upon our friendship.

"This is a great opportunity, and I'm letting you in while it's still early. You actually own your own business, and you get other people to sell for you, and you just sit back and watch the checks come in."

"Hmm. Really," I hedged, but he didn't even flinch.

"Jane and I started doing this and we already have a few people lined up, so we wanted to offer it to you two since you're getting pretty serious, and…"

I felt like I had just been called "Sport" by my best friend. Ugh!

Product catalogs followed, along with the visionary descriptions of double-ruby dealers at the top who were making a HUNDRED THOUSAND A YEAR JUST WORKING A FEW HOURS A MONTH. It went on and on, and my girlfriend and I politely sipped our sodas and listened until a pause finally came. The script had ended, and all the literature was in the client's hands. All that remained was to ASK FOR THE BUSINESS.

"So what do you think?" a self-satisfied Carl asked. It might have been the way he delivered that line. Although the day had begun with all the proper soft selling techniques – the fun, the food, the friendship – it had culminated in an obvious hard sell.

"I think it's stupid!" was my stern reply. "Let me know when you make your first hundred thousand."

I had always been quite accepting of his false starts and his wild hare ideas. When he had told me that he was thinking about becoming a walk-on to a local university's football squad, having never touched a football in the years I had known him, I was nevertheless willing to hear him and support his goal if that's what he wanted. But this? Multi-level marketing?

It ended there.

That very night marked a fork in the road. Carl and Jane took their so-called commodities business one direction, and months later my wife and I started our new life, both with steady jobs. I never saw Carl again, although I did once receive a family Christmas card from him. He was no longer with Jane, but had picked up a new wife and child. I didn't read what work he was doing or whether he had ever achieved that lofty life's goal of becoming a multi-level marketing king, and whether those who had joined him in Pocatello those many years ago had gone on to the beneficial life he promised. It didn't matter.

What did matter all those year later was that the priceless friendship had been sold cheap, although no money had ever changed hands. Perhaps my friend had only operated out of a genuine sense of wanting what he believed was best for me. I'll never really know. It doesn't matter now anyway. I have learned to recognize when I'm being sold.

"Hey, I'm having a little get together at my house next week and thought you might come over. I'd like to tell you about something I'm considering as a new business venture."

"No, thanks. I wouldn't be interested."
"Hey, maybe we could meet for lunch sometime and share some ideas?"
"No, thanks. I wouldn't be interested."
"If you ever have time, I'd like to send you something about…"
"No, thanks. I wouldn't be interested."

So next time you listen to the pitchman who tells you there's no harm in contacting a few of your close family members or friends and convinces you that really you're doing them a favor by offering them something that they would naturally want anyway, please reconsider. And if you're a friend who feels you've been sold out or betrayed to a multi-level marketing infected friend, consider giving them one more meeting before you walk away forever. You might not get apricot-glazed scallops, but you might find that weathering one more hardship makes your friendship even stronger.

61

THE HUNTER BECOMES THE PREY

Credit cards are a necessary evil, and for some who like to go on spending binges, the plastic partying eventually ends and the purging begins. A monthly minimum payment is missed, and reality sets in quickly. Usually the over limit fees kick in, annual percentage rates spike, and then the collection calls begin, and the hunt is on.

I was a hunter. One of my first real career jobs was working for one of the largest credit card firms in the Collections Department. The company had just recently moved into their newly-leased space, and I was among the first of several hundred phone collectors to be hired. I was in Level 1 Collections, which were the accounts between 30 and 90 days delinquent. My job consisted of being logged in to an automatic dialing system and calls were routed to me for the duration of my eight-hour shift.

It wasn't such a bad job. Unlike the much-maligned telemarketing jobs, we collectors had a known person on the other end of the phone who owed us money, an enviable position for anyone trying to keep the customer on the line. We called simply to remind the person of the overdue status on their account, and tried a friendly, customer service approach to collections. Most of the time it worked, and these early delinquent customers – as if they were all some kind of juvenile delinquents smoking on the corner – paid up, or at least made promises to pay.

After a few weeks of working these accounts, I was promoted to a Level 2 Collector, responsible for 90 to 120 day accounts. Our calls became a little more serious at Level 2. Gone was the sing-song voice of the customer service rep, and we began to take on the role of the hunter, looking for the weak among the herd, and quickly dispensing of them before moving to the next prey. We used to have an award, an inflatable shark that was passed to the person who could collect an entire account balance in one call.

In those early days, skip-tracing, the ability to look up details about the person you were calling became more readily available, so we were able to know about the person's household, number of kids, model and year of automobiles owned, whether they were current on other bills. This intelligence gave us much more leverage on the call, and we used this to persuade the customer to pay. I'll never forget a particularly impertinent call I made to a woman in New Hampshire one afternoon. She was refusing to pay, and claimed that she had no assets and it was impossible to squeeze blood from a turnip (an expression well-known to any collector). While the discussion of turnip gore was going on, I had looked at some details and found that the person lived in quite a nice home and owned three cars, including a late model pick-up truck. I made a suggestion,

"Well, ma'am, I see that you own a truck. Maybe you could earn a little extra cash by driving around neighborhood and offering to pick up some brush or garbage for a price..."

Did I really expect that to work? No. In fact, as a hunter, I expected to get a severely negative reaction, and I did. The customer's volume increased and she got quite heated. I didn't. This was essentially a tactic to tire the prey. It was amazing how the best arguments and heated debates served our purposes. We sat calmly and listened to the vitriolic rants, and when it was over, the fatigued delinquent would still be on the phone, only more submissive than before – like being backed into a corner with no weapons – and they would make a promise to pay rather than having to go through the humiliating chase again.

Still, there was something sinister about the collections game. I was married, striving to put food on the table and thought about starting a family. I couldn't imagine getting myself into that kind of financial hole, being so strapped for cash that I would have to decide whether to pay the credit card or the energy company, or having to float a check hoping that when my paycheck did come, I would have enough so that the check wouldn't bounce. That was the life of the prey, and it was a very real game of survival.

During this time in my life I worked the late shift, and on my way home from work I would tune my AM radio to the soothing voice of Bruce Williams, a tough-talking New Jersey man who offered plenty of advice to those who had mismanaged their money and were in the same desperate state as many of my customers. Often a caller to the show would describe the debt that he had piled up, and the expensive car he couldn't live without, and was now turning to this gruff guru for advice whether to apply for bankruptcy or find some other solution. In his typical fatherly way, Mr. Williams would respond something like this,

Well, you've got a serious problem there. Listen, young man, you're looking for an easy solution, but there isn't one. If you take the bankruptcy option, your credit will take a blow for the next seven years, but you may recover not having to pay for the debt you have caused. But let me tell you something else, he would say in a calm and frank way, *If you stick it out, and pay your debt, you'll be better for it. You'll not only dig out of your credit hole much faster – you'll have something that you won't have the other way: personal integrity.*

That was his typical solution for the financial difficulties people faced. Reduce expenses, pick up additional work and then work hard until the debt was fully paid.

Several years passed, and I had left behind the collections job, and was in a new home enjoying my marriage and life with three small boys. My wife caught me after I was doing the dishes and said she had something to tell me, and that it was very important. Her serious tone had me worried. What was it? Another man? Cancer?

She then laid out the financial realities that we had both denied for too long. She shared her secret credit card debt, one credit card after another with most of the credit limits reached or exceeded. I also came clean with additional credit card debt I had accumulated. The sinkhole we found ourselves in was overwhelming. It was more than my total gross income for a year, and with a mortgage, student loans, and three small kids, we were close to the edge already. We had both been living in denial – partying with the plastic, running from the hunters; and now, we were cornered.

The hunter had become the prey.

In the days following our full financial disclosure to each other, we began organizing our bills according to which card we could pay and still retain some remaining credit balance. We were on the phone with collectors raising our voices, sounding defensive, begging for mercy at the hands of greedy profiteering credit card companies.

The treadmill was spinning faster than our best pace could manage, and we knew the inevitable fall was coming. We had to take other measures, or else it would mean losing the house and declaring bankruptcy. I remembered the woman from New Hampshire those many years prior, and I thought of the callers to those late night talk radio shows. I was one of them. We were desperate too. I knew what it felt like to owe more than I could possibly imagine paying, and the wish that it could just all go away. Why had we been so foolish? Where were the goods we had purchased? It was as if the goods had turned to air, vanished into the carpet and walls of our house.

We survived. We met with a credit counseling service and they helped us work out agreements with the creditors to pay back the amounts we owed at reduced fixed rates. We worked hard, and over six long years, we paid off all the balances owed. If we would have declared bankruptcy, we wouldn't have had to pay all that money back, and we would have only suffered the loss of another year's worth of damage to our credit. But that man from Jersey was right, we came out of that quicksand better than before, and clawing our way back to credit worthiness was worth the feeling that came in knowing we did it together, the right way.

I also learned a lesson about debts and forgiveness. *And forgive us our debts as we forgive our debtors, was the Lord's exemplary appeal.* As the hunted I have known the anguish of debt, of the need for compassion and understanding when we find ourselves trapped in the jaws of our own greed. As the hunter I ask forgiveness of the woman in New Hampshire for sporting with her, and I don't think I'll ever hunt again.

62

CHEAP THRILLS

Today everything seems to have a price. It seems we can't do much without paying for it. Learning? Well, just listen to the politicians and they'll tell you that it's simply a matter of applying more money to the scale, and on the opposite side of the scale learning somehow rises. I've never really seen that, but they keep saying it and taxing us for it, so someone believes it. But enough of politics; what about play? Well, play costs between $199 and $399 for the game system and games of your choice. That's it. If you don't have one, you can't have friends over to play. If you want to go "out" and play, then it's going to cost you roughly $50 to $200 for a squirt gun or air gun, or the same amount to go to lunch and shopping at the mall with friends.

Play has become so narrowly defined and pre-packaged that our kids may be losing the ability to really play – that activity where you and your friends get together and make up something out of thin air, set your own rules, and do together every day when school is out. No parents intrude to enforce the rules or to ensure that everyone is treated fairly – good play is self-enforcing.

Living just up the street from my cousins, we always had five boys and two baby sisters to start something. Here's a little history lesson about a few games we played. By today's cold metrics, if you were to estimate an average cost per kid, you could take the cost of materials, multiplied by the number of kids, and divided by the number of games played, and you could come up with a cost that would be miserly, but when added to the memories made, the return on investment would be priceless. Next time your kids or grandkids get together, inspire them to make up their own game with their own rules – but be ready for hurt feelings, physical injury, and pouting – that's what really made games worth playing after all. When the stakes are high, play is meaningful and unrelenting.

Blue Blob

Blue Blob was inspired by sleepovers at our cousins' house when someone put a blue down sleeping back over his head and started crashing into people and things. We thought this was great sport, so we all did it. The rule was simply to put a sleeping bag over your entire body and run around, blindly crashing into each other and into furniture. This meant that eventually a big pile of blue blobs would accumulate somewhere in the room as one tripped, then another, and another, like some sort of amoebic crash test dummies. The one on the bottom got smothered, but you had to get off the pile within a reasonable period of time. In Blue Blob there was no winner, but usually someone would get hurt or would whine about always getting smothered, and then we would all join in blaming that person for "ruining another game." Ruining it for everyone else was a capital offense, so we played as long as we could, through rug burns, near suffocation, and bumped heads.

Ball in the Hall

Like Blue Blob, Ball in the Hall was another game with very simple rules. This involved any ball smaller than a basketball – preferably one that was a little soft, like a volleyball or playground ball (for you youngsters out there, a playground was where kids in school used to go during recess, usually a 15-20 minute break in the morning and afternoon for kids to just play). This two-player game involved stationing each player at the end of a long hall in the kneeling position, and they would proceed to hit the ball back and forth until it got by one of the players. If the ball made it clean by the other player, no touches, it was 3 points; a deflection was worth 1 point as long as it went through the player to hit behind them. Ball in the Hall was great, but it did have a bad impact on the light fixtures. No problem, we just made up a rule that to score, the ball had to remain on the ground (carpet).

Spot

Moving up in complexity there was Spot, a game our neighbor invented so that we could have more people play on their trampoline. If you have ever jumped on a trampoline, you will know that three is a crowd, so Spot allowed for two jumpers, one on each half of the rectangular trampoline, and a third person seated on the side of the trampoline, back to the jumpers. This "it" person had to call out a particular move, like "seat drops" or "back drops" and both jumpers had to comply or they were out if spotted by the person on the side doing the move incorrectly or attempting to do a flip. The jumpers could "earn" freedom from getting out by doing five flips without getting caught – little tiny ones from the crawl position or backward from a backdrop, or grand forward or back flips from the standing position. Spot masters could even do a suicide flip, which was a forward flip where the jumper looked at the mat and didn't tuck their head in until the last minute. Injurious? Oh yes. But we played Spot in the summertime from mid afternoon until the floodlights came on and parents finally "ruined another game."

Frozen Tag

Of course everyone knows the game of tag, but what about Frozen Tag? In our neighborhood there was a triangle where three roads intersected, and the patch of grass on the triangle was about half the size of a football field, and it was perfect for Frozen Tag. In this game, if you got touched by the "it" person, you had to stand in place, legs apart until someone who wasn't "it" crawled through your legs to unfreeze you before the "it" person could freeze everyone.

Other Diversions

We had so many other diversions: We made stop-motion movies using an old Super 8 movie camera and dress-ups from hand-me-down clothes and garage sales; we made radio shows on old cassette tape recorders, complete with sound effects; we wrote the rudiments of a script and then ad-libbed the rest; and we had drawing contests to see who could create the best architectural drawing of a futuristic house or a space ship. If we got tired of those things, we reverted back to playing "Big People" – usually a process of dressing up and adopting roles of spies, soldiers, police, and other admired characters – or "Little People", which involved pooling all of our small army men, cowboys and Indians, knights, and creating villages made of Legos and Lincoln Logs. I suppose if we had been properly indoctrinated back then, we would have celebrated the multicultural aspects of our village, but instead we spent afternoons carefully orchestrating attacks from different sectors of the village to see which group would win. These precision attacks would occasionally be undone when the call for Kick the Can came, and you had to do Godzilla attacks, stomping through wide swaths of town to wipe out the losers immediately, in order to make it outside in time.

Kick the Can

We also played a lot of Kick-the-Can. A game of Kick-the-Can was a neighborhood-wide call to action, and we could usually round up ten to twelve kids who were willing to play this advanced version of hide-n-seek. The ritual was well-known by anyone who was part of the game, and it always began with a round of My Blue Shoe to pick the "it" person. Some new kids called it My Blue Show, but they would be wrong – it was blue because Keds were blue, as all kids knew. Everyone put one foot in, like the nucleus of a Hokey Pokey song, and one person – usually the oldest – recited New Blue Shoe while tapping each shoe in turn:

"New blue shoe how old are you?"
"I'm ten."
"One, two, three, four, five, six, seven…" and eventually one kid was eliminated. This continued until all kids but one – the "it" – had been eliminated. As you can tell, just getting through New Blue Shoe was a bit time consuming, but it's how it worked. Next we set the physical boundaries for the game. It had to be at least three houses together.

"Okay, I say Peterson's front yard, our front and backyard, and Roses' front and backyard."
"No backyards, only front yards."
"Okay, but window wells are in."
"Right, but no climbing trees."

Kick-the-Can always started at dusk; that way, your degree of difficulty in finding your hidden friends went up considerably, and you really got creative so you didn't have to be "it." After all the kids had been found, and the seeker was making his rounds, the tension built.

"Do you know where Jeff is?"
"Shh. He's right over there, under Petersons' car. Don't look at him!"

Then, just as the seeker was closing in, the final hidden person would make a break for the can, and the seeker would join the sprint to the can to say the imprisoning words "over the can on (name)", locking away the final hider and giving up the "it" title for a turn. But no, the hider would make it there a step ahead, and kick the can down the street, freeing the prisoners and sending the "it" back into counting mode while everyone scattered for new hiding places.

So when I see kids stuck in front of a video game, I mourn the loss. "Why don't you guys go out and do something fun?" I plead.

Their reply hits me like a boomerang from my childhood, "Thanks Dad, you ruined another game!"

63

CHAOS AND CLARITY: THE TOKYO EARTHQUAKES

Friday afternoon, March 11, 2011 marked the ending of another long week in Tokyo for me. It had started with the same 14 hour flight from Chicago on Tuesday, and was marked by two full days of meetings Wednesday and Thursday with my project team culminating in a presentation made to our corporate officers on Friday morning. We had a bit of a scare on Wednesday just before lunch when our building began to rumble, and then swayed back and forth from what turned out to be a 7.3 earthquake that had hit off the northeast coast of Japan. The next morning, I was awakened sometime around 3:00am in my hotel room by what sounded like a rake being scraped along the wall opposite my 15th floor room. When the room began to sway, I realized the noise was the sound of the building reacting to another earthquake, and five minutes later, another, both in the 6.0 magnitude range.

Our project team was happy to have just finished up preliminary designs for an upcoming two-year executive development program, and we had begun our final agenda item for the week. If we could finish by 3:30 or 4:00, we could still catch the trains over to Asakusa, on the other side of Tokyo, where we planned on doing some souvenir shopping. I was at the end of a small conference table, surrounded by Kathy, my colleague from our Chicago office, Sean, our "mate" from the London office, project leader Chad, an 18-year resident of Tokyo, and Sasaki-san, our other team member from the Tokyo office. We had complained for three days about the stifling heat in our windowless conference room, and the remnants of empty soda cans and cookie wrappers signaled we were near the end.

Then it hit. At 2:45pm, our room began to pulsate vertically, not like the swaying motion on Wednesday. This felt as if the building were going over speed bumps. I looked to Sasaki-san on my right, and he said, in Japanese, "This is different…it's big…it's big…it's HUGE…" and then we all got under the conference table. The bumping, rolling, and swaying became more severe and it took some effort just to stay on hands and knees. We could hear people down the hall in another conference room scream. The jerky motion kept going for what must have been about a minute. I wondered what it would feel like to ride a building from our eighth floor conference room to the ground floor. Would the floor collapse? Would the ceiling collapse? or would the whole thing just simply teeter over? At that moment it seemed inevitable, but then it stopped. We got up, and I went to the doorway and looked down the hall. Nobody. Then the shaking started again, as bad as before. I came back in and got under the table with the others, and I noticed the door to our room swinging back and forth wildly.

Another minute or so, and then it stopped. Now what? We had survived, but what had the damage been?

Sasaki-san checked online and saw that first estimates put the earthquake epicenter near Sendai, about 150 miles north, and it was a 7.9. This was later updated to 8.9. He said a fire was burning at a telecom office building, and several people on our floor reported that the building across the road had several broken and missing windows. A tsunami warning was issued for the entire east coast of the main island of Honshu and on up to Hokkaido island. We were far enough inland, and Tokyo harbor sits over an isthmus that protects it direct exposure to the open Pacific, so we weren't too concerned about possible tsunami damage where we were.

We discussed options while various announcements came through the loudspeaker in our office. Everyone was asked to stay inside for fear of falling objects outside, although other buildings were being evacuated around the city. Chad decided to go down one flight of stairs to recover some earthquake emergency kits for us, and when he returned we donned our helmets and took some relief in having penlights for later on, although later that night I opened my penlight and found that it didn't work – no batteries. We all marched down the stairs to the seventh floor where we saw employees seated at their desks, many of them checking information online and others watching a TV monitor that had been set up to watch the updates. Some had their hardhats on, others didn't. From what we saw, there hadn't been any damage, although a report from another American working in our Tokyo office said that a ceiling had collapsed in his area, but no one had been injured.

We decided to make our way back to the hotel, determined that there was nothing more we could do in the office, and we also wanted our colleagues to go tend to their families rather than worrying about the three of us. They were somewhat reluctant, but relented, and we walked down the stairs and out to the street, accompanied by Sasaki-san, who walked with us until he was comfortable that we could go the rest of the way on our own without getting lost. We walked about ten blocks back to our hotel, and I was amazed that there were no significant signs of damage. We saw a few broken windows, but nothing else. Crowds were moving on the sidewalks, but no one appeared to be panicked, and others had already gone back to their tasks.

When we arrived at the Royal Park Hotel, our twenty-story home for the week, we saw that the spacious lobby was occupied by hundreds of people sitting under blankets, and the center area had been roped off. This was done as a precaution because of the possibility of falling glass from the crystal light fixtures overhead that spanned about 30 feet wide and 70 feet long. The hotel staff informed us that no one was allowed up to their rooms or down to the basement restaurants and shops. They were inspecting our rooms for damage and would inform us once we were able to return.

The lobby of the hotel consisted of guests and others who were looking for shelter. Businessmen tapped on Blackberries and laptops while others gathered by a small radio set out by the staff, and others tried to work out their plans for getting home. Sean, Kathy and I sat on the floor and took turns sharing a hotel chair. A whiteboard was set up by the reception desk and on it the hotel updated information in English and Japanese about trains and busses, all of which had stopped operating, and also gave the latest about the expressways, which had also been closed. The two airports serving Tokyo were also closed. Later a TV was set up in the lobby, and chairs in rows were set out to watch. During our wait, the aftershocks had continued. Every few minutes we would feel the hotel move, and we would look up at the chandeliers to confirm the occurrence. No one acted panicked, and most were calm and waited patiently.

After about three hours in the lobby, the hotel staff announced that they would begin bringing guests to their rooms, so they asked us to come up to the large ballroom on the second floor. Those who showed their room keys were allowed inside, where tables had been set and long banquet areas were readied to serve. This impromptu buffet was such a relief for us, and we were able to sit and have some time to fill our stomachs for an hour or so until room numbers started to be called. One by one, the hotel staff announcer would read off a number, and a staff member would write the number on a whiteboard, and we were taken in groups to the one working elevator.

When I got off my floor and went to my room I noticed some rooms had yellow post-in notes on the doors and others did not. I assumed this had to do with rooms that had been inspected and were ready for occupation. When I entered my room everything was in order. I couldn't tell that anything had occurred. Then I noticed that the hanging lamp over my desk was missing half of its shade that had obviously been broken off. This fixture was at least a foot from the nearest wall, and it was a pretty heavy material, so the room must have been rocking pretty badly for it to swing with enough force to break it. The staff had already cleaned up the debris, and I suspect they had to do more than that to ready our rooms.

The three of us had agreed to go to our rooms, change into our street clothes and meet back in the lobby, and the aftershocks that continued to sway the hotel provided a bit of additional motivation to change quickly and walk down the fifteen flights of stairs to the lobby. We didn't really have much of a plan, but we decided that walking around outside in the fresh air was more appealing than either the lobby or our rooms. Most businesses had closed by that time, and even the twenty-four hour McDonalds down the street was closed, either due to damage or perhaps to let the staff return home. The streets were congested with traffic as far as we could see, and the sidewalks were also jammed with people scurrying to get home. Several subway lines began operating again, and people headed into the stations to start their journeys home.

We decided to stop in a convenience store to buy a few drinks and snacks, thinking that we might want to have a few things on hand for ourselves. I noticed that some of the shelves were already empty. Without much left to see or do, we concluded that going back to our rooms and hunkering down for the night was probably a reasonable thing to do, although it was clear that none of us felt that a sound night's sleep was really going to happen.

Friday night I stayed up late into the night sending emails and checking information online from the various news sources. While my Japanese is generally pretty good for news programs, I had some deficiencies about nuclear power plant vocabulary, and that story started to become a more serious threat. Kathy, Sean and I continued to email each other during the night, and we would send each other messages after a major aftershock, sometimes calling each other's rooms to hear the reassurance of another friendly voice. Finally I nodded off with the news station still on and woke about four hours later. It was ironic that the earthquake that had stirred me from sleep on Thursday morning was probably not of enough magnitude to wake me on Saturday morning.

Although our flights were likely to be cancelled on Saturday (originally set for 11:30am), we three agreed that getting to the airport, closed or not, was probably the prudent thing to do so that we could rearrange flights and still have a possible way to get out that day. Busses were still not running, so our best option was to catch a taxi to the airport, and the sooner the better, we judged. We gathered our things, checked out of the hotel, and went outside to the taxi stand around 6:15am. No one was there, and no taxis were lined up waiting for guests. Sean and I went out to the street to hail taxis. One driver I stopped said he had been up all night and was going home and not taking any more fares. Just then, a lone taxi pulled into the hotel.

The line at the taxi stand had grown to about twenty people, but fortunately Kathy was still at the front of the line with our bags. A woman exited the taxi and told us that she had been in the car for thirteen hours. The driver, an older gentleman, looked haggard and said he wasn't going to take any more passengers. Others were trying to convince him to take them to the airport, but the bellman and another guest farther back in line signaled to us that we were first in line and should take the taxi. Another man had stepped over to the driver and I could see that he was offering several ten thousand yen notes to him, a bribe to jump to the front of the line; but the driver agreed to take us; and with some trepidation, we stuffed our belongings in the small trunk and pulled out of the hotel around 6:45am.

The first hour was spent traveling maybe one mile, maybe less, in traffic as far as we could see. The second was about the same. As we made our way in the line of traffic, we texted our office, Kathy on her Blackberry, and me, on my iPhone. We were able to secure back-up accommodations at the Hotel Nikko, close to the airport, so we had our office cancel our arrangements at the Intercontinental in Tokyo. It was our commitment to leave the city and take our chances at the airport. Flights were booked for us the next day, Sunday, once we realized we were unlikely to make it to the airport in time; but we hoped to secure another flight out. Any flight.

As we continued our serpentine track toward the airport, Kathy and Sean both fell asleep, and I quietly surveyed the sights outside the window. Although I didn't say it out loud, my tension increased and decreased as we went up hills and then down by the river, thinking that if another earthquake hit, and if it generated another tsunami, we could be caught in a dangerous low lying area. Here and there I began to notice evidence of the earthquake. A sidewalk running parallel to an ocean inlet had sunk nearly a foot for several hundred yards. In one small town, black sandy mud covered the sidewalks, and in some places had been shoveled away like black snow. Hillsides bore the cracks and crevasses of recent movement, and at one point our driver said that the bumpiness of the road was due to the earthquake.

Arriving at Narita airport around 2:00pm, we were encouraged to see that it was bustling with people, and we had seen at least one flight take off as we approached. Our driver handed us the bill, about $300 since the meter ran solely on distance rather than time. I handed him my credit card, but he said he needed cash. This man had taken a chance on us, and in the process he had also missed a neighbor's wedding that was scheduled for noon. I felt terrible that the three of us didn't have enough cash, so I ran into the airport and tried, without success, to access cash at an ATM. Returning, I told the driver I wasn't able to get any cash, and he finally took my card. I asked Kathy for 5000 yen, and I combined it with my 5000 cash, so we ended up charging the fare and giving him an extra $120 on top for his trouble. He was surprised and grateful.

Sean had been able to secure an earlier flight from our taxi on the way to the airport, and as soon as we arrived, he headed off; and he emailed us that he had made his flight and was on his way. We were so relieved that he had made it, and our spirits were lifted as we waited in line to try our chances at rebooking. We waited in line for an hour or so, and we were able to see people at their best and worst. Two businessmen tried to cut in to the front of the line, and they were roundly criticized by the gentleman next to me, but their crass response was, "You'll have to take it up with the airline." The agents at the reservation desk were professional and courteous as ever. Kathy and I discussed our strategy. We would try to change to one of the flights going to the US, either the direct Chicago route, or San Francisco or Washington D.C., and if that didn't work, we might try another route to get to the U.S., such as through Seoul.

Although there were fewer aftershocks, the real threat remaining was north at the Fukushima Nuclear Plant, where the earthquake had cut power, causing their initial cooling station to fail; and then the tsunami hit the plant, causing the back-up diesel cooling system to fail, leaving only a third option for the engineers, pumping sea water directly in to cool it. There had already been an explosion at the facility, and although the reports from the local news said there was no danger, it was clear from some of the foreign press that it was a matter of doubt about how much radiation had leaked into the atmosphere. So in our minds, the biggest threat was of a nuclear meltdown or other catastrophic event that could have sent a radioactive cloud our direction. However unlikely, this gave us the additional motivation to find any flight out that day.

Despite our most polite and patient requests of Miss Sato, our agent, she wasn't able to book us on another flight for Saturday, so we made sure we were on our flights for Sunday, and we resigned ourselves to stay at the Hotel Nikko for the night. After having lunch at McDonalds (where there were only a handful of items that weren't sold out), and stopping at a book store in the airport for a few minutes, we called the hotel and learned that they had an airport shuttle bus we could catch. It was only about ten minutes away, so we were confident that we could get there and still make it back the next day to catch our flights, Kathy's at 10:30am and mine at 5:00pm. The hotel had a convenience store in it, so we stopped and picked up a few items, noting that the shelves were emptying. The aftershocks continued, and after one especially rude tremor, Kathy called just to check in. Somehow, being on the third floor of the hotel gave me a false sense of security. After the long day of travel, I was so tired that when I got to my room I sent a few email messages and then laid on the bed and fell asleep with the news still on.

Sunday morning was another sunny day, and the plan was that Kathy would catch the first shuttle to the airport at 5:45am, and that she would call to let me know that she had made it to her flight. I waited until about 7:30am, but still hadn't received any word, and I was worried both that she might have had trouble and that I might do well to get on my way. Hearing of power outages and fuel shortages on the news, I worried that the shuttle bus might not be running later, so I gathered my things and checked out, making it onto the 8:00am shuttle. I decided that I would try to get through the check-in process and security, and try to find Kathy at the gate.

The airport was packed with people, and I waited to check in, hoping that I wouldn't have any problems checking in so early. When I got to the counter the agent said that I was only on stand-by for the flight, but I told him my flight was confirmed. I tried, somewhat frantically, to find my itinerary on my laptop to show the agent, and as I searched and found it, I immediately lost battery power to my laptop. I texted my office and luckily

279

I was able to get the itinerary sent to my personal email address, so I accessed it on my iPhone. After a few more conversations with another agent, they were finally able to issue my boarding pass and I was on my way.

By this time, I was learning to anticipate my next moves. The airport lounge was closed (it was mostly surrounded by glass, which isn't so good in the middle of an earthquake and aftershocks), but they gave me a food voucher to use. I decided to stop, grab something to eat, and not risk that the shops closer to the gates could have run out of food. If for some reason my flight wasn't leaving, I would have had at least a good meal that day, I reasoned.

I went to the gate and met Kathy, and also ran into our CEO, Seigo, and the CEO of our R&D division, Steve. We were all glad to have made it, and we were catching up on the events of the last two days when another aftershock hit. It was big enough that the windows rattled and the whole building shook fiercely. We were sitting by large windows, so I called out that we should move, and I grabbed my bag and ran across the gate area. Only a couple of others had moved, and I felt foolish, the only paranoid one in a crowd – great. Obviously I was still a bit jittery.

My three colleagues made their flight out, and I was left pulling up the rear, so I found a place to charge my laptop and my iPhone, and waited at the gate reading a book until it was time to go. The situation at the nuclear plant appeared to be growing worse as I prepared to board; and when the plane finally lifted off the tarmac, I leaned back into my seat with mixed feelings. I was happy to be going home, but sad to know that others were left, and I couldn't help them. In my bag were a few snacks and treats I was taking home, and I worried that in my eagerness to bring home food, I might have taken from someone back there who needed it more than I.

I flew to Los Angeles, where I glumly went through customs. The officer noticed I was coming from Japan and he asked how it was over there. "It was bad," was all I said. I transferred to another flight back to Chicago. The TSA agent checking our boarding passes must have seen it on my face. He asked what kind of day I was having, and I just said, "not real good," and he said he hoped it would get better. I smiled at that.

On the way home I had time to think about the last couple of days, and I resolved a few things in my mind. First and most importantly, I resolved that I would never be in an emergency situation without food and water. I was also struck by the fact that in the middle of a disaster, you have to balance being calm and cool with being appropriately active and engaged, focused. A calm focus is something that I hope to cultivate. I recalled a conversation that Kathy and I had as we were going through the experience. I commented how funny it was that we were making decisions in some cases judging not whether it was the safest thing to do, but based on how it might be perceived twenty-four hours from now. For example, if we had flown to Seoul or Shanghai because we couldn't get a flight to the states, and if the nuclear problem had prevented us from getting out of Japan, or worse, then getting that flight – no matter the cost or time delays – would have been a brilliant decision. But if the threat didn't materialize, it would be viewed as overreacting and foolish. That's the paradox we found ourselves in.

As I continue to watch the news reports, where so many reporters have descended on the destruction in Sendai, and have intentionally put themselves in harm's way nearer the still overheating plant in Fukushima, I wonder if they see the paradox. Will it be the greatest event to lift their inflated career ambitions, or will they regret having put themselves in danger if it comes? Only time will tell whether they made the right decision.

64

MY FATHER THE PHOENIX

What defines a man's success? We might look at his collection of goods – the house, the car, the suit of clothes – as one indicator. We could examine his family, the strength of his marriage, the nature of his children, and observe whether his wife treats him lovingly and whether his children are coarse or refined in manner. We might further look at the man's professional life and determine his title, his ranking among his peers, and the extent to which well respected leaders defer to his judgment and employees place in him their trust and their livelihood, and speak of him in tones of respect and warm regard. We could examine other parts of his life, and find in him harmony of purpose, an alignment of will, and a devotion to those qualities that define his character: honesty, integrity, faith, kindness, and so on. These would resonate not from his spoken words, but from his daily example as he responds to the tests of life.

By these simple criteria, my father had achieved success by the time I had reached my teenage years.

Our sprawling one-level house had been gradually remodeled, and finally conveyed the warmth my parents wanted to provide for their children, extended family, and friends they entertained in the formal living and dining spaces or out on the expansive back porch. We had a tennis court in our backyard which doubled occasionally as a square-dance floor for the church's summer party. We had two driveways – one leading to the garage and another arcing gently behind a flagstone wall – another source of contention between my brother and me when the snow fell, to see who would have to shovel the long driveway. Parked in the garage was a large luxury car my dad bought, and he sometimes joked about the absurdity of it – the Daddy Warbucks car. Luxury both suited his refinement and insulted his humility.

He was vice-president of a successful family business, a chain of upscale clothing stores, and he was the head buyer for the men's department. His closet – actually *closets* – burst with the finest suits, dress shirts and slacks, and a colorful array of ties and pocket silks. The musky scent of leather, cedar and a hint of work-worn odor hung in the air inside his closet, reminders of his vast shoe line-up that rivaled or bettered my mother's collection. He was a snappy dresser, even on weekends, when he traded the professional wear for more casual knits and a golf hat.

He and my mother had been married forever and raised six children who were – with a few exceptions – trying to emulate the good life they had been shown in their formative years. My older brother and I were still at home finishing our high schooling and picking up summertime jobs at "the warehouse," the corporate offices and distribution center for our father's business, or helping out in one of the stores on special sale days.

Life at the warehouse was a familial extension of my father's home and church life. Wherever I went with him, I was always greeted warmly by the receptionist, who knew my name, and as we arrived at my father's office in the executive row, his secretary would bring him up to date on the day's business and hand him the latest sales reports. If he needed to check on-hand inventory, we would go through the heavy steel door to the warehouse, and for me it was like flanking a celebrity. Line workers would call out welcomes to my father, and he might stop and catch up on their families and introduce me. Often, as I trailed behind him, workers would stop me and comment on my father's goodness, his personal concern for them, or the soundness of his character.

And then one day, the sun went down on his prosperity.

Through a series of financial missteps and ill-timed events, coupled with changing consumer trends, the family business began to crumble. The signs were slow at first. Now implanted as an assistant manager in one of the largest stores, I watched as merchandise flowed in with less regularity, and the goods landing on the loading dock were less and less impressive in their style, price-point, and hand – that unmistakable touch of quality that someone in the business feels between their fingers when introducing themselves to a new garment. Racks once bulging with leather coats and walls that had strained under the weight of men's and women's suits were now neatly spaced at larger increments both as a result of reduced inventory and increasing spare time for the salespeople.

In my pre-teen years, I had trailed along on store visits, where my father would check displays and talk with salespeople. I remember him gathering the selling staff in the shoe department and instructing them on some new brand of suit, pointing out the quality craftsmanship, knowing that these talking points had to be clearly translated to customers. Then he would make his challenge: Find two suits and build a wardrobe around them in five minutes. Ready…go! The salespeople would scramble throughout the department searching for the right combinations, the right accessorized complements, and then return to home base to display their selections.

Novices would make valiant attempts with a well matched suit, shirt, tie, and shoes; but the more experienced salespeople found two suits, four shirts, a selection of ties – with the faux-knot slipped under the collar and the shirt and tie laid under the lapel – matching belt, shoes, and yes, even shoe polish, consummate up-selling veteran showmanship. As each one displayed and described the selections and customer options for appealing to tastes bland and bold, my father beamed and gave honest and gentle commentary while the energized crew sat back in the store like horses ready to bolt at the sound of the gun when the store opened.

But years had passed, customers changed, and so did the buying-selling repartee, from "I need some help with a suit for a job interview," to "can someone ring this up for me?" The fire had gone out and the business simmered. As rumors about the business started, salespeople sulked and customers walked away, from a steady stream to a trickle of the merely loyal.

Chapter 11 bankruptcy was announced, and the slow decline accelerated. Outside of the stores, my father spent more time in bankruptcy hearings and depositions, and I saw something for the first time in my life, disparity. He had avoided it as long as I had known him, but now it slipped out on occasion when he would confide in me his detestation for the bank's lawyers or face his most faithful employees who were themselves facing uncertain futures. He aged by years as the days rolled on; his walk slowed, and his shoulders visibly slumped as the weight of events appeared to crush him.

But the court must have seen his integrity because he was appointed to be the last man standing among the executive team, the one to bring in the liquidators, the one to convey the waves of bad news to employees. In the midst of this, I recall another visit to the warehouse. New merchandise was flowing in from the liquidators in an attempt to squeeze some additional profit from the dying business, like a defibrillating shock before inevitable death. The old-timers were still there, processing merchandise, driving trucks, answering phones; but the lights were dimmer, whether literally as a result of expense slashing or from the depressive mood, I wasn't sure. My dad told me that those who had counted on retirement funds would fall to the back of the line behind creditors, and likely would never see a dime of what the company owed them. He didn't acknowledge at the time that the same was true for himself. His office, once stately and dignified – with the Lincoln painting and family portraits greeting visitors – was littered with reports and invoices, and the lanky liquidation boss peered over the business like the Reaper come to collect his corpses. But he was a merchant, and so was my dad, and they somehow related like friends peering over the same tombstone in a graveyard.

I witnessed the great decline from inside the company's flagship store, and watched as the business folded in on itself, receding racks, declining staff, and buzzard customers in for a quick bargain – and the occasional kind word for "that really kind man with the white hair who helped me once." Sometimes I admitted to being his son, and at other times I identified the man and shared in the admiration anonymously.

At the end I went to the warehouse and found him there hawking the last remnants of racks, conveyor belts, computers, desks, carts, and making the last buck that would justify one more day's pay. He was ever the optimist, and I was struck with the absurdity of it – he had lost everything!

But no, he had something left on which to build. He had experience as a premier buyer and a solid reputation with good friends who knew of his hardship. Above all, he had a wife and family who were ready and willing to rally if given the chance. I don't know at what point he began to plan his next move, his revival; but I'd like to think it was in the middle of those scraps of the old company when ambition stirred again.

If could have been a Coppola movie. Friends came to his aid lending money on a handshake, and many with a no strings attached clause implied. Wholesalers and manufacturers began to line up. A small space opened up just down that hall from that flagship location of the old store, and a lease was consummated. The family rallied around him. My mother, who had taught piano for decades, increased her load of students to put food on the table. I remember tearing out old aluminum studded walls with my brother

285

and clearing space for The Sock Box. Others worked behind the scenes helping with shipments, pricing guns and spreading the word. In quick order the place was assembled, display windows were prettied, and he was open for business behind the classy wooden entrance and the brilliant neon sign.

This was not the grand scale enterprise he had known, but it was everything a merchant needed: a store front, goods to sell, and available customers. He practically wore the store as a part of him. Fast-food shoppers in for a pair of socks would be greeted by the kindly gentleman who was ever willing to up-sell them with an extra pair, or a t-shirt, or novelty pair of skivvies. If he didn't have the socks the customer casually mentioned, he would take their name, place a special order, and call them when the socks arrived. That was for socks – not cars – socks.

When most men who had worked decades at their craft had settled in for a sedentary retirement, my dad was in the throes of starting a business, generating his own income, and staying ahead of creditors. There he stayed for twelve years, working well into his seventies.

Eventually it became time for him to liquidate his business. Redemption complete, he brought in his own bargain items and held a blowout event to extract from this vibrant business one last race. It was his choice, his time, and he went out with head held high. When loyal customers came to express their condolences regarding the store's untimely demise, he warmly thanked them for their patronage and acknowledged the good fortune that he had experienced in the intervening years.

And so we might ask again what it is that defined this man's success, his rise from the ashes, and the answer is clear. Certainly gratitude extends to supportive family, and friends willing to place a bet on the man's reputation. But the measure of success begins at the inflection point from despair to hope. Despairing, he could have rested, waited, depended, and reflected. Instead, he explored, searched, confided, and wagered on himself. How sure was that bet?

Well, a younger, less experienced man might have cautiously questioned his own ability, casting in against an unknown opponent: himself. The wise man knows his heights and depths, has scaled the walls out of the pit on many occasions, and looks in the mirror differently. The young man searches for answers he does not know, the old man searches for will to do what he knows. But with time running out, the competition growing ever fiercer, he lopes to the starting gates, this time with four pairs of socks, a selection of ties, some novelty underwear, and probably a lone shoe polish, ever the showman…the phoenix spreads his wings.

65

FIDDLING ON THE ROOF

Climbing onto the roof of a house produces an instantaneous magical shift of perspective. In that awkward moment of transition from the ladder to the shingles you consider the distance of the potential fall, the steadiness of the ladder under your last step, and whether the gritty hold provided by the shingles is enough to stop your gravitational pull over the edge. Standing upright on a rooftop is the closest many of us come to that feeling of reaching the summit of a great mountain. We stand above all others, looking down from our royal vantage point like a king surveying his kingdom. Straddling the peak of the roof is a bit like posing atop a large beast just slain on life's safari – ah yes, snap another photograph of the victorious hunter.

Of course, even monarchs and great hunters have to face the gathering mongrel forces arrayed against them or thundering herds of charging pachyderms. At such times, I would like to think of the monarch shriveling in the corner of the castle in fear. I want the hunter to dive under the Jeep clutching his elephant gun spitting prayers into the dusty savannah. That would somehow justify the position in which I found myself one day atop grandpa's roof.

My enemy? The swamp cooler.

I had grown up in a part of the country where humidity was low, and when temperatures would rise in the summer months you had two options, to power up the central air conditioner through the quaint click of the thermostat from "heat" to "cool," or you could reach the weighty decision of launching the swamp cooler. This bayou box was about the same size as a regular air conditioning unit, and usually sat atop the roof in some central location for the house where it could force cool air down to the impatient sweaty dwellers. Swamp coolers functioned by sucking air through water-cooled straw panels on four sides and blowing that air into the home.

Of course, proximity to the swamp cooler in houses cooled by them meant either you were subjected to the roar of the wind tunnel with the welcome arctic blasts of air or the faintest whirr and wisp of a cold front somewhere in a distant part of the house. Since starting up the cooler involved going topside, it had an interesting way of moving down the "to-do" list until the combination of nagging and whining virtually propelled the reluctant climber onto the ladder.

At summer's end, the homeowner had to again venture roofward to winterize the swamp cooler. This meant accessing the proper panel in the unit, shutting off the water line, and draining the swamp, the housing that held about four inches of water when the unit was fully functioning. Procrastinating this task meant climbing onto the roof in cold, or possibly freezing, temperatures when the swamp water was particularly fetid and the shingles were slick with rain, sleet or snow.

I know this from personal experience.

There I was, scaling the ladder to winterize the swamp cooler at grandpa's house after the first snowfall of the season. My wife and I were living in her grandfather's basement while I attended university just a few miles from the tidy little bungalow that had once known house payments of a hundred bucks or so in the post war boom. What sent me into the clouds was not so much the incumbent shame of constant nagging, but the guilt of sending an octogenarian up the ladder to certain death. Of course, the mind rationalizes. If Santa and all these reindeer can do just fine up there…and he's a pretty old guy…well, you can see the futility of vocalizing that line of reasoning.

So up I went. I found the old ladder in the detached garage, its rungs looking more like aged driftwood, and leaned it up against the house. I sunk the bottom end of the ladder into soft ground and remnants of snow that had begun to melt despite the chill in the air, and the top of the ladder just cleared the roofline by a foot or so. That last transition from ladder to roof was tricky, but I pushed off the last rung and hugged the roof like a human gecko, only to watch the ladder fall away, dipping under the roofline and out of view like a sinking vessel into the vast ocean. My heart sunk, but in my state of clinging to hope, the ladder was not an immediate concern.

Having experience as a winterizer, I knew it wouldn't take long for me to complete the task, so I hadn't taken the time to don a parka or gloves. Climbing onto the roof, I suddenly faced several other realities that had not occurred to me before leaving mother earth. First, I was on a roof that was partially covered in snow; second, I was wearing sneakers meant for gym floors, not snow-topped peaks; and third, even if the ladder were still in place, the angle of the roof and the slight clearance of the top of the recently departed ladder would have made my descent a gripping backward creep of faith. I decided that I might as well take care of the swamp cooler – since I was up there anyway, and might be for some time – and then I would deal with the other unfortunate circumstance.

Getting to the swamp cooler was a bit of a challenge, because in front of it was a patch of snow. If I had brought my toboggan up with me, it would be a gloriously quick slide down the roof, with a predictable nose dive at the end. Luckily, I was in jeans, and they had a solid grip, so I crab-crawled backwards up the roof incline to the side of the cooler where I removed the panel and the plug to the housing, draining the water down the icy shingles. The task completed, I turned my attention to the next great challenge, getting off the roof without breaking a limb.

What were my options? Like some urban scout, I began mulling the possibilities. I could climb over the roof to the other side and hope that it's clear over there, but that meant moving when the footing was unsure at best already, no. I could try for a controlled slide down the roof and hope that the ground was soft enough to prevent broken ankles, but that seemed too desperate. After all, grandpa was inside.

Should I yell to him? Does he have his hearing aids in, and would he freeze to death trying to save me? If I screamed, would the neighbors hear and come to my aid? Would I want them to find me there, the procrastinating idiot who didn't bother to wear any winter gear and headed up a ladder after a snowfall? The broken ankle was looking better, I concluded.

In a MacGyver-esque moment, I removed my belt and looped it around one of the support legs of the swamp cooler, and held on to the end thinking it would help slow my descent so that I could slide only a few feet after releasing the belt before I continued sliding past the roofline, and then I could attempt to grab the rain gutter before reaching the inevitable conclusion, like my toboggan fantasy moments earlier. Of course, the other possibility was that instead of landing on soft wet ground, I might land atop the fallen ladder.

Just then, grandpa came outside. It must have been that time of day when he went to the store to fetch his beloved Danish cringle. That meant that he would have his hearing aids in, and he would be dressed like he was entering the Iditarod, a stark contrast to my dressing for the wrong occasion.

"Grandpa!" I yelled. The top of his head twisted left and right, but not up.

"Grandpa! Up HERE!" I yelled again, looking to see if any neighbors were stepping outside at the calls for help.

Now looking up, but not catching my view quite yet, he called, "Well what are you doin' up there? And no coat?"

"Yep. Umm, listen, if you could help me with something…" I began proclaiming.

After listing off the error of my ways that left me stranded on the roof, he heard my public confessional and soon grasped that the ladder had fallen and needed to be replaced. Soon I saw the rise of the ladder again, as if grandpa were one of the marauders about to scale the castle walls; but no, he misjudged the height of the roofline and the ladder fell against the side of the house out of reach. This brought up another interesting dilemma, the window was directly below that area, so it was now possible, if not likely based on his first attempt, that the ladder would fall into the window and send shards of glass into grandpa's kindly face, and leave a carpet of shiny daggers on which I could gently fall. It was like an episode from Looney Tunes.

After several attempts on his part and my chilly encouragement from above, he finally got the ladder in the right spot where I could make my attempt. Grabbing the end of the make-shift belt-rope, and crawling backwards on my belly, my foot touched the welcome top of the ladder. I released my grip on the belt, went into gecko cling mode, and inched backward to the ladder. Grandpa stood there at the bottom of the ladder holding it steady. Luckily, he had placed the ladder so that more of it was visible above the roofline, but this also meant that the angle of incline was steeper, so I could only imagine stepping onto the ladder and falling backwards on top of him, crushing him into perfectly square pieces like some kind of onion dicing gadget.

He stood his ground and I descended, clinging to the worn rungs. Oh, I forgot to mention that the rungs were starting to pull away from the sides of the ladder, so it might have been my final fate to see the ladder suddenly split apart and turn into stilts – another Looney Tunes bit fit for laughter when, as a young boy, I might have been found lounging comfortably in my bean-bag chair eating cereal rather than hanging from rooftops. Spared this final insult, I set foot back on solid ground, hoping that grandpa's poor memory would erase this unfortunate incident from his mind and limit the risk of this swamp cooler tale being told over Thanksgiving dinner. Whether by his poor memory or simply by his own conscious choice, as a man who had seen far worse in his day, he never repeated the incident. The belt was recovered the next spring.

James Taylor once wrote a song about being up on the roof, where all your troubles would melt away. Having spent time on the roof, where the snows were not melting away and where troubles only multiplied, I could add a few stanzas to his tune. Needless to say, buy central air, don't hang Christmas lights by going up there, and leave the fiddling on the roof to someone with boots and scaffolding.

66

A LESSON FROM THE NEEDLE PICKERS

Once, when visiting an ancient Buddhist temple in Japan, my wife and I came across a group of workers unlike any we had seen. We had been walking down a winding dirt road on our way to the main temple complex when we passed through an open area where several walkways met, surrounded by many evergreens. Nearby was a stand of bamboo with tiny white wildflowers covering the ground below. But what caught our attention were several large blue ground cloths at the base of some of the largest evergreen trees. The royal blue cloths were stark against the brown dusty roads and the green of the grass and shrubs.

As we approached the area, we saw that the drop cloths were covered with pine needles. Why would someone want to catch the falling pine needles, I thought. Then I heard a stirring overhead, and looking up, I saw a man cradled in the crook of the tree, perhaps fifteen feet above, about halfway up the tree's trunk. It was hard to tell at first, but as we looked around, we saw others in surrounding trees, with similar drop clothes full of needles. They were leaning out from the trunk to each branch and pulling off the needles one at a time. They appeared to be thinning out the evergreen branches because on the opposite sides of the trees the branches and foliage were slightly denser and uneven.

Watching them work, I noticed that each one seemed focused on his or her task so intently that no one was looking at us on the ground. When I was in school we used to study research papers about "time on task," that ability of research subjects, usually small children or starving college psych students, to remain working on a problem, solving puzzles, or – often just for contrast – engaging in playtime. From my own experience I can confirm that at two ends of the continuum you have teenage boys, whose time on task for video games starts at infinity and goes up, and at the other end are the same boys seen cleaning their rooms. This time on task begins at the touch of the first article of clothing and ends when the closet door slams shut on the vast pile of articles tossed in at chipmunk-like speed.

If these needle pickers were measured on quality of work as well as time on task, they would be the Olympic gold medalists. More than the awe-inspiring beauty of the trees, I was agog at how intently they looked at those spiky clumps, studying and then selecting which needle to pull in order to convey the most natural appearance in a most unnatural way. Couldn't there be a machine or a robot that could do as well? The thought passed from my mind the more I studied the workers. It was as if they had actually become part of the trees upon which they perched. I had seen pictures of sloths wrapped up in tree branches before, but they just sat there, not really doing anything – how slothful, and how unlike these workers.

As I think about the many tasks that fill my day, I wonder if I spend as much concentrated effort as these needle pickers. At work, my mind sets sail as I sit in meetings waiting for another hour to pass, wishing I could be somewhere else…maybe on a beach or hiking in the mountain air…and then I'm snapped back to the next droning speaker. At home, my attention scatters across several cable channels only to land on two shows that fight for my viewership every time a commercial break comes along. I'm a sloth, slow-moving, dim-witted, and I only stir from my perch to forage.

What if I applied the needle picker's meticulousness to other aspects of my life?

Maybe treating my email at work the same as a needle picker would force me to concentrate on those emails that were truly worthy of my attention, sending the emails with the subject line "FYI" falling to the ground. If I were to wrap myself around my work in a way that would allow me to spend several undistracted hours focused on the most important tasks, perhaps I would find new appreciation for what I had accomplished. I wonder if my boss would nip at my ankles like a herding dog if he could see my progress more clearly and observe my time spent on more worthy tasks. Maybe I could convince my colleagues to climb into the trees with me, and leave behind the mundane needle gathering on the ground for more elevated work. I might even ask for their opinions on my work more often. Does that branch look right to you?

What if I looked at my relationships with as careful an eye as those tree dwelling un-sloths? I would spread out my ground cloth, ascend into position in a comfortable nook where I was visible to all who entered, and then I would devote complete attention to the needles. I would start by thinning the browned and withered needles first by finding some obvious and undesirable task that made that clump in front of me ugly or out of place: empty the garbage, clean off the counter, put away something left out, do the dirty dishes, reduce the pile of dirty laundry.

Next I would search for the most vibrant, lightest green needles and make sure they weren't being crowded out by asking a few questions to my wife, "How was your day?" might be followed by "Anything I can do?" and then perhaps sharing a memory like, "Remember when we were in our first apartment." If we are lucky, she might climb onto the branch with me and we could prune the needles together for an hour or so, recalling the joys and sorrows of a life that grew this majestic tree.

With my boys I might lock eyes with them when asking how well their day was spent at work or school, and search in the needles for an opening. An unenthusiastic "It was okay," might lead to a bit more attentiveness on my part. What was it in their voice – boredom, discontent, concern? Let me pick...that one...there, and see if it might let in a little more light. Needle picking is not nit picking, and it involves pulling out the unnecessary to get to the necessary, not inserting more needless needles to clutter the conversation and disharmonize the branch. If I can help my young apprentice preserve the right needles, this young tree can gather more light, and continue its reach heavenward uncluttered and unfettered.

Beyond our woods lies an evergreen forest awaiting our touch, our attentiveness, and our shaping influence. So if you see an unkempt group of trees along your path, put down your blue drop cloth, climb into a comfortable nook, and start your needle picking. The task is large, the tree is tall, and the forest looks endless; but look there, right in front of you. What's that needle doing there but making the rest of your tree look ugly? Pull it, let it fall, and when you do, you'll find there's a bright green one behind it – let's have a look at that one.

295

67

SORRY I HIT YOUR CAR MONEY

Years ago, before my wife and I started our family, we took a year-long honeymoon sabbatical to Japan, where I taught English at a small high school. Getting around in Japan was a simple combination of riding the train, pedaling your bike, or walking, and in the metropolitan areas this suited the commuters just fine. But where I was stationed, out in the country, the distances were greater, requiring a bit more time or horsepower to get to the destination. To ease the burden a bit, my host school granted me the use of an old motor scooter.

We were first introduced, my scooter and I, when the teacher assigned as my mentor took me outside the colorless walls of the school beneath a set of stairs where old milk crates were stacked and an unused water hose sat coiled near the tires of my new transportation. It sat there, not quite fallen, but listing deeply into the wall, held up by the hand grip. The contrasts were immediately apparent. Scooters today are made of sleek, molded plastic components that convey speed, art, and personality, none of which was present in my vintage ride.

Rather than small sporty tires mounted on solid rims, my scooter had full-sized spoked tires that were only slightly wider than most bicycle tires today. The olive drab frame was solid aluminum that must have been forged in some ancient foundry with monks dedicated to producing the most functional and least aesthetically pleasing piece of metal on their way to nirvana. Only slightly more embarrassing to the rider was the large white plastic shield out front. Sure it kept the rider protected from wind, rain, and mud; but it did nothing to ward off the stares of the townspeople or to turn back the pointing fingers of teasing children. Function over form – that was my scooter.

Since there was no pride of ownership – or ridership, for that matter – I was nonplussed when, at the scooter store, I was forced to buy the only helmet that fit my bulbous foreign head, a solid pink helmet with a chin strap that was just long enough to keep the pink pompadour in place while only moderately restricting the breathing function of the rider. Why the largest helmet in the store was pink, I'll never know. Somewhere in the outer townships of Japan was there a mutant race of large-headed women? Perhaps there was a gang of large-boned tuffs who were founded on the principles of pink power, and this helmet was a symbol of intimidation to their enemies.

In any case, it was my lot to ride around town, the absurd picture of a pink-headed alien astride his noble green chariot. When I wasn't riding to school or to the grocery store, I donned my exercise gear and rode to the town's recreation center where I liked to jog. I wore my sneakers, gray sweatpants, and a light blue t-shirt, and no one mistook me for anyone else in a twenty kilometer radius. I had been stopped by a policeman once and was asked to produce ID and a driver's license, a completely unnecessary act given my reputation as the town idiot.

It was in this constant state of embarrassment that I was riding one particular day to my jogging site, following a delivery truck. The truck turned, and I swung wide, just missing his tailgate as he slowed and entering the lane of oncoming cars momentarily. That's when I was introduced to the hood of an oncoming Alto. To call the Alto a car would imply something of great mass moving toward me and my green steed, but really the Alto was more of an almost car, with four tires, two doors, and all the makings of a car, but I think the engine compartment housed small furry rodents that powered the vehicle because when I hit, I think the car actually jumped backwards. As if reluctant to join the fun, my scooter had stayed behind while I was launched onto the passenger's side of the hood, where I made a sort of metallic snow angel impression, and then I traveled down the side of the car – a very short journey with the Alto – removing the rear view mirror in the process.

I came to rest lying face up on the pavement, and a gaggle of townspeople began to gather on the sidewalk. The scooter was missing the front shield, which had shattered on impact, and on my skyward journey my shin caught the jagged edge and left me with a gash that needed some work.

Lying there on the ground I thought I must have broken something – my back? Collar bone? Nope. Apparently the soft metal of the Alto had absorbed most of the shock. I wonder if one of the national safety laboratories in Japan had studied the impact of a large-headed foreigner launching into an Alto at 50 kilometers per hour and found that the driver could get through without sustaining any injuries.

There I was, not wanting to look down at my limbs, certain I would find something at an unnatural angle, and not wanting to move, fearing a spinal cord injury. I was able to remove my helmet, and it had a large crack, and the *suchiro-ru*, or Styrofoam, was exposed. It was an improvement, I thought. Just then, one of the teachers from the high school where I taught drove by, and seeing my sprawled on the ground, blocking traffic, he stopped to inquire.

He approached, smiling, and with a smothered laugh in his voice, greeted me with, "Wow, you're so fat!"

I might have taken more offense at his comment if I hadn't already spent some time in Japan, and had come to grips many times with people commenting openly on my size, shape, sound, scent – it's more of a factual accounting of things than a condemnation. I suppose the workout clothes accentuated my less flattering features. Maybe I should put the helmet back on to distract attention from my neck down. His comment reassured me that my body must have been intact, *en masse*. He helped me to the curb where I was able to sit and gather my thoughts, and any remaining pride.

By this time police and an ambulance had arrived, and I was whisked away to the hospital where my leg was stitched up. Fat comment aside, my teacher friend remained at my side throughout the ordeal, and he helped me call my wife to explain how I had just crashed into a car, and how the car had sustained more damage than me.

In the days following I had two very strange incidents. First, while recovering in our little apartment, a knock came on our door. It was the women driver of the Alto. I thought it highly irregular, but she seemed genuinely concerned, or possibly afraid. After all, the last time she saw me, I was beating up her car. She introduced herself and slipped a box into my hands, and then bowed deeply and apologized for my unfortunate injuries. Had I known the right words to say in English, I might have attempted them in Japanese, but there I stood, dumbfounded, but touched by her compassion. She hurried off, and retreating to our bedroom, I opened the box.

Hand towels.

Befuddled, I attempted reason, but perhaps I was still suffering the after affects of a mild concussion, because logic failed. I had hit her car, and she was giving me hand towels. Sorry-you-ran-into-me towels? I was unfamiliar with the cultural dynamics behind this kind gesture. Or maybe she was suggesting that I tie the towels together and hang myself from our second story hovel. Perhaps like my smiling teacher's greeting she was really saying, "If I had a knife, I would plunge it into your lumpy chest, but since I don't have a knife, I'll give you these towels instead."

The second incident began when my teacher friend informed me that I had to come up with the equivalent of fifteen hundred dollars to pay for the damage to the Alto, and I should pay that to the school. Perhaps the cultural nuance I was missing here dictated that the offender pay the equivalent of a hundred times the gift given by the damaged party. In these days of my languishing confusion, I was called down to the principal's office during one of my non-teaching class times. Principal Dei was a diminutive, wiry gentleman in his seventies, who had always treated me with the kindest regard. I actually feared for his life on one occasion when the teachers went out for the year-end party, and I saw him drink enough *sake* that he could have spontaneously combusted if he had fallen into one of the candles on the tables. The tradition on such occasions was to pour beer or sake for your superiors as a sign of respect, never letting the glass go empty. They had nearly killed him with respect.

Entering his office on this occasion, he had a most somber tone, and he told me that they were bringing in the woman driver to accept his apology. Next to the mayor, I think the principal held the most esteemed position in town, and I had damaged his reputation because of my carelessness. The woman was escorted in to the dimly-lit, spartan office by one of the office staff workers who was wearing a look of concern. Principal Dei and I stood, and he made a bow of deep respect and personal subordination to the woman, and I followed his lead. He gave a most eloquent apology and quietly handed her an envelope that looked suspiciously to be the same thickness as the fifteen hundred dollars I had given him earlier.

Sorry-I-hit-you-money.

That was it. I gave the best apology I could manage in Japanese, and the woman was shown the door. I don't know if the money went for repairs to the car, or was simply a way to rebuild some of the damage I had brought to the school's reputation. It was then that I realized I had not just made a big metallic impression and ripped off the rear view mirror of the Alto, I had abused the trust placed in me by the school and its austere leader. They didn't have to say it, but as I observed the envelope exchange and saw the pain in Principal Dei's eyes, it was as though I was back on the pavement looking up.

And the fat comment didn't seem quite harsh enough.

68

POLICE BULLY MEETS FLOWER POWER

As a college student I was always on the lookout for opportunities to supplement my income. In those pre-Internet days, I used to rifle through the classified ads in the local paper and circle jobs that I could do. Sometimes the jobs I circled were a bit of a reach, such as the red marker around Financial Planner when I was scrounging for every dime, or thinking I might be a great Parts Runner when I knew less about cars than just about anyone on the planet. Then my eye caught something I could do:

Temporary Help Wanted selling flowers for Mother's Day. Must have transportation and customer service background.

I called the number, and explained my experience working part-time in retail sales. Apparently I had just passed the interview process because I was told to bring a folding chair and meet at the address I was given.

So there I was, Mother's Day weekend, waiting in my car in a dirt parking lot with several other flower people, when our boss drove up with a truckload of flowers. We gathered around the back of his truck for our lightning-quick training session; after all, we were selling flowers to people who were impulse buyers, our temporary boss explained. We didn't need to explain the variety of the flowers or how they were grown, we just needed to transact cash for flowers and guard the goods from grab and go thieves. Yes, apparently flower sellers were easy targets for shoplifting, although given the temporary street locations it might more properly be called carlifting – an impressive name for someone so crass as to deny mothers everywhere the joy of flowers on their special day.

My colleagues and I were given shoe boxes with some seed money for making change and handed maps marked with prime selling locations, busy corners where customers could easily drive in, pay, and drive out, without leaving their cars. I was assigned to a corner near a popular shopping mall. I set up my folding chair on the sidewalk in front of a gas station, and lined up several 5-gallon buckets of flowers. The flowers were packed in so tightly that from a short distance it looked like a rich carpet spilling over a cheap white plastic trunk below. I leaned my hand-painted sign with the three-tiered pricing plan next to my chair, pulled out a novel, and waited.

As the morning sun moved overhead, business was still pretty light. Customers from the gas station would wander over periodically and some would buy, but the boss had said to expect the biggest rush to come late in the day as men were driving home from work. The weather was beautiful, and the novel, Kafka's _The Trial_, was engaging although I might have chosen a less weighty read, since I was to be interrupted throughout the day. Kafka's main character, K., was a sympathetic figure. He had been arrested as he sat doing his bank job, and he never learned of the accuser or the charge, only that his fate had been somehow pre-destined by the court.

It was at this precipitous time, at the height my literary enlightenment and tuition-induced impoverishment, that I was greeted by an officer of the law. I saw the police car pulling into the gas station and caught him in my peripheral vision as he stepped from the vehicle, dark blue, thick at the waist, sunglasses accentuating his blank disregard for the aesthetic life I had set up on the corner of Highland Drive and 4800 South. I pretended to continue reading until he stepped closer, and then, feigning surprise, I asked what I could do for him.

"You're gonna have to move. You can't conduct business here," he sternly said.

"But I'm on a public sidewalk," I meekly contended.

"The owner of this establishment called to complain, and he doesn't want you in front of his store," he said, and then added, "You're also endangering others who might look out their car windows at your flowers and have an accident. This is a busy intersection. So pack up your things and get on your way."

"What law am I violating, officer?" I asked, trying to make eye contact, but facing my own reflection in his bug-eyed shades.

Sensing my silent resistance, his volume increased and I heard in his tone a growing exasperation at the inconvenience he had been caused by a complaining store owner and this flower power student who refused to go quietly.

"It's improper use of streets. I can show you the ordinance," he offered like a bully who pulls back the sleeve of his t-shirt to reveal a bulging bicep.

Owing to my Kafka-induced victimhood, slow sales, and bored curiosity, I responded, "Sure, I've got time. I would like to see the ordinance." How the officer resisted giving me a nightstick taste-test I'll never know, but I was gratefully shocked to see him withdraw to his unit. He must have called for backup earlier, because a second police unit had arrived, and another sunglass-wearing blue man joined the first officer.

I had never really been a bully, despite my large frame, but I had defeated bullies who pushed me too far. No, I had never raised my fists to a bully. I learned from previous encounters with blustering bullies that they feed on intimidation, so you have to starve them by filibustering their reason and postponing their ability to act. So I went back to my book, not reading a page, but keeping my head forward while trying to catch what the officers were doing from the corner of my eye. If only I had sunglasses.

What I saw next both surprised and disappointed me. These two officers were sitting in the first one's vehicle thumbing through a large binder. Could it be that they were actually looking for the ordinance for "illegal use of streets"? I had expected more from them, a forceful takedown to the sidewalk, cuffs behind the back, and perhaps strewing the flowers over me for my impertinence. But time passed, and the stalemate continued, and passersby must have wondered why two police cars were parked behind a novel-reading flower salesman. I felt a new solidarity with my older brethren of the 70s who placed flowers in gun barrels, and also a sense of shame that my singular resistance hadn't already unleashed the canine units and tear gas.

Eventually the officer exited the vehicle and handed me a citation, with the violation listed, but without an ordinance code number next to it. He almost sheepishly explained that there was such an ordinance, but they couldn't take any more time looking for it, so I was getting the violation and would have to pack up or face arrest. His hands went to his hips after he gave me the citation, so I decided it might be time to drive on. I packed up my car and drove around for a few minutes before settling in an area a mile or so up the road where there was an abandoned movie house, and easy access to drivers. I sold all my flowers that day, and pocketed nearly two hundred dollars after explaining the day's events to my boss, who seemed unconcerned about the violation. He told me to go fight it. Temporary boss pulled away.

I did have my day in court, and I drew a picture of the corner while I explained to the judge what the officer had said.

"There is no such ordinance," he pronounced from his wooden pulpit before he dismissed the ticket and excused me. The officer never showed for the hearing – probably embarrassed at his failure to find the ordinance and unwilling to face the mocking of his fellow officers because he couldn't come up with something better than "improper use of streets."

But rather than feeling an air of victory, I came away thinking that this had been the best possible resolution to the situation for both parties. The officer had convinced me to move, resolving the situation with the gas station owner; and whether such an ordinance existed or not was ultimately rendered immaterial in the officer's absence. Was he a bully? No, I think he gave me the ticket just to get me out of the way. Had I intimidated him? Well, let's just say that if you're going to play the intimidation game with a seasoned and fully-armed law enforcement officer, I think you'd better leave Kafka and the buckets of flowers out of it.

69

DEATH BY CORPORATION

Having spent a good deal of my career working with employees, managers, and senior executives inside corporations, and seeing the rise and fall of talented people from the ground level, I can only conclude that corporations are killers. A popular book among academics who study organizations metaphorically describes them as machines, political systems, psychic prisons, and instruments of domination, among others (Morgan, 2006). This multifaceted analysis of organizations provides important insights about structures, systems, the perpetuation of a cultural identity or brand, or the formal and informal power wielded by leaders.

Rather than those convenient metaphors, I'd like to focus on the corporation as an instrument of death. So let me field-strip the weapon and lay out the key parts that once assembled, yield a potentially lethal force.

What is a corporation? Others define corporations in terms of their market capitalization, share, or as a domestic or multi-national business entity. Surely an individual can be a corporation – the Supreme Court said so, as it relates to that noble cause of the campaign contribution – and corporations can be designated as fulfilling different purposes and receiving unique tax statuses, but it's all legal vocabulary laundering that has no basis in the real-life experiences of workers. Does the hot dog stand operator qualify as a corporation? What about the church around the corner? My dog breeding business? My son's lemonade stand? Tax code wonks salivate as they consider the possibilities for revenue by classifying them all as institutional executioners. No, they're not corporations.

In my definition, a corporation consists of a number of artifacts that define it: a full color annual report, a headquarters or administrative building (preferably with lots of glass walls), someone on staff who writes speeches for the president, rows of cubicles that continually shrink as the business grows – an ironic consequence of something positive (growth) turning into something insidious, a claustrophobia inducing garbage smasher like something out of Star Wars. A corporation has an on-site cafeteria, not vending machines and card tables.

Corporations have tax departments of highly-compensated analysts exploiting the proper loopholes to reduce the corporation's tax burden. Corporations have gates for all to pass under as workers drive onto the manicured property and enterprise resource planning software teams who are the only ones who know or care what ERPs are, catalogs showing the selections of logo wear – you know, hats, polo shirts, mugs, water bottles, lanyards, mouse pads – all bearing the company brand, and corporate meetings have themes, you know, cheesy ones like "One Giant Leap for NewCorp," or themes that highlight the alliterative banality induced by continuing to come up with annual themes, such as, "NewCorp: People, Products, Power" or "Building a Better, Bolder, Brighter Business for Beetles". Well, okay, maybe not beetles; but chances are, if you've got these things, you're a corporation.

So what is death? In my corporate metaphor, it is the absence of life or passion for life, a vacancy of the soul, an incremental subtraction of *art de vevre*, the "art of living" as the French say. But how is life extracted, depleted, or routinely snuffed out? How does the factory of death function, where healthy subjects enter the front door, and corpses are hauled out the back? To better understand this, we must go back to the seventies, to an apocalyptic movie about the coming over-population apocalypse – a big theme of the seventies that somehow never materialized – and the scarcity of food. In the movie, one enterprising firm had learned how to turn people into food and labeled the innocuous little green chips soylent green. Of course, our hero, Charlton Heston, was able to learn the truth that soylent green is people only after following his friend, Luther, on his final journey to the glass-fronted building with the spacious lobby and friendly receptionist. A corporation.

Hestons' friend Luther pays his fee and is placed on a gurney and wheeled into multi-media room reminiscent of an IMAX theater without the seats where he is connected to death inducing IV drips, but first he gets to enjoy his favorite music and show of fields of flowers while listening to Grieg's *Peer Gynt Suite*, as a sort of going away present. Death.

I'm not suggesting that corporations would actually manufacture people chips as a way of dealing with mass starvation – I'll leave that to some enterprising MBA student's winning business plan – but the extraction of life really is a similar kind of surrender, a capitulation in which the only meaningful choice left is whether the beneficiaries listed are up to date in the system, so the death benefits can be properly processed. Properly Processing Passing Progenitors – corporate meeting planners swoon at the poetic possibilities for new themes. Bright young people enter to a warm receptionist, are securely tagged with the appropriate access badges, and sent on to the promise of a meaningful career and secure retirement. They are plugged into the mainframe of work, with a boss, a steady flow of caffeine, and a series of beautiful programs to relieve that stinging needle in the vein and the distant tinge of toxin entering the blood.

Of all the instruments of death within the corporate arsenal, the boss is the most effective at inflicting pain, stress, and hopelessness. It's too bad that they can't just be honest about death by micro-management. At least it would be more interesting to hear your boss confess,

"Hey, this is a well written piece, but if you could just add something about the history of flying pigs – I know it's not at all relevant to what you've written, but I played a major role in flying pigs back in the day, so if you could just add that part in, I could claim credit or blame you if it doesn't go well," or,

"Hope it's not too much to ask, but if you could drop everything to do this completely menial task that I really don't want to do, I would be able to claim that I've delegated. Be a sport!" or,

"I know you have just spent the last five years studying this in school, but I think you should do it my way, you know, the manual way. Sure it increases errors, but it also increases your dissatisfaction and uselessness to the corporation."

The office environment can be another purposeful means of death. If you occupy one of the inner honeycombs, you are a worker, and you are there to make the queen, that one in the corner office, well regarded and well compensated. Of course, you can bring pictures from home to dress up your cubicle, but please don't bring anything that makes anyone else uncomfortable around you; that would be any pictures of kids (not everyone can have them), quotes from the Bible (you know how intolerant religious people are), that art project your son made (it's just kind of not "in keeping" with the professional décor after all), or that award you won last year (it might make the low performers feel unappreciated).

The cafeteria is helpful in keeping employees at work, and fattening them for the kill. Monday's breast of chicken becomes Tuesday's chicken salad, and eventually, Friday's chicken soup as passed over food enters the cafeterial cycle of death, a gumbo slosh of the week's castaways. Employees who venture outside for lunch also risk breathing fresh air or feeling the warm sun on their skin, and no one wants employees obsessing about long vacations, distracting them from work. Corporations, particularly the ones who win awards as best places to work, often have walking paths or on-site workout facilities, and this provides helpful ways to activate blood flow and stimulate endorphins useful to what – that's right – accomplishing the work. Work here, eat here, exercise here, send out your laundry here, and when you die at your cubicle here, they'll get someone to cart your body away, tomorrow's soylent green gumbo.

Corporate programs become the final drop in the vein. Indoctrination sessions on appreciating diversity, preventing sexual discrimination, or recognizing workplace violence threats infuse division, suspicion, and trepidation on a workforce that had been disinclined to intolerance, misogynism, or intimidation before the session. It's death by policy, rather than a courageous and aggressive removal of offenders. Exposing and marginalizing employees' eco-ignorance and social movement illiteracy through company-sponsored recycling and volunteer programs helps the corporation invoke conformity of thought and action to a new religion – the newspeak of corporate belief systems. Drip, drip, drip.

Orwell had it right about Big Brother. Sending an email on corporate assets, it's not "your computer", and you're watched. Badge in, badge out, and every movement is traced. You can imagine corporate security, ever vigilant, and watching…

"Uh, subject just left premises…pick up camera 7…"

"Right, I've got him. He's carrying something, unclear what it is, possibly keys…and he's heading towards a number of cars…okay, I've lost him now…"

"Pick up tree camera 4, and let's get a closer look. It could be something *disguised* as keys – don't jump to conclusions. It's alright; he's entering the vehicle he came to work in this morning. Code green."

And then there are the poor naïve honeymooners fresh from

orientation, who see the hive of activity around them and want to be a part of it, but they are uncertain where it all leads, like steak into the sausage grinder they ask the simple but unschooled questions as they read through the litany of corporate rules.

"Hey Jim, you've been here a long time, can you tell me why they only give you the day before and the day after a family member's death as time off?"

"Shh, keep your voice down. And it's not just any family member's death, it's only for immediate family, can't you read?! Now stop talking over the cubicles. They'll hear you, and I'm already on a performance action plan for failing to attach a taxi receipt to my last expense report."

"Oh, okay. Hey, how come we have an onsite Mental Health Clinic?"

What can be done to slow the rate of death by corporation? Considering that many of the benefits offered to employees ring similar to those of every other corporation, I would suggest just a few things that, if adopted, would resuscitate many corporate death camps today.

1. Be aggressive in disciplining managers who intimidate, harass, micro-manage, or take credit for someone else's work.
2. Divert all money spent on Corporate Social Responsibility programs to annual bonuses for your top performers as voted on by management and co-workers.
3. Divert all diversity, inclusion, and harassment funding to a budget that teams can use for fun events out together to build camaraderie and communicate with each other.
4. Allow workers to give a day of service to help a co-worker who may need help.
5. Require top executives to spend one week per year doing an entry level job in the company.
6. Select top performing employees to shadow senior leaders for one to three months as a way of learning more about the business.
7. Increase employee ownership in the company.
8. Remove the annual performance appraisal and increase pay only when key milestones of performance have been met.
9. Allow children over age 14 to serve as summer interns, from 2-8 weeks, based on the job the age of the child.
10. Create programs that allow the frequent movement of employees from one department to another so they see the

company from a wider perspective.

70

THE CHOICE ADDICTION

I guess it's the result of too many choices, I thought as I stared at the menu. It was as though my tolerance for choosing had run out, and I couldn't speak the words to order my food. I was sitting at a long table with my co-workers, and we had just concluded a day of meetings on my first visit to Chicago. This restaurant was notorious for giving the customers a little ribbing when they ordered – a little bit of diner banter – it was part of the charm that kept customers lining up. I guess they figured that if the staff could blow off a little steam at customers by saying what they really felt, it was less likely that something bad would end up on your plate or in your drink by a vengeful kitchen saboteur.

So around the table, one by one, the orders were spoken and dutifully noted.

"I'll have the Caribbean salad with the dressing on the side, grilled chicken not Cajun, and no croutons."

"Hey Bill, we got a SALAD PRUDE here – get out the doilies! Okay m'am, would you like the homemade bread with that salad? We have homemade French bread, sourdough, wheat, multi-grain, or rye."

"Is it my turn now…?"
"Let 'er rip honey!"
"Right, I'd like the double bacon burger."
"Fries with that?"

"Ya, sure."

"What to drink?"

"Coke."

"Regular Coke, or Diet, Zero, or Cherry?"

"No, just Coke."

"Do ya want the burger with some pink in the middle or well done?"

Ugh, this was going to take all night. And while the friendly banter was amusing, I got more anxious about ordering – what if I couldn't choose, and what if I didn't have a crystal clear idea not only what I wanted but how I wanted it cooked, primped, and delivered?

It was my turn, and I scanned the menu for the fourth or fifth time. Nothing looked particularly good, and nothing looked particularly bad, so I blurted out, "Y'know, why don't you just pick something for me?"

The self-confident Lil or Flo actually looked up from her writing pad.

"What?!"

"Ya, that's right, you can pick anything on this menu that you think I would like to eat, and just bring it out however you want to serve it." I was ranting, but it quickly became my shtick, and this was good. "Knowing what you know about me," I pontificated in a now royal tone, "bring me anything and I will eat it. I don't even want to know what it is – ANYTHING AT ALL will be absolutely fine."

Looking at me like my sons do when I tell them they can order anything on the menu, Lil or Flo said, "Really? You don't want to order?"

"Nope," I said with an air of relief. "It's all up to you – you pick and I'll eat."

The Salad Prude at the end of the table nearly fell off her chair. Shocked and overcome with concern for my choiceless stance she pleaded, "What if they bring something you don't like?"

My boss half-whispered to me, "Is this just an act, or are you really not going to order?"

"I just did!" I smiled, closing the menu and stared back at the poodle-skirted waitperson.

And that was it. When my order came out and I saw that it was a pulled pork sandwich I was a little disappointed that it wasn't something more exotic. Before my food was served, everyone at the table sat and discussed with eager anticipation what would be served to me. I had become the life of the party. Eureka.

Of course, there was no way my co-workers could have known that my food tastes had little or no refinement. When I was in junior high I had experimented with mixing cold cereals for breakfast, I had put just about anything and everything in the omelets I had cooked up, and I had gone through my teen years like many boys, experiencing the food challenge. I had eaten loaf-of-bread peanut butter and jelly sandwiches – the whole loaf at once – and I had eaten the eight-patty burger at the Mrs. Robinson's restaurant in my hometown. My best friend, who had a vegetable garden in his backyard, used to get me to eat all kinds of raw vegetables right out of the ground, from carrots to red potatoes and turnips – you just wipe as much of the dirt off as possible, and put a little salt on. And his aunt, just a couple of houses down, used to make her own pickled peppers – yes, like the ones in Peter Piper's tongue twister – and I could eat a whole mason jar of those in one sitting.

So whatever was on that menu was going to be pretty safe by comparison.

I wonder if sometimes the number of choices we have are really necessary, and have we become so conditioned to make choices about such superficial things – what to watch on the several hundred cable stations, what blend of gasoline to put in our car, what shape of ice we prefer in our glass, and which of the multitude of ties, shoes, or shirts are we going to wear – that when a grave and consequential choice comes along, we want to decide quickly and move on rather than weighing it out, thinking it through, or seeking friendly advice.

Maybe there was something grand in the routine that my grandpa-in-law kept when we lived with him. He didn't wonder what to eat for breakfast – it was a Danish cringle, always. After breakfast, Grandpa watched TV, and he wasn't one to use the remote much. He seemed to get as much enjoyment watching the infomercials about chicken roasters and mops as he did from the police dramas and game shows. TV was his Lil or Flo and he had learned to just accept TV as it was – bring me whatever you've got. That was Grandpa's TV watching – it was the absence of choosing. When he went to the grocery store, he could have worn a path in the shiny floors at all his favorite stops, the bakery aisle, the butcher counter to buy some brains – no, the butcher wasn't the Wizard of Oz, Grandpa liked to eat brains – ugh! – then on to the in-store bank where he would chat up the teller over his account. He was on auto-pilot once he hit the automatic entryway.

I wonder if he just ran out of choices after making so many after eighty some-odd years. What I experienced in that one night at the Chicago restaurant may have been the precursor to some naturally-occurring wall in human development in which your choices have all been made. Black or brown shoes? Doesn't really matter, just cover the feet. Plaid or plain shirt with those striped pants? Sure, whatever. Beef liver, beef tongue, beef brains? Hey, as long as it's beef something that's probably fine.

How liberating. What would the world look like if the majority cared less about this or that? Maybe the new tagline for your favorite cola beverage would be, "Hey, it's a cola, what's the fuss?" Or maybe the search engines online would just return one answer to your query. Imagine!

Of course, in a world of Salad Prudes, it would be difficult to achieve choicelessness in all areas of life, but let me just offer up to a world obsessed with the array of choices before us a few helpful credos that I think everyone should adopt as a way of freeing the rest of us from endless choosing:

Food is just to help you live.
Clothes will keep you warm and hide your squishy parts.
Vacuum cleaners perform one function, sucking.
Cars just move you from here to there.
Houses are just shelter.
Shoes are just to keep your feet safe when you step on glass.
Chickens don't know they're free range.
Teenagers hate everything you buy anyway.
All tires are made of rubber.
Shampoo pretty much works the same.
Any gum loses its flavor after five minutes.
All mechanics charge too much.

So next time you face a difficult choice, like which college to attend, who to marry, where to raise your kids, or what your career will be, you can sit back, think, ask a friend to come over and help you discuss it, go to your clergy for guidance, or do an online search – go ahead, take your time. I've got to get back to my Danish cringle.

314

71

THE ART OF OVEREATING

"Oink, oink, I am a pig," said the heavy-set man who was the center of attention as he stood above his conquered foe, a silver trough now swirled with the psychedelic remains of a dozen ice cream scoops. This man, the adoration of the local Farrell's Ice Cream Shop, had just beaten the Pig's Trough, a challenge not only of quantity, but of speed, and there he was having his Polaroid posted on the wall for others to admire and kids – like me – to simply aspire.

The food challenge has always been the same, and it consists of several key elements: First, a cool name, like the Pig's Trough, the Brownie Tower, the Bathtub of Death, or the Flaming Firepit. After all, no one would eat six pounds of fries if it was just called Fries Extra Large. But call it The Brick, and you've got something. Second, there has to be a promise of instant fame and notoriety, a photo on the wall, a t-shirt, a certificate, or some other way of saying to others, "This guy could do it, so what's your problem?" Third, there must be the all-or-nothing hook, either you finish everything in the allotted time, or, in addition to that feeling that you're about to burst forth in full color spew, you have to pay for the food as the final insult to your audacity.

I'll admit, my first few attempts at fame lacked the necessary enticements, but I was still training for the big one. The other very real problem as a kid was not having your own money to blow on a food challenge. After all, if you're going to do the Pig's Trough, you have to have a parent willing to back you, a manager, someone in your corner to front the money if you fail. Parents, in my personal experience, are reluctant – if not downright hostile – to the idea of an explosive bloated child riding home in the car or to the idea of shelling out twenty bucks for some leftover melted ice cream.

Scout camp was the answer.

I was at a scout camp one summer and every day our little patrol of four guys would get a loaf of bread, a tub of peanut butter, and a jar of jelly. That was our lunch allowance from the quartermaster. Of course, we wouldn't always consume the entire loaf, and soon we had excess loaves piling up after a few days. Out of pure boredom and bread came the Loaf of Bread Sandwich Challenge. The name needed some work, I'll admit. I came up with the idea, and my buddies sort of agreed it would be a cool thing for me to try, but none of them felt particularly invested in the outcome. It was as if I had called a race, invited my cheering section, set the distance marker at the end of the track, and I was the only runner. Despite the lack of a catchy challenge name and the all-or-nothing hook (after all, we were due for another bread delivery in the morning), my attempt proved successful, and a thousand flashing Instamatic cameras vaulted me into the history books and a hundred conversations that began with, "Remember when you ate that loaf of bread sandwich?"

Ah, fame.

Next was the Two Pound Burger Challenge at Mrs. Robinson's, a restaurant that had been alternatively a dry cleaner, a quesadilla stand, and a sandwich joint all within a few years. Mrs. Robinson's deserved a chance at survival, so I did my part. My friends, Jeff and Mike, rode their bikes with me over to do the challenge. Of course, talking about the challenge and actually doing it were not always compatible.

"I'm going to do the challenge today," I announced to my friends.
"There's no way you're going to eat a two-pound burger," chided my doubting friend, Jeff.
Not to be overshadowed, Mike exclaimed, "I'll do it too, no problem."

So Jeff went along to witness the event and attest to my failure. Mike went along for moral support, and we had ourselves a challenge. Of course, Mike was about half my size, and kind of a picky eater, so it was no surprise to the other two-thirds of our group that he backed out once we hit the restaurant doors. He claimed that he couldn't pay for the burger if he didn't finish it. I offered to front him the extra cash not out of a sense of generosity, but merely to see him squirm to come up with another excuse besides the I'm-only-skin-and-bones-and-I-just-don't-think-I'm-man-enough-to-eat-two-pounds-of-beef one.

I ate all eight patties and that extra large bun, reminiscing about the loaf of bread sandwich challenge and cackling my way to victory. I had fame in the eyes of my friends, and I ate free – that was a win.

I was becoming an over-eating master, and soon I would face my greatest challenge. Several years later I found myself sitting in a fast food Chinese restaurant in Osaka, Japan. My friend, Frank Wolthius, had convinced me to try the Osho's Juninmae Challenge, or Ten Portions Challenge. Osho's was like the McDonalds of the Kansai region that encompassed Osaka, Kobe and Kyoto. It was the place to go for cheap food prepared right in front of you – mainly because the restaurants were usually a single counter and a few tables. The untrained patron could simply order by pointing to the picture on the wall, no need for much language skill.

The Ten Portions Challenge consisted of sixty potstickers, or gyoza, served in ten neat rows. The challenge? Eat all sixty in less than thirty minutes, and you could crawl out for free. Oh, and you could write your name on the wall with a short phrase of encouragement to other diners. Even in Japan, all the elements were present.

Frank and I choked down our last gyoza at about the twenty-three minute mark, and although the last dozen had been a little shaky, we were already thinking about the next time we would take the challenge. The kind woman behind the register handed us each a marker and she instructed me what to write: "Oneesan wa bepin da" (My older sister is a beauty.) Of course, it was a compliment to the woman to be considered my sister rather than my mother or grandmother, so I obliged and signed my name after the complimentary tome.

That was the first of many gyoza challenges to come.

In Mikunigaoka I cut my time to eighteen minutes. In Sakai, I did it in just over twelve. And in Hirano, I cut it to just under eight minutes. By now I had become accustomed to several variables, and had learned how to master each one. If the gyoza were served all at once, I would start eating from the end they plated first, to avoid burning my mouth. If they were too crispy on the ends because they had been fried a little too long, I would dunk them in sauce to soften the ends. But I had a new plan I was ready to test on the next challenge.

The next challenge was in the town of Hirakata. I forgot to mention that I had to keep moving to new venues because the restaurant owners would become upset if you completed the challenge and then came back another time. It was an unwritten rule that once you conquered the restaurant, you weren't supposed to rub it in a second time – it must have been part of the samurai way, I imagined.

So there I was in the Hirakata Osho's with three other guys who were strictly there to have lunch and watch me beat the time of eight minutes in that restaurant. I vowed I could do it in five. I ordered the Juninmae Challenge, and carefully instructed the cook to only start counting time once the platter of gyoza was served in front of me.

"Hai, wakatta…" he said, confirming my request.

I quickly sprang into action, unstacking five small saucers from the table and filling each with the special gyoza sauce and several drops of sesame oil. I then lined up four small glasses of water, no ice, and prepared my chopsticks.

The platter of gyoza dropped in front of me and time started ticking. With all the calm deliberation of a seasoned overeater, I carefully pulled two gyoza into each of the waiting saucers to cool, and then came back to saucer number one. Grabbing both gyoza in my eager chopsticks, I tossed both in my mouth and chewed only once to test the texture, and gulped them down with a sip of cool water – enough to cool the remaining burn of the cabbage, garlic and pork centers exposed by my single chomp.

In rapid succession I cleared each saucer and the first ten were down in under a minute. Refilling the saucers, I repeated the same order – soak, chomp, sip, swallow – and nearly half the platter was gone. It was actually pleasant to be eating the gyoza, despite not really tasting them. With the encouragement of my comrades, and to satisfy the incredulity of the cook and the other guests, I kept up the blistering pace and swallowed the last golden fried dumpling at five minutes twenty-five seconds. It was a new record. The restaurant cheered, and with pride I wrote my name and winning time high on the wall above all other competitors.

I had done it. I had won my place in food challenge history, and settled any doubts about who was the greatest gyoza eater in Hirakata that day.

After that, I did the gyoza challenge a few more times, loping across the finish line at fifteen minutes, like the sprinter who turns to mock the field of runners behind him as his chest cuts through the finish line tape. The cheering crowds were gone, and my friends had grown tired of my eating games.

Twenty years or so later, I returned with my wife to a newer Osho's restaurant near my old apartment in Hirano. It was spacious, and the tables actually matched. It had menus and commercially-produced napkins bearing the restaurant's logo. It was as if the arena had been swept clean of the blood and sweat of a past generation of gladiators. Oh well. I ordered a few portions of gyoza and asked the teenage waitress if they still had the Juninmae Challenge. I thought my pronunciation was good, but she shook her head as if to say, "I don't know what you said, and even if I did, there IS no challenge." I didn't push it.

Like the fighter past his prime, I sat in happy reflection of the five and a half minutes of glory, and I swallowed a dumpling without chewing – just for old times.

72

WE COULD ALL USE A TRANSPLANT

It was 5:00am Thanksgiving morning, and my wife fumbled for the phone, answering it in speaker mode by accident. What? A liver? Yes, get to the hospital as soon as you can. It came in an instant, but it had taken many more years of wondering if, then when, and when the call came, it set off a mad rush in the house.

As we had done for much of our kids' lives, we had invited our best friends over to spend the holiday with us, but here we were, packing up in the dark hours of the early morning in hopes of a gift that might – or might not – come. If it was going to be today, at least she was going to take a shower, knowing that it might be several days before she might feel its welcome warmth again.

While she made preparations for the transplant surgery, I tried to think. How could I solve the problem of our guests coming for Thanksgiving and having a miserable time? After all, it's one thing to excuse yourself from someone else's feast, but it's bad form when you're the host and hostess. And was it okay if they were miserable as long as my wife had the hope of a new life? It seemed such a pointless argument, but there I stood in the kitchen as the minutes ticked away – cook the turkey or don't cook it? With the ingredients for stuffing sitting on the counter staring at me, and with a decent win-loss record for turkey baking, I decided to go for it, and I dressed and stuffed that bird and put it in the oven just before carrying our things out to the car. At least our friends could come on over and eat to our good fortune.

Sparing the medical details, transplantation is a big deal, not only for the complexity of the surgery, the inherent risks to the recipient for organ rejection, or the possible return of the once-vanquished symptoms, but for the mental conflict that it causes.

When my wife first went on the list it was with the expectation that a year or two would pass and her health would decline to the point where her chances of transplantation improved. Unlike some other organ transplants, liver transplant patients move up and down on the list, not by being more tenured among the listed, but by the worsening of symptoms and the progression of the disease. Endless blood tests mark the peaks and valleys, and the long roller coaster ride begins.

In the midst of this physical ride, the patient begins to wonder at their own bad health and good fortune as their listing position improves and health declines. They also wonder about the justice of someone dying in order to enjoy the chance at a new life. How could it be that we found ourselves for months wishing for her own poor health and hoping for another's premature demise? Summer weekends and motorcycles made for a morbid hope that this might be the time.

But there we were, waiting to see if this liver would become a match, waiting in the pre-op queue, and suddenly, the question on my wife's lips was, "Why me?" I paused and looked at her eyes – she was breaking, not bitter. Then she added, "Why do I deserve this?" to which I answered nothing. Having passed the silver wedding anniversary a while back, I have learned that often men like to give answers when the question didn't really require one. This was one of those times.

So I tried to formulate the answer in my head.

What makes us deserving of goodness, of compassion? What makes us worthy of another's dying wish, that fortune would smile upon us while the lights go out for another? I realized that I do not have the answer why, any more than I have the answer as to why a person dies who we think might better live.

I was still stuck on the question that I had heard so many others spew at Heaven, not in grateful humility, but in desperate confusion. Why me? Then it occurred to me that transplantation could be of the mental and spiritual kind as well as a physical organ.

What is it that could bring about our transplantation of hope for despair, of optimism for grief, and of misery with assurance? Where is the donor who will give to our souls the chance at a second life? Where is the death of the cynical victim, he who denies the hope that awaits him? What price must be paid for the disease to be rooted out and cast aside so that the new part can be implanted in us?

The discomforting answer, the difficult dilemma, and the unsettling reality is one simple word: faith.

Faith is hope without proof, the ultimate test of man's ability to reach out beyond his own grounded, empirical blindness. We see the orderly stars, the majestic mountains, the family of animal life, and the bounties of the harvest, and we deny the verity of the divine handprints surrounding us, and we strain to comprehend them all.

Why us? Why do we belong among and above these greatest of all creations? Because we are in His image, we are His children, and though we may shake the fist or prostrate before Him, it does not change the undeniable truth – we exist as evidence of His love. Imperfect so that He may teach us, flawed so that we might seek Him, damaged so that we might be humble before Him, and weak that we might trust in His unfailing might.

ABOUT THE AUTHOR

Robert Kjar, PhD, is a husband of twenty-seven years and a father of three boys and two dogs. From a New Zealand tree house to the quiet Rocky Mountains, and from Japan corporate life to his home in the mid-west, he incorporates the places and people from his life in his writings.

Made in the USA
Columbia, SC
07 September 2020